W9-CMP-849

Religion and the State in Turkish Universities

Middle East Today

Series editors:

Mohammed Ayoob
University Distinguished Professor of
International Relations
Michigan State University

Fawaz A. Gerges
Professor and Chair of Middle Eastern
Politics and International Relations
Director of the Middle East Centre
London School of Economics

The Iranian Revolution of 1979 and the subsequent Gulf Wars, along with the overthrow of the Iraqi President Saddam Hussein, have dramatically altered the geopolitical landscape of the contemporary Middle East. This series puts forward a critical body of first-rate scholarship that reflects the current political and social realities of the region, focusing on original research about the Israeli-Palestine conflict; social movements, institutions, and the role played by nongovernmental organizations such as Hamas, Hezbollah, the Taliban, and the Muslim Brotherhood; Iran and Turkey as emerging preeminent powers in the region—the former an Islamic republic and the latter a democracy currently governed by a party with Islamic roots; the oil producing countries in the Persian Gulf and their petrol economies; potential problems of nuclear proliferation in the region; and the challenges confronting the United States, Europe, and the United Nations in the greater Middle East. The focus of the series is on general topics such as social turmoil, war and revolution, occupation, radicalism, democracy, and Islam as a political force in the context of modern Middle East history.

Religion and the State in Turkish Universities: The Headscarf Ban
Fatma Nevra Seggie

Religion and the State in Turkish Universities

The Headscarf Ban

Fatma Nevra Seggie

palgrave
macmillan

First published in 2011 by
PALGRAVE MACMILLAN®
in the United States—a division of St. Martin's Press LLC,
175 Fifth Avenue, New York, NY 10010.

Where this book is distributed in the UK, Europe and the rest of the World,
this is by Palgrave Macmillan, a division of Macmillan Publishers Limited,
registered in England, company number 785998, of Houndmills,
Basingstoke, Hampshire RG21 6XS.

Palgrave Macmillan is the global academic imprint of the above
companies and has companies and representatives throughout the world.

Palgrave® and Macmillan® are registered trademarks in the United
States, the United Kingdom, Europe and other countries.

ISBN: 978–0–230–11037–3

Library of Congress Cataloging-in-Publication Data

Seggie, Fatma Nevra.
    Religion and the state in Turkish universities : the headscarf ban /
Fatma Nevra Seggie.
        p.   cm. — (Middle East today)
    ISBN 978–0–230–11037–3
    1. Education and state—Turkey.   2. Religion and state—Turkey.
    3. Universities and colleges—Turkey.   4. Islamic education—Turkey.
    5. Hijab (Islamic clothing)—Turkey.   I. Title.   II. Series.
    LC94.T9S44 2010
    379.2′809561—dc22   2010035159

A catalogue record of the book is available from the British Library

Design by Integra Software Services

First edition: May 2011

10 9 8 7 6 5 4 3 2 1

Printed in the United States of America.

This book is dedicated to the two women who helped me
become who I am today:

My grandmother,
Müzehher Sargut
and
My mother,
Aliye Belkıs Ergin

Contents

List of Tables

Foreword

Ann E. Austin

Dr. Fatma Nevra Seggie has written a book that gives readers across nations and cultures greater understanding about higher education, the lives of a particular group of women, and the intersection of religion and public policy. This book began as Dr. Seggie's dissertation in the Higher, Adult, and Lifelong Education program at Michigan State University, where I had the pleasure of serving as her advisor. I can attest to the careful thought and probing questions that led her to the topic, the sensitive approach she took to the research she conducted in her home country of Turkey, her diligence in analyzing and interpreting the results, and, ultimately, her continuing commitment as she developed her study into this book. In a world where religion plays an important role in individual lives, national contexts, and international developments, Dr. Seggie's work deepens in important ways our awareness and appreciation for the ways in which national policies and personal experiences pertaining to religious practice interact within higher education institutions.

While each reader will find specific aspects of the study of interest, I highlight three thematic areas in which the book makes important contributions. The primary focus of the book is on the experiences of covered women in Turkey who must unveil to pursue their academic degrees as a result of the higher education headscarf ban policy. Second, the book highlights the kinds of issues that emerge when public policy, higher education, and religion interact, and the complex, sometimes unexpected, outcomes of public policies. Third, Dr. Seggie's work sheds light on issues that emerge in the process of doing qualitative research, especially pertaining to sensitive issues in the lives of individuals and nations.

As she explains early in the volume, Fatma Nevra Seggie was inspired to study the experiences of covered women who unveil in order to pursue higher education in order to understand "the other," in this case, women who share her Turkish citizenship but whose experiences by virtue of their specific religious commitment and background are quite different from hers. She sought out covered women who would talk with her about the decision making in which they engaged to reach the point of unveiling, and the impact of unveiling on their educational experiences and identities as Muslim women, Turkish citizens, and females. The narratives she provides of five women as well as the extensive quotations from the larger group she interviewed open to readers many aspects of the lives, thoughts, and dilemmas facing these women. We learn that, in deciding to unveil, they grapple with family pressures (in some cases, strong encouragement to unveil, and, in other cases, resistance to unveiling) and are motivated by the promise of preparing themselves to enrich their family lives, to educate their children, and to contribute as talented, competent women to their country. Some also believe that unveiling in order to pursue higher education is a political step toward advancing and supporting the overall situation of covered women in their country.

We learn also, often poignantly, about how they experience unveiling in order to pursue their education. We learn that many of the participants in the study feel "different" from other students, sometimes fearful and unsafe, and often less confident than they would like. The students are diverse in the strategies that they employ to help them handle unveiling as the necessary route to participation in higher education. Some spend as little time on campus as possible, skipping classes when faculty members are insensitive to their situations, choosing electives on the basis of the reputations of faculty members for tolerance, eschewing extracurricular activities, and refraining from unnecessary conversation with other students or faculty members. The research particularly probes what the women believe is the impact of unveiling on their identities as Muslims, Turkish citizens, and women. Some feel they are giving up some of their Muslimness, while others find their religious commitment as Muslims deepens, even as they recognize that they are trading strict adherence to religious expectations for the opportunity to study and learn. In terms of their identity as Turkish citizens, some of the women indicate that the unveiling policy makes them feel like second-class citizens, while others have become more involved politically in response to the policy. In regard to the impact on their identity as women, some report feeling "naked" and discriminated against. In contrast to those who try to become as invisible as possible, some of the women report an assertive reaction, becoming even more motivated and ambitious in response to barriers to their educational process. Reactions and coping strategies vary depending on the personalities, choices, and circumstances of each particular woman.

What stands out, however, as Dr. Seggie notes, is that these students share many characteristics with students everywhere—delight in learning, eagerness to interact with friends, concern about and commitment to their families, nation, and beliefs. Yet, one cannot but be moved by the challenges and barriers they must overcome in order to learn and pursue an academic degree. Dr. Seggie expresses, and I share, a sense of respect for their strength and resilience. As a faculty member in a university, although in a different national and cultural context, I am reminded as I read about these women that the lives of students are complex. Often what we as teachers see and are aware of as we interact with students is only a piece of the multifaceted, demanding pressures, expectations, and aspirations that each learner brings to class. Remembering that students' lives are complex and often challenging helps me bring more compassion to my work as a faculty member.

A second theme in the book pertains to the policy issues and implications associated with the ban against veiling within higher education institutions in Turkey. The analysis shows that the environment for teaching and learning within a university is always situated within a broader national context. In the case of higher education within Turkey, the clash between secularists and Islamists and the relationships between politics, religion, and democracy within the nation have an impact on university life. While perhaps an obvious observation, this situation does serve as a reminder that, while universities share similarities across countries, they also must be understood within their specific national contexts. Additionally, we see in this book how policies can lead to unexpected consequences. For example, if the intention of the headscarf ban policy is to ensure a secular environment within universities, an unexpected outcome seems to be the enhanced religiosity experienced by some of the students as they unveil to participate. Dr. Seggie's analysis is particularly interesting in highlighting such outcomes that are different from what one presumes the policy was intended to achieve.

At the policy level, the book also raises questions about the role of Islamic women within contemporary Turkey. The women studied clearly are highly committed to education, and aspire to futures that include active careers, economic reward, and opportunities to contribute to the well-being and future directions of their country. What the role will be, in the national arena, of women as motivated as those studied—sufficiently motivated to overcome significant personal challenges—is a question one cannot help but consider after reading this book.

Finally, I commend Dr. Seggie for sharing some of the challenges she encountered as a researcher. We learn about her difficulties in finding participants willing to talk with her and the skepticism with which she was met, even as a Turkish citizen and a Muslim, because her doctoral study was occurring in an American university and because her life experiences and expressions of faith take a different form than those she was studying.

She shares the difficulty of finding friends or colleagues who could fully understand the sentiments she was experiencing in doing the research and the resulting feeling of solitude as she proceeded with the study. Through reflecting on her own perceptions as a researcher, Dr. Seggie's work not only enriches knowledge of the experiences and challenges of covered women who unveil, but also deepens readers' understanding of the process of doing sensitive qualitative work.

This is a carefully researched and thoughtfully written book that will bring fresh insight and understanding about the lives of students and the impact from national policies on individual lives that is often unexplored. While readers are likely to come away with new knowledge as well as further questions about policy issues in Turkey, I suspect they will also close the book with respect for the daily courage of the women who unveil in order to pursue higher education.

Ann E. Austin
Michigan State University
East Lansing, Michigan
United States

Preface

In Turkey, higher education is centralized and regulated by a state-controlled Higher Education Council (HEC). This institution is responsible for decision making in the realm of higher education. The nature of council control of institutions is an important issue and raises critical questions, such as institutional control of budgets, curriculum, and the faculty tenure system. The Council formulates national policies to meet the needs of Turkish higher education stakeholders, to address issues of concern, and to further improve the quality of higher education in Turkey. Even though these policies are formulated for the public good, at times their outcomes might become troublesome. One such policy is the higher education headscarf ban policy.

The higher education headscarf ban prevents Muslim women who cover their hair from entering Turkish university campuses. As such, Muslim female students who choose to cover their hair need to remove the headscarf to gain access to higher education institutions. The ban was introduced by the Higher Education Council as a response to "a perceived threat posed by the encroachment of Islam" (Human Rights Watch, 2004, p. 1) into higher education in the 1980s. Furthermore, the ban was introduced to ensure the stability of Turkish higher education and preserve its secular mission (Human Rights Watch, 2004).

A Turkish public university is tightly controlled and regulated by the Higher Education Council and thus responsible for strictly adhering to national educational laws, including the headscarf ban policy. To achieve this goal, the public university is obliged to ask students to uncover their hair to grant them access to its campus. A Turkish public university also has an obligation to ensure that students have positive educational and cultural experiences to help them succeed in their studies. A positive educational and cultural experience could be best described as a campus life that is inclusive, engaging, and supportive, where everybody feels welcome and comfortable, and is granted opportunities to construct or reconstruct individual character habits of mind, establish identities and affective domains, and become intellectually and socially engaged to gain growth, development, learning, and success. However, forcing students who cover their hair in their private lives to take their headscarves off and act against their cultural values and religious beliefs to receive a higher education may create challenging educational and cultural experiences for these covered students.

Guiding Questions

This study on which this book is based examined the educational and cultural experiences of "part-time" unveilers during their degree programs in public institutions in Turkey. A part-time unveiler is a woman who covers her hair in her private life in line with her understanding of the tenets of Islam,[1] but who removes the veil while at a Turkish university as a result of the higher education headscarf ban policy. Although not all Turkish women wear a headscarf, those who do must remove it, often against their wishes, if they wish to study in postsecondary institutions. The subset of the part-time unveiler studied here comprises undergraduate students.

Religion and the State in Turkish Universities: The Headscarf Ban explores the impact of the headscarf ban policy on the educational and cultural experiences of part-time unveilers during their undergraduate programs in public higher education institutions in Turkey. The following questions are addressed:

- How do part-time unveilers understand and decide to comply with the headscarf ban policy?
- What opportunities does unveiling bring to part-time unveilers on campus?
- What challenges are part-time unveilers faced with on campus and in their lives as a result of unveiling, how do they deal with these challenges, and how do these challenges affect their educational progress?
- How does complying with the policy affect their sense of identity?

Why Does This Matter?

Since the ban was implemented, the headscarf ban has resulted in the exclusion of thousands of Muslim women from Turkey's higher education system. The ban has forced veiled female students to make a choice between their religious convictions and higher education. They either take their veils off and continue their education or insist on wearing the headscarf and terminate their education. Faced with this dilemma, some veiled female students have refused to uncover their hair, claiming that they wear the scarf to follow the tenets of Islam (Human Rights Watch, 2004).

Of these noncompliers, many of those who can afford it go abroad to continue their education, but those who do not have this option lose their chance of receiving a university degree. On the other hand, there have been some others, the part-time unveilers, who have complied with the policy. These part-time unveilers uncover their hair by either taking their veils off or wearing wigs or hats.[2]

Of these two groups of female students, compliers and noncompliers of the policy, the media and researchers have generally focused on the hurdles of veiled undergraduate women who have been denied access to postsecondary education as a result of their resistance to the policy. However, few studies examine the educational and cultural experiences of Muslim female students who comply with the ban during their undergraduate studies. This book is intended to fill this gap. I examine how the policy has impacted these students' academic involvement and multiple identities as Turkish Muslim women, thus helping student affairs professionals, faculty and higher education policymakers understand the needs of this special group.

Overview of the Book

The structure of this book is as follows. The first chapter introduces how and why I undertook the research, frames the topic of the study as a sensitive area of research, explains research sites, emphasizes what I learned from the pilot study, explains how I did or did not reach the part-time unveilers, describes who the part-time unveilers were, and documents the challenges in conducting the research. The second chapter focuses on the background information by (1) presenting the macro-drivers of the headscarf ban policy within the political context of Turkey; (2) exploring the micro-drivers of the headscarf ban policy within the Turkish higher education arena; and (3) analyzing the background, language, and institutional enactment of the policy. The chapter concludes with the conceptual framework used in the study. The third chapter discusses the background of the 30 part-time unveilers who took part in the study. Then, it presents case narratives of five selected part-time unveilers to help readers make better sense of the perceptions of the 30 part-time unveilers regarding the headscarf ban policy and their educational and cultural experiences. Chapter 4 explores how these 30 part-time unveilers understood and negotiated the headscarf ban policy. Chapter 5 presents their opportunities and challenges associated with unveiling at universities. This chapter also examines the strategies used by the students when confronted with challenges related to unveiling. The chapter ends with a discussion of the ways in which the challenges affected the educational progress of the part-time unveilers. Chapter 6 explores how complying with the headscarf ban policy influenced the sense of identity of the part-time unveilers as citizens, Muslims, and women. The book concludes with a final chapter, which discusses and interprets the findings.

Notes

1. Some debate exists in Turkey as to whether or not the headscarf is compulsory for women to wear according to Islam. Some parties argue it is compulsory, others say it is not.
2. As an alternative solution to exposing their hair, some students wear a wig or hat in a way that completely covers the headscarf and/or their hair. This way they look unveiled to the outside world when in fact they keep their real hair and/or headscarf unexposed underneath the wig or hat.

Acknowledgments

This project would not have been possible without the support of many people. Many thanks to my doctoral thesis adviser, Ann E. Austin, who read my numerous revisions and helped make some sense of the confusion. Also, thanks to Mohammed Ayoob, James Fairweather, and Reitumetse O. Mabokela, who offered guidance and encouragement. I would like to thank Soli Özel, Tuğrul Katoğlu, and Murat Önok for reading the manuscript and offering useful suggestions. I would also like to offer my appreciation to my editor and to Robyn Curtis from Palgrave Macmillan, who answered my thousands of questions patiently during the writing of this book.

I would finally like to thank my family for all the support and love that they gave me during this long and, at times, arduous process. I am especially thankful and grateful to my husband, Steven H. Seggie, for reading several drafts of this work and editing and reediting them with helpful suggestions. Without his support, I could have never achieved to complete this manuscript.

The research discussed in this book was partially funded by the Middle East Research Competition (MERC) program.

List of Previous Publications

Refereed Journal Publications

Seggie, F. N., & Austin, A. E. (2010). Impact of the headscarf ban policy on the identity development of part-time unveilers in Turkish higher education. *Journal of College Student Development*, 51(5): 564–583.

Seggie, F. N., & Sanford, G. (2010). Perceptions of Muslim international and Muslim American female students: Campus religious climate. *Race, Ethnicity & Education*, 13(1): 59–82.

Mabokela, R. O., & Seggie, F. N. (2008). Mini skirts and headscarves: Undergraduate student perceptions of secularism in Turkish higher education. *Higher Education*, 55(2): 155–170.

Seggie, F. N., & Mabokela, R. O. (2006). Impact of secularism on undergraduate core curriculum: Perceptions of Turkish students and faculty. *Education and Society*, 24(2): 5–24.

Book Chapters

Seggie, F. N. & Mabokela, R. O. (2009). Unpacking the Turkish undergraduate core curriculum: A comparative textbook analysis. In Fatma Nevra Seggie & Reitumetse Obakeng Mabokela (Eds), *Islam and Higher Education in Transitional Societies* (pp. 83–98). Rotterdam: Sense Publishers.

Seggie, F. N. (2007). Perceptions of graduate students towards the manifestation of secularism in Turkish higher education. In Reitumetse Obakeng Mabokela (Ed.), *Soaring Beyond Boundaries: Women Breaking Educational Barriers in Traditional Societies* (pp. 37–54). Rotterdam: Sense Publishers.

Edited Books

Seggie, F. N. & Mabokela, R. O. (Eds) (2009). *Islam and Higher Education in Transitional Societies*. Rotterdam: Sense Publishers.

Other Writings

Seggie, F. N. (2009). Başörtüsü yasağının bir başka yüzü, *Feminisite*, Temmuz 9, http://www.feminisite.net/news.php?act=details&nid=657.

Seggie, F. N. (2008). (Mis)understanding of secularism among higher education students in Turkey. *Turkish Daily News,* January 3, p. 15.

Seggie, F. N. (2008). The impact of the higher education 'turban' ban policy on part-time unveilers, *Turkish Daily News,* February 4, http://www.turkishdailynews.com.tr/article.php?enewsid=94971.

Book Reviews

Seggie, F. N. (2004). *Putting the University Online: Information, Technology and Organizational Change.* Cornford, J. & Pollock, N. (2003). London, UK: Open University Press. *Education Review.*

Austin, A. E., & Seggie, F. N. (2007). *Evaluating Faculty Performance: A Practical Guide to Assessing Teaching, Research, and Service.* Seldin, P. & Associates (2006). Bolton, MA: Anker. The Department Chair, 18(1): 30–31.

Encyclopedia Entries

Seggie, F. N. (2007). Challenges of Contemporary Turkish Higher Education: Issues of Gender. *Encyclopedia of Women and Islamic Cultures.* Volume IV Economics, Education, Mobility and Space General Editor: Joseph, S. Associate editors: Najmabadi, A., Peteet, J., Shami, S., Siapno, J., Smith, J. I., Assistant Editor: Horner, A., Koninklijke Brill NV, Leiden, The Netherlands (pp. 330–331).

1

The Research and the Researcher

This book presents the research I conducted in 2006 in Turkey for my doctoral dissertation, "The Headscarf Ban Policy in the Turkish University: Educational and Cultural Experiences of Part-Time Unveilers" (Seggie, 2007a), when I was a Ph.D. candidate at Michigan State University in the United States. This chapter gives a brief overview about the research and the researcher, including some information about the methods and procedures of the research. Comprehensive and detailed information about the methods and procedures, including research design, data collection techniques, interviews, and data analysis, can be found in my doctoral dissertation.

Almost everybody who learns about this research wonders why an unveiled and "privileged" woman studies a veiled woman, who is so "different from her." They wonder why I did not undertake a piece of research that was more in keeping with my personality and/or lifestyle. My answer is always short and simple: a desire to learn about the "other" in my own country.

Why and How Did It All Start?

My husband and I took the plane to East Lansing, MI, to start our doctoral studies in January 2004. I was accepted to the Higher, Adult, Lifelong Education (HALE) program in the Department of Educational Administration at Michigan State University. Coming from the English Language Teaching area, with some work in Teaching Training, my plan was to specialize in the area of Professional Development in the context of higher education.

Throughout the course of my doctoral studies, I made new acquaintances and formed new friendships. These new people I met were from all over the world, but mostly American. They were polite, friendly, and eager to know more about where I came from. As an individual who has lived most of her life in Istanbul, Turkey, I thought I knew enough about my country and its most prominent issues and could answer questions about my country without any problems. I soon discovered that this was not the case. I found myself bombarded with questions about the headscarf ban policy, a topic that had appeared in the *Chronicle of Higher Education* several times and thus had become a matter of interest for academics in the United States. I realized that I did not really know much about this policy, and I set about learning as much as I could.

Who Was the Researcher?

Born and raised in Turkey, I have always been surrounded by family members involved in education and service to secular Turkey. Both my maternal grandfather and my uncle were officers in the Turkish Navy. My maternal grandfather later became the Governor of the Turkish province of Zonguldak. My paternal grandfather was the head teacher of a high school.

My mother is a retired high school teacher, and my father is a retired businessman. When my grandmothers were growing up in Istanbul, women usually married at an early age, so only very few attended higher education. This did not mean that they did not value education, however. When my mother was born, her mother was determined that she would receive the best education possible and attend university if she so desired. My mother attended university and earned two bachelor's degrees, one in Archaeology and another in English Language Teaching. After graduating, she worked as an English Language teacher in a high school in Istanbul.

My paternal grandmother and her background had an influence on my belief system. As a devout Muslim, she practiced Islam all her life. She received her religious training at a very early age. I hear that some of her relatives who I only know of and have never met are practising Muslims and follow Islam closely. My paternal grandmother taught me the practices of Islam when I was a child.

My parents, secular in their lifestyles, practice Islam by reading the interpretation or translation of the Qur'an, praying, and fasting from time to time. Of all the women in my immediate and extended family, only my deceased paternal grandmother and one paternal cousin veiled. Even though they wore a headscarf, they never insisted that other female members of the family veiled. Thus, even though I practice Islam in multiple ways, such as praying and fasting, veiling has never crossed my mind.

I grew up in a secular environment where I did not have many chances to have contact with veiled women. I had a comfortable and relatively easy life without many hurdles or challenges. My friends were primarily male and female Muslim or Jewish Turks who had comfortable lives. I had an active social life and enjoyed drinking, going out, and partying. During my high school and undergraduate years, my main concern in life, as the concern of my friends, was what to wear, where to go, and what to do. I read a lot, but mostly read about French literature and culture. I read particular newspapers and novels, listened to certain talks and discussions, and joined clubs. They all shaped me in a particular way as a person. In my teenage years and early 20s, I was like many other adolescents in my surroundings. I never felt privileged or part of any elite group since everyone else around me was like me and I did not know about or of the "other." In my late 20s and early 30s, my extensive traveling to other parts of the country and reading on different topics helped me mature intellectually and realize the privileges I had. My doctoral studies contributed to my personal and intellectual growth since I investigated the political and social context of Turkey in depth from a researcher's perspective. This helped me gain a clearer and perhaps more accurate understanding of who I really am and where I stand in my home country and in the Muslim world. Meanwhile, my international experiences while living in Britain for two years and in the United States for almost four years contributed to my growth as a cosmopolitan person and clarified the meaning of what it means to be "the other". Before I began to conduct the research for my dissertation, I was well aware of all the nuances that I needed to know about different ethnic, racial, socioeconomic, cultural, social, and political groups. Even though I became very conscious about myself and "the other" in relation to the headscarf ban policy, until I started the research, my closest interaction with veiled women had been with my mother's cleaning lady, who wore a traditional headscarf. And the headscarf never became a point of discussion and the policy a topic of debate in the surroundings in which I lived in Turkey until I came across the questions about the headscarf ban policy in America.

What Was the Research About?

When I realized I was not able to answer most of the questions directed at me related to the headscarf ban policy, I knew I wanted to find answers to these issues not only to satisfy my friends' curiosity about the ban, but also my own. Then I started reading about it and soon discovered the complexity of the issue. What perplexed me most was that even though the ban was exercised through female university students who covered their hair, putting them at the center of the issue, academic and political discussions and debates were always framing the issue from political and social perspectives, leaving the education perspective aside. However, the ban was taking place in the context of higher education, impacting universities in various ways. I found this paradoxical and decided to study the issue in depth. My doctoral dissertation was born.

The more I read about the issue, the more I realized the paucity of research in this area and the more I realized the importance of conducting research into the part-time unveilers. This is how I finalized my area of interest and decided to focus on who these students were, how they lived in general, and how the ban impacted their educational and cultural experiences. Nevertheless, I knew the research was going to be challenging as it would cover a sensitive issue. The reasons why the topic is sensitive is twofold: (1) "there are potential consequences or implications, either directly for the participants in the research or for the class of individuals represented by the research" (Sieber & Stanley, 1988, p. 49); (2) research becomes challenging when "it impinges on political alignments, [the word 'political' used to] refer to the vested interests of powerful persons or institutions, or the exercise of coercion or domination, [making] researchers often trespass into areas which are controversial or involve social conflict" (Lee, 1993, p. 4).

Which Research Design Did the Researcher Use While Conducting the Research?

During my initial readings, I discovered that there was limited empirical research on the educational and cultural experiences of part-time unveilers. So my research was going to be an exploratory one, aimed at understanding who the part-time unveilers were and what was the impact of the headscarf ban policy on these students. In order to decide how to conduct this exploratory research, I considered both quantitative and qualitative research designs. I concluded that a qualitative study would be best for the following reasons: (1) I could explore some hidden issues related to the headscarf ban policy not easily explored in a quantitative study, (2) I could unpack the complexity of the act of veiling as a social issue and its embedded relationship with the Turkish political and educational system, (3) I could help uncover inconsistencies and conflicts (if any) built into the policy, and (4) I could provide a rich and detailed description of the part-time unveilers as well as an interpretation of the policy and its impact on them.

In this exploratory qualitative research, I wanted to bring out the unheard voices of the part-time unveilers and explore the headscarf ban policy through their eyes and their reality. To this end, I followed the theoretical perspective that socially constructed knowledge occurs when "individuals seek understanding of the [environment] in which they live and work. They develop subjective meanings of their experiences—meanings directed toward certain objects or things. These [personal] meanings are varied and multiple [and define the knowledge of individuals]" (Creswell, 2003, p. 8). In other words, the approach in this book is that knowledge is constructed and evolves through the interactions between people and the world in which they live. This knowledge provides an opportunity for members of society to create their own truth, thanks to ongoing social interactions within cultures (Derry, 1999; Ernest, 1999; Kim, 2001). So, in my research, culture and context played crucial roles. Another premise of my study was that "reality is constructed through human activity. Members of a society together invent the properties of the world (Kukla, 2000). [So] . . . reality cannot be discovered: it does not exist prior to its social invention" (Kim, 2001, p. 1).

In short, the underlying goal while conducting the research was to understand the context, culture, and perceptions of the individuals under study. As a researcher, I was primarily concerned with the perceptions of the part-time unveilers regarding the headscarf ban policy in the context of higher education in Turkey. By investigating the impressions of part-time unveilers, I intended to discover salient categories of meaning for part-time unveilers and how these categories were linked with each other. This way I hoped to generate hypotheses for further research. I gathered information through visits to universities and personal interactions with individuals and then inductively generated "meaning from the data collected in the field" (Creswell, 2003, p. 9), which is an interpretation "shaped by the researcher's own experiences and backgrounds" (Creswell, 2003, p. 9).

Where Did the Researcher Conduct the Research?

In this book, the names of the cities, higher education institutions, and participants are concealed with the use of pseudonyms. Some participants requested that the names of their universities not appear in the written documents or oral presentations. Thus, not only did I have to conceal the names of the higher education institutions, but also the names of the cities where they are located since some cities have only one or two universities.

Cities

I conducted the study with 30 part-time unveilers in five public institutions in four different cities in Turkey: two big cities and two small cities. Of these four cities, I would argue that two big cities are more cosmopolitan in terms of the political and religious beliefs of their citizens compared with two small cities, which are relatively conservative and have citizens with more uniform political and religious beliefs leaning toward the right wing of the political spectrum.

Public Higher Education in Turkey

The research was conducted with part-time unveilers who were pursuing their undergraduate studies in public institutions. In Turkey, there are 164 (102 public and 62 nonprofit, private foundation) universities. They host around 16 percent of the total student population (around 18.2 million) in a country where the total population was around 71.5 million in 2008 (National Education Statistics: Formal Education 2008–2009, 2009). To enter a university, students need to pass a national university entrance exam. Of those who take the higher education entrance exam, on an average, 50 percent are successful and continue in higher education (associate and bachelor degree programs). For example, in 2009, of the 1,451,350 applicants for higher education placement, 786,677 were placed in higher education programs, including the Open University and universities in other parts of the world (2009-ÖSYS Merkezi Yerleştirme Sonuçları, 2010). Full-time student enrollment (excluding the graduate student population) in public universities in Turkey accounts for 90 percent of the full-time student enrollment in all universities, both public and foundation. Thus, public universities carry the burden of Turkish higher education vis-à-vis foundation universities. In numeric terms, for the 2008–2009 academic year, of the 1,589,292 full-time undergraduate students (associate and bachelor degrees) in Turkey, 1,441,463 students (516,927 in associate degrees and 924,536 in bachelor degrees) attended public universities. The breakdown by gender for bachelor's level students is 46 percent female and 54 percent male (2008–2009 öğretim yılı vakıf üniversitelerinde okuyan öğrenci sayılarına ilişkin bilgiler, n.d.; 2008–2009 öğretim yılı devlet üniversiteleri öğrenci sayıları, n.d.).

Public universities are the oldest and largest higher education institutions in the country, and their students and faculty have always been on the front line of political movements. Compared with foundation universities, public universities have been the venue of many student movements, including resistance to the headscarf ban policy.

Public universities include four-year schools, offering bachelor's level programs with a vocational emphasis, and two-year vocational schools, offering pre-bachelor's level programs of a strictly vocational nature. Compared with foundation universities, they charge very low tuition fees. To compete with the foundation universities and overcome underfunding, since 1998, they have been given the authority to raise funds through partnerships with the industry and corporate world.

Universities

I recruited students from University of South, University of Center, University of North, University of West, and University of East. The total full-time pre-bachelor's and bachelor's level student population of these five universities was around 110,000. The reason why I chose these universities was that they had a high number of female students. In addition, these were the universities where I had professional contacts that helped me find participants for my study.

Reaching the sites was not challenging: Turkey was the country from where I came and had lived for most of my life. Reaching the universities was hurdle free as well. I was quite familiar with the settings of University of South, University of Center, and University of North. In addition, I had various contacts at universities of West and East, enabling me to recruit students. I have known many colleagues on all campuses for a while now. Furthermore, in all institutions, I was acquainted with several administrators, professors, and students.

Pilot Study

In June 2006, I decided to conduct my pilot study in a small city since I already had three volunteer students eager to participate. They were recruited through the Dean of a public university, thanks to my father's social network. I talked to the Dean on the phone, explained my research, and requested help for the pilot study, to which he agreed. He assigned a graduate assistant to find some female students meeting the research criteria in the college where he worked. The graduate student made the initial contact with these students and explained the research project to them, asking if they would like to participate. Those interested were asked to see the Dean for any questions or concerns they had. The Dean arranged a day and time for the students to meet me on campus.

I was keen to make a positive impression on them, build trust, and establish good relations. As such, I was challenged by the decision of what to wear. I felt I had to wear something formal to meet the Dean, a close friend of my father, but something casual to look like a university student and break the ice more easily. I decided to dress in business casual. Since I was meeting the students on campus, I knew they would all be unveiled. The next day, I traveled to the university with my interview questions in English and the consent form both in English and Turkish. My father accompanied me to introduce me to the Dean. The Dean allocated one of the meeting rooms for me to meet with the students and had refreshments served for us during the meeting. When I met the students on a one-to-one basis, I spent some time with each of them and explained who I was and discussed my project in a detailed way. I described the rationale behind the study and told them the reason why it was an important study for Turkish higher education. I explained to them I needed to conduct a pilot study at the beginning of the project to make modest changes or adjustments to the interview protocol as necessary, based on the findings of the pilot study. I told them I would also welcome their input regarding the interview process and the protocol. I went over the consent form and asked them to read it. The consent form specifically mentioned the issues related to confidentiality and anonymity. I explained that students would keep a copy of the Turkish and English versions of the consent form, and tape recording would only be used should the women give permission. Finally, I asked them if they would like to participate in the pilot study. After they expressed willingness, we set a date and time to meet, on campus, since it was easier and more comfortable—they were going to be on campus on those days, and I had access to a conference room thanks to the Dean.

In general, the interviews with the students went smoothly. They were conducted in Turkish and I made notes. I had copies of the consent forms. Some part-time unveilers asked me if it was OK for them to write their initials instead of their full names. None of the students wanted to be tape-recorded and asked me to write (and sign) "I conducted this interview without using a tape recorder" on the copy of the consent form they were going to keep. The interviews lasted between 150 and 240 minutes. At the end of each interview, I asked the interviewee to provide some feedback. On the basis of my observations and the feedback received from three part-time unveilers, I made the necessary changes and revisions and finalized my interview questions and the rules and procedures for the interviews.

Even though the pilot study was fruitful and helped the research design and interview protocol become more solid, it was a little misleading. Reaching the three part-time unveilers for the pilot study was relatively easy, thanks to my father and the Dean. These three students were eager to participate, and I established a good rapport with them. The interview logistics in terms of the conference room and service were comforting, stimulating a positive environment. This led me to think that I could find the participants easily, even perhaps on my own, and they would all be eager to participate. However, this turned out not to be the case and caused some distress and discouragement for a short while.

How Did the Researcher Select the Part-Time Unveilers?

The students who took part in this research were part-time unveilers, who covered their hair in their private lives but unveiled on campus as a result of the headscarf ban policy. These were students who exposed their hair or used wigs or hats in order to look unveiled on campus. Inclusion of these categories allowed me to explore the similarities and differences in their experiences. In this study, the hat included the hat, beret, hood, and bandana.

Since the study was conducted in the summer of 2006, part-time unveilers who would start the second, third, and fourth (fifth and sixth in the health sciences) years of their studies in the 2006–2007 academic year were chosen. First year students have no experience with higher education. The second, third, and fourth (fifth and sixth in the health sciences) year students are more familiar with their institutions and have more experiences to share with better grounded opinions.

On the basis of these criteria, I interviewed 30 part-time unveilers from five public institutions in four different cities. I was able to obtain a breadth of part-time unveilers, with diversity in age, type of veiling, discipline, and socioeconomic status.

How Did the Researcher Reach the Part-Time Unveilers?

As I mentioned earlier, after the pilot study, I was under the assumption that I would be able to recruit participants on my own. The day after the completion of the pilot study, early in the morning, I went to the main gate of University of Center. Under the heat of 100°F, I waited all day and used trees as shelters to protect myself from the sun. As soon as I identified the students approaching to the fitting room to take their headscarves off, I walked toward them with a smile on my face. When I approached and asked them if I could have five minutes of their time, they looked at me either in an uninterested and oblivious way or in a terrified and unnerved manner. I could tell their discomfort and anxiety from their face, gestures, and body language. Some looked at me directly in the eye and said they did not have time for me. Others said they only had five minutes. While I was trying to explain who I was and my research, they constantly checked their watches anxiously. Some interrupted me and said they were not interested. Others were more polite and waited until I finished what I had to say and then rejected my request. One student asked me who I was *really* working for, and another inquired whether I was a journalist or a government member. At the end, they all rejected taking part in the study, and in the late afternoon, I decided to go back home—disappointed and unsuccessful, with some sunburn, but no recruits. The perceived political sensitivity of the topic and the "culture of suspicion" (Clark, 2006, p. 418) existing in the society were evident in the students' nervousness and the mistrust I felt all day. This state of affairs discouraged me, and I thought I would not be able to complete my research. What encouraged me again was to consider strategies to overcome the challenges and use the help of administrators, professors, and others. As such, I turned to personal contacts for help in recruiting part-time unveilers.

I identified the participants through my friends and professional connections—administrators, professors, and ex-students, and participants referring their friends to me as potential participants. Via these two chains of referrals as vehicles to identify the part-time unveilers, I was able to refer to a common contact and thus establish some degree of rapport and trust. This at least gave me a chance to explain who I was and what my research was about, over the phone or face-to-face, before students made a decision about their potential participation in the research.

I contacted over telephone or through campus visits administrators, professors, and ex-students I had known for many years. I explained my work to them. Due to the sensitivity of the research topic, I was clear and detailed about the research project and the criteria for participant recruitment, including how I planned to ensure anonymity and confidentiality. Some of those contacted, mainly administrators and ex-students, agreed to help; others, mostly faculty members, did not wish to reveal the names of their students without asking their permission and/or explaining the situation. Faculty members thought the interviews might lead students to feel "unsafe" on campus, which could result in some decrease in trust between teacher and student. Another concern was that they did not want to be associated with the study due to its sensitivity as a research topic as well as its potential higher education policy implications. Colleagues who agreed to help identified some students and provided me with the students' phone numbers for me to reach them. One male ex-student of mine was especially helpful. He, with numerous contacts with veiled women and part-time unveilers, put me in touch with six or seven friends of his who met my criteria. In addition, I asked my friends for help. They used their own professional or nonprofessional contacts to identify a couple of part-time unveilers meeting the criteria.

The second strategy I used to identify and contact potential participants was part-time unveilers directing me to others. Some were generous in providing names and directed me to three or four of their friends. The chain of referrals was interrupted if these part-time unveilers refused to participate in the study. I only contacted referrals after the first set of part-time unveilers contacted them and told them to expect a phone call from me. This strategy eased my job in the sense that they were already expecting a phone call from a Fatma Nevra Seggie when I contacted them.

Through these strategies, 72 potential interviewees were identified. In most cases, I contacted them over the telephone. In some cases, I met them face-to-face if they specifically requested. I explained who I was as a researcher, described my project, and helped them understand that the findings would inform policymakers in the context of higher education. Procedures were reviewed and assurance of confidentiality and anonymity given. I then answered any questions and concerns they had. Each initial contact lasted approximately 30 minutes. In one or two cases, rapport was established in such a way that an engaging discussion took place where I was on the phone for 90 minutes.

Of 72 students, who were the initial contacts, 38 agreed to participate in the study. However, five of them changed their mind either later during the day or the next day. In one case, the woman changed her mind at the last minute—when I was on my way to our meeting point. She sent a text message to my cell phone and luckily my phone was not turned off, which is what I usually did on the way to interviews. As for three students, despite their eagerness to participate in the study, I could not meet with them because they had already returned to their hometowns for the summer holiday. Thus, I interviewed 30 students. An aggregated overview of the participants is given in Appendix A and an individually charted profile of all the participants in Appendix B. In the following section , I will highlight the demographics, educational characteristics, and general outlook of the participants.

Some Demographic Information About the Part-Time Unveilers

The 30 part-time unveilers included in the study ranged from 19 to 30 years in age. More than half of the participants came from a big city, a city with a population of over one million. Twenty-one students had mothers who were housewives. The fathers of almost one-third of the respondents were businessmen. Twenty-two part-time unveilers came from nuclear families in which all women were veiled. Twenty-four women started to veil at some point in their education before university. One started using the headscarf in the first grade, one in the fifth grade, nine in the sixth grade, three in the seventh grade, two in the eighth grade, four in the ninth grade, two in the tenth grade, and two in Grade 11. Fourteen of the students covered their hair voluntarily to follow the tenets of Islam. Two part-time unveilers wore a headscarf as a result of paternal pressure, and one student started veiling to receive a scholarship from a test center. Of all the part-time unveilers, 16 exposed their hair, 11 wore a hat, and three used a wig as their type of unveiling while attending universities.

Educational Characteristics

Twenty-four participants were traditional undergraduate students earning various bachelor's degrees. Six students were returning students who dropped out of college as a result of the headscarf ban policy and chose to return to college to receive a bachelor's degree. Twenty-seven students were single, and three students were married, two of whom were returning students. Twenty-eight students were in four-year institutions, and two students were in a two-year institution. Three students were studying social sciences and eight students were studying applied social sciences. Almost all part-time unveilers lived off campus, with the exception of two part-time unveilers. One-third of them were in their third year and one-third in their fourth year. Thirteen part-time unveilers had high GPAs and 11 average GPAs. Thirteen part-time unveilers attended İmam Hatip schools at some point in their education before university (see Appendix C for a detailed description of the Turkish educational system). Of the 30 part-time unveilers who participated in the research, eight mentioned whether the schools they attended before university were coeducational or only for girls. Of these eight women, five attended high schools only for girls and three coeducational schools.

General Outlook

Part-time unveilers gave off a variety of impressions. Some appeared more nervous and anxious, with perceived feelings of distrust, than others while talking to me. Observing part-time unveilers during the interactions helped me perceive the covered women's fashion and clothing trends of summer 2006. On the basis of the accounts of the part-time unveilers and my observations, I found out that all part-time unveilers used the türban style of hair covering, which completely covered their hair, their neck and/or shoulders (see Chapter 2 for more information). The most noticeable feature of their attire was the perfect match of the headscarf with the rest of their clothes. Some part-time unveilers wore headscarves and long coats that were plain black, dark blue, or brown and made from cotton or polyester, which implied a low or average socioeconomic status (Navaro-Yashin, 2002). Other part-time unveilers had colorful Vakko (a premium Turkish clothing shop), Valentino, or Christian Dior headscarves in silk. Their clothes were bright and expensive looking. They wore gold or diamond jewelry, which implied a higher socioeconomic status (Navaro-Yashin, 2002). Some part-time unveilers wore tight jeans, trousers, skirts, and tops with long sleeves that exposed the frame of the body. Others wore loose clothes that hid the shape of the body. Some overcoats were long, others short; some loose, others tight; some plain, others colorful with patterns. Not everybody wore an overcoat. They all wore a bonnet under their headscarves that covered their hair and neck (and sometimes their shoulders). There were a couple of part-time unveilers who wore fashionable long lace-knitted scarves as opposed to traditional square headscarves. Few part-time unveilers wore makeup. Generally, their fingernails (and toenails) were short without nail polish. Some wore sandals without socks; others wore closed toe shoes with different types of socks. Nobody had high-heeled shoes. All in all, other than their most distinctive features, headscarves (in the türban style) and long coats (in some cases), they appeared as any other young women in the street.

Interview Protocol

The interview protocol I used during the interviews with part-time unveilers was originally designed in English and then translated into Turkish. During the translation of the interview protocol, I referred to the help of various colleagues in Turkey. I met with a couple of assistant professors who are either in the field of political science or follow politics closely as a personal interest. My aim was to ensure the accuracy of the terms I needed to use while conducting interviews in Turkish. They guided me through the translation process. The challenge was with the choice of words. In Turkey, the ban is usually referred to as either the headscarf ban or the *türban* ban. Since the word *türban* has a political meaning attached to it within the context of Turkey, as I will explain in the following chapter, I was advised to use the Turkish word *başörtüsü* (headscarf) while referring to the headscarf/*türban* ban to avoid any impression that I was making political statements and to ensure a more comprehensive term—the word "headscarf" refers to all types of hair covering, including the *türban*. In addition, translating the word "policy" and using it together with "ban" posed a challenge. At the end, I decided not to use them together as I do in English. I either translated the word "policy" as *başörtüsü yasağı* (the headscarf ban) or *üniversitelerin başını kapamayı tercih eden kız öğrencilere karşı uyguladıkları politikalar* (policies that universities exercise for veiled female students). After consultation sessions with the faculty members for a final approval of the Turkish version of the interview questions, I conducted interviews with the part-time unveilers.

Interviews with the Part-Time Unveilers

The interviews started with a series of short-answer questions to get some demographic information about the part-time unveilers. This included questions about age, year of educational study, parents' job, GPA, the university they were attending, the discipline they were studying, the place they resided in while going to university (dormitory or off campus), the city they were from, and the type of unveiling they used on campus (e.g., wig, hat, or exposure of the hair). This section ended with a question asking students to briefly explain their educational background and how they started veiling.

After these background questions, I asked six open-ended questions to explore the perspectives of the part-time unveilers about their educational and cultural experiences with regard to the headscarf ban policy. In broad terms, the interviews focused on part-time unveilers' goals in going to university, their understanding of the policy, the reason they had chosen to comply with the headscarf ban, the way in which the ban was implemented in their institution, and the ways in which unveiling impacted their experiences on campus and in their private lives. Furthermore, part-time unveilers described their identity as they perceived it and then explained how unveiling affected it.

During the interviews, in addition to the open-ended questions, I used more specific, probing questions based on the components of my conceptual framework. That is, when answers to the open-ended questions were brief and general, I used specific, probing questions to give the part-time unveilers an opportunity to talk about their experiences in a more specific, detailed way.

The interviews, conducted in Turkish and hand-recorded, were semi-structured (Berg, 2001) and let me interact face-to-face with the students in natural settings (Marshall & Rossman, 1999). The length of interviews ranged from 150 to 240 minutes, depending on how much information part-time unveilers had or wanted to share. Usually, a short break of ten minutes was taken partway through the interviews.

I interviewed the students only once, with the exception of three women. In the case of these three part-time unveilers, interviews were interrupted due to emergency calls or other commitments. Second interviews were conducted the following day. This way I had the opportunity to conduct two interviews as opposed to only single interviews. One main advantage of interviewing a woman twice was that the second interview gave her an opportunity to come back and discuss the points she thought she had left out. In addition, during the second interview, the women seemed to be more comfortable with me. Interviewing twice seemed advantageous in terms of trust building, and two part-time unveilers wanted to develop a friendship after the second interview. They invited me out for lunch or dinner and introduced me to their parents and friends. On the one hand, it was a very enriching experience for me and I was particularly happy to cultivate acquaintances with these young women since, in my own life, I had not known very many veiled women. On the other hand, with my researcher hat on, I struggled with their desire to befriend me since I did not want to compromise issues of confidentiality.

While I was recording the data, I asked part-time unveilers to check what I was writing so that they could warn me if I misreported a piece of information. This type of data checking during the interviews proved invaluable since it allowed students to validate and ensure the accuracy of data recorded. I then translated the interviews into English.

Where Did the Researcher Meet with the Part-Time Unveilers for Their Interviews?

Part-time unveilers had the liberty to choose the meeting points for their interviews. Thus, I met them in different settings. Some invited me to their houses; others wanted to meet outdoors in a coffee shop or restaurant. A couple of them felt more comfortable having the interview in organizations for which they did volunteer work, while two others requested on-campus interviews.

Five university locations were used for conducting two of the interviews and reaching administrators or professors. Other than two, all interviews were conducted outside a university. Two students preferred the campus because of logistical reasons and time constraints. They had classes in between the interviews and did not want to go through the hurdle of leaving the campus and then entering the campus again, which meant veiling and unveiling again. In addition, since they were returning to their hometowns after the final exams in a couple of days, they wanted to be interviewed as soon as possible. All other women preferred to be interviewed outside the campus. By the time the interviews were conducted, most of them had finished their final exams and started their summer holiday. Thus, they did not want to meet on campus and go through the unveiling process when, as many part-time unveilers pointed out, "there was no pressing need."

I also think students selected the meeting points for the interviews on the basis of where they thought they would be most "comfortable" and "safe."

Position of the Researcher

As a researcher engaged in an inductive research process with the intention of generating meaning from the data collected to develop a pattern of meaning (Crotty, 1998), I knew that my identity and background were going to shape my interpretation of the data. Thus, I positioned myself as an unveiled secular Turkish Muslim woman while interpreting the views part-time unveilers had about the world.

Challenges of the Research

The piece of research explored in this book proved challenging for me at various levels. I went through personal and interpersonal challenges that had numerous social and political implications. As a researcher, one of my challenges was in the area of recruitment. There were three important reasons for this:

1. First, the headscarf ban policy was a sensitive topic in the Turkish higher education system and was intertwined with Turkish politics. The ban had a history of almost 30 years, impacting the lives of covered women in one way or another at different levels. The history of the ban included campus riots, police harassment, arrests, student protests, court cases, classroom violence, student discrimination, dropouts, and other events ("Mazlumder," 1998). It was a

topic that had been discussed widely by the opposing political factions in the political and educational context of Turkey and had been one of the mostly hotly debated topics in the media. The constant battle for or against the ban cultivated feelings of mistrust and bitterness in society ("Mazlumder," 1998).

2. Second, as a researcher, even though I was a Turkish Muslim woman and an insider within Turkish society, I was an outsider to the covered women's community. As being in the position of "the other", I felt I was perceived as if I was one of the representatives of the headscarf ban in the eyes of the potential participants.

3. Third, in many instances, I was perceived as a researcher affiliated with America rather than a Turkish researcher. The perception of most students, administrators, and faculty was that I was a doctoral student affiliated with an American university. In their mind, since I was studying in America, socializing with American students, and working with American professors, my frame of reference would be formed by American higher education. This seemed to be threatening to some administrators and potential research participants because they were not sure if a researcher with an American frame of reference would be objective in the piece of research she was conducting. This type of perception challenged me on a personal level as well since while in my home country, I never identified myself as a student/researcher from America, but rather as a Turkish woman who was unveiled. Being thought of as an American affiliate challenged my identity while I was conducting the research.

These factors made me struggle while locating the participants, making initial contacts, and convincing them to participate in the study. My colleagues, administrators, and professors sometimes directed me to other colleagues who they thought would be helpful in identifying potential interviewees. When I contacted these colleagues, some of them wanted to meet with me and have a little "chat" about my research before they agreed to help me. These people were professors from various departments in the universities of South, Center, and West. When I met them in their offices on and off campuses, they asked me detailed questions about my personal and educational background. Then, they inquired about my philosophy of research, the research paradigm I was using in the study, and the data collection methods. They challenged the research paradigm I had chosen and argued that inductive studies were more journalistic rather than scholarly and not well grounded in the theory. Thus, they were not entirely convinced about the rigor of the study. In addition, lately they had come across a couple of qualitative researchers asking for their help to conduct research.

They perceived that qualitative research was full of subjectivity and thus could be biased. This was not how they believed research needed to be conducted. Thus, they refused to help me.

Potential interviewees asked me various questions about my personal and educational background, including my study. There were a couple of questions that were asked systematically, and I struggled answering them since I had not expected such questions or comments. Almost all potential students I talked to over the phone or face-to-face wanted to know why I chose this topic. They inquired whether it was the "United States" that wanted me to pursue this research or not. In addition, they asked for some explanation on the direction I was planning to take while presenting the results. Some of their comments stressed that I was a student working for American professors in America. They believed the study would be framed by American mind-sets and findings published in America. All the potential interviewees wondered about the kind of goals and objectives I had in studying this sensitive topic. Some asked me if I thought my dissertation would enable "America" to solve the headscarf ban problem. Others asked me directly whether I was working for the American media or government besides going to school. They expressed concerns about U.S. foreign policies and the war in Iraq, and they made inquiries about potential "hidden agendas" of professors in my department. Clearly, the perceptions of potential interviewees about the international political climate and the role of the United States in the Muslim world had an impact on their decision to take part (or not) in the study. In addition, considering the questions asked, it was obvious that I perceived as a student researcher from America rather than a Turkish woman living in the United States, attending an American higher education institution. I believe this influenced the way students reacted to me as a researcher and to my work.

Some potential interviewees challenged the benefits of the research findings due to my status as an unveiled woman. Their argument was that as an unveiled woman, a privileged Turk, I would be working from a perspective of someone who would be in favor of the existing headscarf ban. They wondered about the value of this type of research since they did not understand how their participation in a study conducted by an outsider might benefit their lives. I also struggled with answers when a couple of women wanted to know how I perceived the life of a veiled woman in Turkey, because I was not sure of the extent to which I wanted them to know my perceptions of them.

On a more personal level, my challenges stemmed from how I felt and carried myself throughout the research as I heard part-time unveilers' remarks during interviews. As an unveiled secular Muslim woman, the visible part of my self that would shape potential interviewees' perceptions of the researcher before and during interviews was my clothing; in other words, the dressing style of the researcher as explained in McCosker, Barnard, & Gerber, 2001. It was summertime, over 100°F in most parts of Turkey. I wear clothes that are not necessarily liberal but not conservative either. Especially in the summer, I wear light clothes such as short-sleeved tops, short skirts, and V-neck blouses. As a researcher, this is who I am and I did not want to change that. I considered wearing more conservative clothes, but I felt it would be a deception. On the one hand, I wanted to show them I had respect for their lifestyle, and on the other, I did not want to change an important aspect of my identity to suit theirs. As an unveiled woman, I was an outsider and did not want to be perceived as an insider by temporarily looking like them. I am not sure how, if at all, the clothes I wore influenced my research, the interviewees' perceptions of me, their decision to participate in the study or not, and the quality of data I collected.

As an unveiled and "privileged" woman, I had challenges at two different levels. First, as an unveiled woman, I was (or at least believed I was) an outsider, one of the "other." I do not know the extent to which their perception of me as an outsider, if that was the case at all, influenced the degree of openness when they answered the questions during the interviews. Second, I was troubled by some terms part-time unveilers used while exploring their understanding of the headscarf ban policy. They constantly used the word "they" to refer to secularists or policymakers who initiated the ban. Every time I asked the part-time unveilers who "they" were, I could feel their discomfort and hesitation. They perhaps did not know how to answer since I was unveiled and possibly, in their eyes, a member of "they." They explained that "they" were unveiled people and added "unveiled like you." Some of their descriptions of "they" included people who did not practice or appreciate Islam. In addition, a few students associated Muslimness with the headscarf and the Islamic way of life. I was very challenged, trying not to react and to stay neutral without making any comments. I felt confronted and challenged as never in my life had I been treated as the "other" or "outsider" or been constantly reminded of this "otherness" as throughout the course of the research. There were times when I almost lost my researcher hat and found myself defending my values as an unveiled Turkish Muslim woman.

Another challenge was the feeling of unease—as if I were in some way responsible for the challenges part-time unveilers were encountering since I appeared (or believed that I appeared) as the representative of the secular elite who had issued the ban. In addition, I was troubled and disturbed when I started to learn more about the "other" Turkey, a Turkey I did not even know existed. I felt feelings of discomfort for having lived my life within the five-mile radius of my apartment and not seeing beyond the perimeter. Another challenge of mine was the solitude throughout the research process. I was gaining new perspectives and learning about new communities, lifestyles, and experiences. Their challenges were puzzling, disturbing, and troubling in different ways. I tried to discuss my feelings and observations with my family and friends, but they did not understand me since they did not know much about my point of reference. This made me question whether I still fitted into the community in which I grew up. I felt like an outsider on the inside.

Finally, the interview process brought some challenges. For example, some interviewees cried during their interview, and this was unnerving. I was not sure what to do or how to respond. There were times when I felt helpless and searched for a piece of advice to handle the situation gently and proceed.

My final challenge concerned the length of time I could devote to the research. When I flew to Turkey in the late spring, the initial plan was to start recruiting some students in the summer and others at the beginning of fall since during the summertime many of them would be gone on holiday. I paced the research accordingly. However, in the weeks to follow after I settled in Turkey, some unexpected issues came up that required me to modify the schedule and return to the United States at the end of August. This changed the pace of the research. I rushed, which was stressful, and I completed the final interview the day before I flew back to the United States.

2

The Headscarf Ban Policy in Its Political, Social, and Educational Context

This chapter describes the political, social, and educational context of Turkey with specific reference to the higher education headscarf ban policy. First, I explore the macro-drivers of the policy—that is, secularism, religion and identity, gender and class, and democracy in Turkey. Next, I move on to explain some of the policy-related features of the higher education system and elaborate on the way higher education policies are formulated, including the challenges policymakers face in Turkey. Later, the chapter provides a historical background about the higher education headscarf ban policy and discusses some of the issues emerging from its existence. I conclude the chapter by presenting the conceptual framework I used in the study.

Political Context of Turkey

Modern Turkey emerged from the Ottoman Empire, which was ruled by Islamic law. After the collapse of the Empire, Mustafa Kemal Atatürk founded the Republic of Turkey in 1923. He led the Turkish forces to victory over the Western armies in the Turkish War of Independence. A series of political, social, cultural, educational, and economic reforms followed this victory, leading to the creation of a modern and strong nation (Cherry, 2003). These reforms brought about numerous changes in the way power was distributed among the population, creating new balances between the elites and the masses (White, 2002).

Modern day Turkey has both a president and a prime minister. Political parties come to power through democratic elections, which take place once every four years. Today, the Justice and Development Party (AKP) rules the country under the leadership of Prime Minister Recep Tayyip Erdogan. The party, which parts of the media identifies as a moderate Islamist party, has had some conflicts and tensions with the secular elite. The differences between secularists and Islamists are explored in depth in the following pages.

Turkey bridges the West and the East not only geographically but also culturally; hence, it has the potential to become a model for the rest of the Muslim world as it is a secular democratic country with a predominantly Muslim population (Cherry, 2003). This puts Turkey in a unique position in the world. Secularism, democracy, and religion are important features of the country, intertwined with issues of gender, identity, and class. Within the context of the study, it was important to analyze these characteristics in depth because they were the macro-drivers of the headscarf ban policy and to depict the background and rationale of this policy in Turkish higher education.

Macro-Drivers of the Headscarf Ban Policy

Turkish Secularism

Traditionally, secularism has meant the separation of religion and state. The system works in such a way that both the state and religion function autonomously. Secularism displays certain differences in characteristics in different countries. The Turkish model of secularism has a separation of state and religion, and religion has no role in the affairs of the state (Ayoob, 2004); however, the model differs on other important dimensions. First, attempts to separate religion and state, especially in the areas of judiciary and education, in the last decades of the Ottoman Empire resulted in the emergence of dual practices. Some groups that had lived under the rules of religion for a very long time could not (or did not want to) adapt to the new system and chose to continue with their religious lifestyle (Avcı, 1990). Other groups accepted the separation of state and religion. As such, secularism and religion became distinct belief models, with separate followers of each. With the foundation of the Republic of Turkey, which chose secularism as the regime of the state, this dichotomous system was eradicated by abolishing all institutions that failed to conform to the ideals of secularism (Berkes, 1998). The move to secularism happened gradually in all areas, including the government, the Constitution, the judiciary, and education (Avcı, 1990). The Department of Religious Affairs—in which *imams*[1] are civil servants and bound to follow the rules of the government—was attached to and still is under the control of the state. Thus, all independent religious representatives and/or symbols were removed from public life and regulated by the state. From this perspective, in Turkish secularism, the state dominates and controls religious institutions at every level, rather than religion being an autonomous unit as in other secular countries such as the United States. Religion being controlled can be exemplified by the fact that mosques are built and led under the direction of the state (Fuller, 2004).

Another characteristic of Turkish secularism is that even though the normative definition of secularism is based on the ideas of enlightenment, freedom of expression, and freedom of thought (Gülalp, 2003) and implies a movement from the grass roots in a society, in Turkey "it is imposed from above and protected in an authoritarian manner by state institutions, including the military" (p. 382). According to Ayoob (2004), "this augments the military's role in the political sphere and creates the Turkish model of 'authoritarian secularism'" (p. 452).

Since Turkish secularism is based on both the separation of religion and state and state control of religion, within the context of the Turkish university, higher education policies sometimes result in outcomes that create tensions because of state domination over religion. One such example is the headscarf ban policy in Turkish higher education, which was introduced by the ruling elite. Research conducted by Seggie (2007b) and Mabokela and Seggie (2008), where secularism in the context of Turkish higher education is examined, indicates that the higher education headscarf ban policy, perceived as jeopardizing religious freedom on campuses, led to conflicts in the minds of undergraduate and graduate students in Turkish universities. What are the roots of these conflicts in the minds of these students? The answer lies in how Turks generally view themselves in relation to secularism and Islam. It is important to understand how religion has inserted itself into secular and predominantly Muslim Turkey and how secularism and religion have influenced the identity of Turkish citizens.

Religion and Identity

The population of Turkey is 99 percent Muslim (Anon, 2008).[2] The country's cultural heritage dates back to the Ottoman Empire and identifies mainly with Islam. After the establishment of the Turkish Republic, founding secularists were guided "by the ideas of the European Enlightenment" (Ayoob, 2004, p. 454) and emphasized "nationalism based on territory and ethnicity rather than religious affinity" (Ayoob, 2004, p. 454) as the milestone in Turkey's progression. The aim was to create a Turkish identity that had a common language, common race, and shared background with a new Western lifestyle. But it took quite some time for large parts of Turkey to have links with the West and to enjoy the opportunities their country provided (Fuller, 2004). These groups remained marginalized. Meanwhile, their identity was shaped around both religion, taking pride in their Ottoman background, and secularism, being loyal to the newly born system (Fuller, 2004). Ayoob (2004) and Gülalp (2003) explained that this happened because the Turkish ethnic identity could not be separated from its Islamic identity: a "non-Muslim can be a Turkish citizen but not a Turk" (Ayoob, 2004, p. 455). Fuller explained that the integration of Islam into the Turkish identity manifested itself in 2002 when an Islam-oriented party won the elections. In addition, Fuller and Ayoob suggested that the majority of the Turkish people do not view being both a Muslim and a secularist as contradictory; rather, they consider the aspects as complementing one another. Despite the fact that Turkish identity is composed of both religion and secularism, over the decades, Turkish citizens have started associating their identity more with either secularism or Islam. From this association emerged two distinct groups in the country: secularists and Islamists. Islamism is a concept coined in the twentieth century as a result of a global discussion about Muslim lifestyle, exacerbated by both mass media and education.

Separate identities: Secularists and Islamists. Secularism was implemented to help Turkey modernize (Fuller, 2004). The nation underwent numerous societal reforms that led to the adoption of Western laws and lifestyle. As a result, the ruling elite marginalized Islam, and religiosity became associated with backwardness (Fuller, 2004). The development process resulted in a society that was polarized along secular and Islamic lines (Göle, 1997; Sunar & Sayarı, 2004; White, 2002).

Secularists consider themselves liberal, progressive, and individualistic and are strongly tied to the idea of modernity, "characterized by an emphasis on the superiority of individualistic, goal-seeking behavior over deference to 'traditional' forms of family and communal authority" (White, 2002, p. 20). In contrast, Islamists are "Muslims who, rather than accept an inherited [religious] Muslim tradition, have developed their own self-conscious vision of Islam, which is then brought to bear on social and political events" (White, 2002, p. 23) in Turkey. Secularists believe that Islamists engage in conservative, macho, and religiously extremist behavior (White, 2002).

Secular-oriented citizens treat Islam as their religion, whereas Islamists have a lifestyle that views Islam both as a religion and as a way of life. These devout Muslims choose to live strictly in accord with the tenets of the Qur'an. This alignment is most visible in the way women are dressed. The Islamist woman conceals her hair and wears modest clothes to cover her body (White, 2002).

The mission of secularists is to protect Turkish secularism and "its guarantees of free choice of lifestyle, particularly for women, but limited choice in the realms of religion and ethnicity" (White, 2002, p. 29). Thus, the secular elite who are in power have determined the direction of the country through the state, the law, and education. Since politics and education are intertwined in Turkey, secularists have played crucial roles in higher education policymaking and have contributed to the formulation of national higher education policies. In the last two or three decades, Islamists have also gained substantial power in the decision-making arena. In 2002, the AKP, a party with political roots in Islam, won the elections.

In the realm of Turkish higher education, from time to time there have been tensions between secularists and Islamists in terms of policymaking and attempts to make changes in policies. These tensions are explained in the following sections. I believe one of the causes of such tensions is the headscarf ban policy introduced by the secularists to the detriment of female students who wear headscarves and are associated with Islamists.

How has religion played itself out in politics when there have been tensions between secularists and Islamists? In the following section I discuss the role of Islam in Turkish politics.

Islam in Turkish Politics

During the Şeriat[3] rule of the Ottoman Empire, Islam played a central role in the governance of the Empire. The Sultan (King) of the Empire simultaneously represented the caliphate of Islam. Religious educators and leaders such as preachers and judges were part of the state elite and enjoyed extensive influence and power (Sunar & Toprak, 2004).

The establishment of the Turkish Republic in 1923, the abolition of the caliphate, and the process of secularizing and modernizing the country pushed Islam from the center to the periphery. The clergy and religious leaders lost their status (Sunar & Toprak, 2004), and Islam was marginalized from the center during the leadership of the early secularists. Even though central Islam lost its power in politics, "peripheral Islam" (Sunar & Toprak, 2004, p. 161) flourished in the rural areas of Turkey. In the late 1940s, when there was a shift from the mono-party to the multiparty electoral system, peripheral Islam was moved toward the center by two competing political parties—the newly formed Democrat Party (DP) and the old guardian of republican values and principles and reforms of

Atatürk, the Republican People's Party (CHP). Both these parties used Islam as a means of attracting voters in rural areas. "As a consequence of party politics what emerged was a period of liberalization—a period of decompression of Islam in which for the first time in republican history, peripheral 'folk Islam' became a participant in Turkish politics" (Sunar & Toprak, 2004, p. 161).

The decade between 1950 and 1960 is considered a period of revival for Islam in Turkey (Sunar & Toprak, 2004; White, 2002). Unlike the early secularists, who excluded the religious masses, the leaders of the DP adopted a populist approach. They used Islam as an instrument to gain the hearts and votes of the masses (Sunar & Toprak, 2004). The DP attempted to "reinstate religion as civic ethics to fill in the ethical void created, especially among those born under the Republic, by the erosion of religious beliefs" (Sunar & Toprak, 2004, p. 162). In addition, party leaders formulated policies to train religious leaders to push Islam to the center. Religious education was reestablished in primary schools. Religious schools called İmam Hatip high schools and departments of theology were opened for the purpose of training preachers, *imams,* and other religious leaders. *Ezan* (the call to prayer) began to be recited in Arabic (Sunar & Toprak, 2004). These activities followed the revitalization of *tarikats*[4] and the establishment of unpaid service groups to teach religion to the masses and to publish religious materials. All of these activities were curtailed by the military coup of 1960, which led to a revision of the Constitution.

In the 1970s, a newly formed party, the National Salvation Party (MSP), placed itself on the radical right and joined the government as a coalition party on a couple of occasions (Sunar & Toprak, 2004). Besides the MSP, there was another party called the National Action Party (MNP). The 1970s were also a time for Islamists at the periphery to gain power. For Islamists to move toward the center and move up socially and politically, the MSP systematically organized and networked Islamists to make their voices heard. The party used Islam as an ideology and advocated a more religion-oriented lifestyle. Its activities were interrupted by the 1980 military coup (Sunar & Toprak, 2004).

During the 1980s and 1990s, Islam continued to take its place in politics through the Welfare Party (RP) and Virtue Party (FP), parties with political roots in Islam (White, 2002). The RP participated in coalition governments and became a means for Islamists to grow and flourish in the country. A community of Islamist businessmen and "young professionals who consciously situated their economic and political activities within a Muslim identity and Islamic principles [was established]" (White, 2002, p. 115). The Islamist movement was strengthened when a group of Islamist elites emerged and contributed generously to the RP, funded Islamist scholars and students, donated to charity, and built schools and residence halls

(Sunar & Toprak, 2004). Islam reached its peak in Turkish politics (and in society) in 2002, when, for the first time in Turkish history, a political party rooted in Islam, AKP, [some of whose members had also been members of the Virtue Party which was banned in 2001] (White, 2002), won the elections and formed the government on its own without a coalition.

In addition to religion and identity, the role of women in society and socioeconomic status are two other factors closely associated with the headscarf ban policy in Turkish higher education. These issues are discussed in the following pages.[5]

Gender and Class

Gender. Through the manner in which they behave and dress in society, women have always represented either a secular or a religious lifestyle in Turkey. The status and appearance of women have symbolized the historical transformation in the country, that is, the abolishment of religious lifestyle and the introduction of modernity (Aksoy, 2005; Arat, 2005; Göle, 1997). When secularism was introduced in the newly founded Republic of Turkey, women began to enjoy equal status with men in both public and private life and gained several judiciary rights such as full suffrage in society (Aksoy, 2005; Göle, 1997). On the path to modernization, they played key roles as students, businesswomen, and civil servants. Photographs of women unveiled and in modern clothes, socializing with men in restaurants or bars, conveyed the new secular and modern lifestyle in Turkey (Göle, 1997). Women also represented the reintroduction of religious activities in Turkey through their headcovering and conservative style of dressing in the 1980s (Göle, 1997).

The Islamist woman and the issue of haircovering: After the foundation of the Turkish Republic in 1923 and until the end of the 1970s, a "religious" Turkish woman was generally defined as an uneducated women coming from the lower or lower-middle class with a conservative style of dressing and lifestyle. Her Islamic identity was formed by her religion, which she followed traditionally (Göle, 1996). Usually a housewife, she obeyed her husband and/or father and wore a headscarf that was loosely tied under her chin or at her neck with the exposure of some of her hair. When the feminist discourse gained momentum and Islam became re-visible in Turkish society in the early 1980s, the "religious" woman moved into the public sphere, participating in grassroots and political movements in which political Islam was at the center. She attended school, worked, and became more active and assertive in society (Arat, 2005; Göle, 1996). She rejected the traditional Islamic female identity, introduced herself as an "Islamist," and argued that she was the new female face, who sought change and reforms in the religious community. As opposed to the traditional "religious" woman, this new female face of Islamists became engaged with Islamic teachings and argued "to know the 'true' Islam" (Göle, 1996, p. 4). To show that she rejected the model her elders represented, she made a change in the most visible aspect of her self-presentation: the headscarf (Arat, 2005; Göle, 1996). She used a new style of headcovering, framing the head with the headscarf tightly covering the neck and/or shoulder. It was not possible to see even one loose strand of hair under this scarf, as opposed to the traditional headscarf, which allowed some hair to be on display. This new type of headcovering was labeled the *türban* by the Turkish media. The word *türban*, "originally from Turkish *tul(i)bend* and Persian *dulband*, refers to a headdress of Muslim origin, consisting of a long linen, cotton, or silk scarf. In modern Turkish, however, it is employed as a French word, one denoting a fashion of headdress, itself adopted from Ottoman Turkish" (Göle, 1996, p. 6). This new veiling style deepened the polarization that already existed between the secularist and Islamist communities because of the meaning each group attached to the *türban*. On the one hand, Islamist women claimed that their use of the *türban* was the accurate way of following the tenets of Islam and symbolized reform and modernity in their lifestyles (Göle, 1996). On the other hand, secularists found this *türban*-wearing movement a threat to the secular nature of the country and claimed that this new outfit, originally uncommon among Turks, was similar to headcovering in other Muslim countries (most of which are governed by Şeriat and/or are ruled by a king or dictator) and hence constituted a political statement. In other words, according to secularists, these Islamist women "politicized religion as an assertion of their collective identity against modernity [and secularism]" (Göle, 1996, p. 4), and *türban* wearing was "a political statement of women, an active reappropriation on their behalf of Islamic religiosity and way of life rather than ... reproduction [of veiling] by established traditions" (Göle, 1996, p. 4).

According to a piece of research conducted by Tarhan Erdem in 2007, the percentage of Turkish women who covered their hair outside the home was 69.4 percent. The majority of these covered women reported that they veiled in a traditional way, tying the headscarf under the chin or behind the head. Of the respondents participating in the research, 16.3 percent reported that they wore the *türban*, covering the hair, neck, and/or shoulders, which was a sharp increase since 2003, when another piece of research by Tarhan Erdem had found that 3.5 percent of the research participants used the *türban* (Türbanin hızlı yukselisi, 2007). This finding contradicted the research results of Binnaz Toprak and Ali Çarkoğlu, who conducted two pieces of research in 1999 and 2006 consecutively and concluded a decrease in the use of *türban* from 15.7 percent to 11.4 percent ("Türban" tartışmaları ve bilimsel araştırmalar, 2007). Although there were differences in the research findings, it was still possible to conclude that more than 10 percent of those who covered their hair used the *türban* in Turkey.

Whether secularists or Islamists, Hooglund (1996) explained, most Turkish men and women, having different values and attitudes, tended to socialize within their own gender group. While some modern urban families may encourage the socialization of men and women, such a practice would be unacceptable among traditional families. Although gender relations may be a complex area, social class is also a defining factor for the structure of a society.

Social class. The structure of social classes in Turkey has evolved over the years under the social, economic, and ideological conditions of the country. The shift from rural areas and agrarian society to urbanization and industrialization has also contributed to the evolution of the social structure. The degree of power and skill and the level of education and income are among the indicators of the social classes in Turkey. (See Kongar [1999] and Mardin [1983] for information about Turkish social class.) Even though there are different criteria to stratify the society in Turkey, for the purposes of this book, I will highlight that values, including religion, create subcategories within the social structure in the country.

Traditional families have a different outlook on life than those with a more modern outlook (Nauck & Klaus, 2005). Since modernization is associated with secularism and traditionalism with Islamism, this creates a conflict between secular modernists and Islamists and between feminists and Islamist women because of differing worldviews and belief systems (Göle, 1997; Marshall, 2005). The perception that women can represent either the introduction of secularism or the reintroduction of religiosity and socioeconomic class differences with regard to modern and traditional values is an important factor in the decision-making process and in the implementation of the headscarf ban policy in Turkish higher education.

In addition to conflicts between Islamists and secularists in the decision-making arena and the role of gender and class in the realm of the headscarf ban policy, it is also important to understand Turkey's democratic nature and the role of democracy with regard to the headscarf ban policy.

Democracy in Turkey

After the fall of the Ottoman Empire, a republican system was established in 1923, which consisted of a secular nation-state with a constitutional parliamentary system. The first republican regime was defined as "state-dominant mono-party authoritarianism" (Sunar & Sayarı, 2004, p. 70). Over the years, various parties took their place in politics. The problem is that the transition from a mono-party to a multiparty system was guided from the top by the ruling secular elite. Although the shift to liberalization and democracy determined from above was smooth at the beginning, over the years, the centralized state structure, "the traditional and weakly pene-trated nature of society" (Sunar & Sayarı, 2004, p. 73), and economic and political problems made the development of democracy problematic for the country (Sunar & Sayarı, 2004). "Competitive parliamentary democ-racy" (Sunar & Sayarı, 2004, p. 66) was cut off several times by the direct or indirect participation of the Turkish military in politics. Nevertheless, despite military coups, Turkey has been successful in keeping multiparty and parliamentary democracy as the norm and in founding a variety of organizations associated with democracy (Öniş, 2006). On the other hand, according to Dagi (2004), this type of democracy—that is, democracy from above—has resulted in the suppression of Islamists and other peripheral forces in the country.

A change began when the AKP won the 2002 elections and formed a single-party government. Furthermore, the government was eager to take steps toward joining the European Union. For Turkey to conform to European Union policies, there have been numerous developments that extended freedom of speech and human rights and freedoms. There has also been further commitment to issues related to social justice and transnationalism (Öniş, 2006).

One might argue that recent democratic developments enabling Turkey to become a member of the European Union have softened, to some degree, the conflict between secularists and Islamists (Öniş, 2006). However, the higher education headscarf ban policy is still in place and continues to cause tensions between these two groups. The policy also creates tensions among secularism, religion, and democracy in the sense that Islamists perceive it as a restriction of their religious freedom and thus a violation of the democratic nature of the system.

All in all, issues of secularism, religion, class, identity, and democracy in Turkey are the main background drivers of the controversial headscarf ban policy that has caused fervent debates in numerous milieus since its imple-mentation in the country. Having presented the pertinent background information, in the following discussion, I explore the characteristics of Turkish higher education since the foundation of the country in 1923.

Turkish Higher Education

Two of the primary aims of higher education in Turkey are to educate students so that they will be loyal to Atatürk and preserve his reforms and principles and to enable students to understand the country's cultural values and develop a sense of national unity (T. C. Yükseköğretim Kurulu, n.d. a). "Equality" is considered one of the core values of Turkish higher education (T. C. Yükseköğretim Kurulu, n.d. b). In addition, Turks believe higher education is a vehicle to a better life and career, allowing one to climb at least one step upward on the social class ladder (Hooglund, 1996). These aims are to be accomplished through the delivery of the Turkish college curriculum.

The undergraduate program usually takes four years (full time) to complete. There are no liberal arts or general education requirements (except in one or two foundation universities), and few, if any, electives are offered. Certain courses are compulsory for all the curricula across institutions for a minimum of two semesters (T. C. Yükseköğretim Kurulu, n.d. b). These courses are the Turkish language, a foreign language course, and Atatürk's principles and the history of Turkish reforms, in which the concept of Turkish secularism is part of the syllabus. These courses were either added to the curriculum or started being offered differently from the way they had been taught in the past, as a result of secularists' demands after 1980.

Turkish higher education has many characteristics. However, within the context of this book, I shall only focus on features that are closely related to the headscarf ban policy. These features are the secularization of Turkish higher education, the Higher Education Council (HEC), higher education policymaking, and the higher education headscarf ban policy.

Modernization Policies

Secularism led to the creation of the modern education system in Turkey (Barrows, 1990; Berkes, 1998; Mızıkacı, 2006). Before the foundation of the Turkish Republic, there were both religious and secular schools. Religious education was abolished in 1924, and subsequently Turkey's educational system was unified and centralized. This was followed by various reforms that drastically affected the higher education sector in the country. With the closure of *medreses*[6] and the opening of secular postsecondary institutions, the teaching and learning of theology as a central component of college education came to an end. The theological curriculum was replaced with a secular curriculum that consisted of various subjects to educate Turkish citizens in different disciplines (Berkes, 1998). The teaching of Arabic and Persian was eliminated from primary and secondary schools. These languages became part of the curriculum of particular departments and came to be taught as foreign languages. With the launching of the Latin alphabet in 1928, higher education institutions started using it as their medium of written and oral delivery (Berkes, 1998). These modernization policies helped to establish secularism in primary and secondary schools and universities.

In the late 1940s, there was a public request for the reestablishment of religious education as part of the school curriculum (Hooglund, 1996). In the early 1950s, an optional course on religious education began; in 1982 it became compulsory for all primary and secondary schools. This decision raised some questions about the place of religion in higher education. The secular elite believed that the best way to teach Islam would be through religious leaders trained in universities controlled by the state. Thus, departments of divinity with their curricula central to religious teaching and learning were established in order to train future preachers and *imams* (Hooglund, 1996).

Until the 1980s, universities kept a strict secular nature without intruding in the private lives of students with certain exceptions that required autonomous actions of universities with relation to the use of headscarf and/or style of clothing as explained in a detailed way in the "The Higher Education Headscarf Ban Policy" section of this chapter, and religion was taught as a separate subject. The 1980s signaled a new era for the Turkish university, in which many changes were brought about. Two such changes were the centralization of the higher education system and the introduction of a new higher education law.

The Higher Education Council and Policymaking in the Turkish University

Turkish universities had academic and institutional autonomy due to the university law enacted in 1946 (Hooglund, 1996), and this autonomy essentially remained until the military coup in 1980. Sunar (2004) and Sunar and Sayarı (2004) explained that this coup was an attempt to stabilize the country, which was struggling both politically and economically. The coup resulted in a revised Constitution constructed in order to keep anti-secular groups on a tight leash. The new Constitution also aimed to depoliticize the society, which had a major effect in the arena of postsecondary education in Turkey. The secularists in power thought that university campuses were arenas for the cultivation of political ideologies not compatible with secularism, thereby jeopardizing the long-term security of the country (Hooglund, 1996). Thus, the government made provisions that would keep higher education institutions from becoming politicized, hence posing less of a threat to Turkish political stability. The higher education law in 1981 and new provisions in 1982 led to the establishment of the Higher Education Council (HEC), which regulates universities in Turkey

(T. C. Yükseköğretim Kurulu, n.d. c). Duties of the HEC include planning, coordinating, and supervising higher education. Public universities are largely controlled by the HEC, which also regulates foundation universities by special provisions. This situation has drastically affected the campus lives of administrators, faculty, and students.

The new higher education law banned all students and teachers from having ties to a political party. The curriculum was standardized (Hooglund, 1996). This means that in higher education institutions "where education is given in the same fields or branches of a discipline, the Council of Higher Education, upon the recommendations of the Inter-university Board, regulates the education, methods, scope, teaching duration, and the principles of evaluation within each academic year in order to establish a uniformity of expected standards and degrees granted as well as of rights and privileges" (T. C. Yükseköğretim Kurulu, n.d. d, p. 1).

The HEC is a state-controlled institution and consists of 24 members "appointed by the President of the Republic from among candidates who are nominated by the Council of Ministry, the Chief of the General Staff, and the Interuniversity Board in accordance with the numbers of posts to be filled" (Barrows, 1990, p. 15). The council consists mainly of members with secular roots (Altıntaş, 2002). The head of the council is selected and appointed by the President of Turkey for a period of four years (Barrows, 1990; Mızıkacı, 2006). The HEC is the institution responsible for centralizing the higher education system. Demirer and Özbudun (1999) explained that this institution intends to create one type of university, one type of faculty, and one type of student and to eradicate "the different" by generating homogeneous groups of university youth. The HEC has become an institution in conflict with many other institutions, and thus its reformation has been on the agenda of political parties (Altıntaş, 2002).

The HEC is the policymaking mechanism for the higher education system (Barrows, 1990; Mızıkacı, 2006). Since higher education policies are determined by small clusters of leading individuals who share similar worldviews (Edmondson, 2005), in the context of higher education, higher education policies are in the hands of the ruling elite in the HEC. The higher education headscarf ban policy, therefore, is a product of the HEC and dates back to the 1980s.

The Clash of Secularists and Islamists as a Result of Education Policies

Since the Islamists' rise in power, conflicts and tensions have arisen between Islamists and secularists with regard to education policies. With the AKP winning elections and an AKP parliamentarian becoming the head of the Ministry of Education, the clash between secularists and Islamists in the political arena has been extended to the context of higher education.

One major clash centers on İmam Hatip schools. These are state-controlled, Muslim, İmam-training schools. The military and the secular ruling elite think that these İmam Hatip schools produce radical Islamist students and threaten the secular nature of the country (Gorvett, 2004). In 1997, as a way of dealing with the threat, a new policy was adopted that included the classification of İmam Hatip schools as vocational high schools. If vocational school graduates choose to pursue a discipline/program that is different from what they studied and specialized in during high school, then points are deducted on the university entrance examination. In other words, as a result of the new policy, the exam points of İmam Hatip graduates get deducted in such a way that they may not have a chance of securing a place in higher education other than in their vocational training area from high school (Gorvett, 2004). This policy is intended to keep İmam Hatip graduates in religious studies fields, by making it difficult for them to study in other disciplines than their high school area of specialization—that is, the teaching of Islam. The clash between Islamists and secularists regarding this policy arose because there are few jobs in religious studies, and many female students attend these schools just to get an Islamic education, but women cannot become *imams* or preachers (Robinson-Fischer, n.d.). Islamists believe that this policy limits the career prospects of İmam Hatip graduates by restricting their access to only religious studies departments in universities. In addition, Islamists argue that İmam Hatip schools are no different from other high schools, in the sense that they follow a curriculum similar to that of high schools rather than vocational schools. The big difference seems to lie in their emphasis on religious subjects (*Turkey, education,* n.d.).

In 2004, the AKP initiated an education reform that would provide vocational school graduates, including those from İmam Hatip schools, an opportunity on the university entrance exam equal to that of their peers from other public or private high schools. This reform brought secularists and Islamists into conflict again. According to Dumanlı (2004), "university rectors reacted severely against the proposal that was aimed at making some amendments in the university entrance system. It was alleged that the government, trying to eliminate the obstacles against İmam Hatip schools, was pretending as if it was correcting the wrongs committed against other vocational high school students" (p. 1). Eventually, the bill was withdrawn.

In 2010, the issue reemerged under the leadership of the head of the HEC. The aim was to first eliminate the "point-deduction" policy for the vocational school graduates. When the Council of State objected to this elimination, the HEC proposed a reduction in the difference of the coefficient vocational and nonvocational school graduates' exam scores are multiplied by. The Council of State rejected the amount of the reduction and the HEC prepared another proposal, which was this time approved by the Council of State. The proposal suggested that if vocational school graduates choose to pursue a discipline/program that is different from what they studied and specialized in during high school, their points will be multiplied by 0.12, which decreased the previous disadvantage substantially (Kotan, 2010).

Another clash happened around the issue of Qur'an teaching schools. Secularists believed that there should be more foreign language teaching schools, rather than Qur'an teaching schools (*Kuran kursları icin anayasal tartışma*, 2005). Islamists wanted to have Qur'an schools teaching five days a week instead of three days. In addition, some Qur'an teaching schools had been established without state permission. Islamists tried to reduce the penalties for those caught running these schools; however, secularists objected to this (*Kuran kursları icin anayasal tartışma*, 2005).

One other ongoing clash between these two groups in the arena of higher education concerns the policy that bans the wearing of the headscarf.[7] This issue, central to this book, greatly diminishes access to university campuses by female students who cover their hair. This policy has caused further friction between Islamists and secularists in the arena of postsecondary education. The higher education headscarf ban policy is described in detail in the following section.

The Higher Education Headscarf Ban Policy

Background. During the 1970s, there were two main political parties in Turkey: the Republican People's Party (CHP) and the Justice Party (AP) (Sunar & Sayarı, 2004). On opposite sides of the political spectrum, the AP leaned more toward the right of the center, whereas the CHP leaned to the left of the center. In addition to these parties, there were other less powerful parties with various political orientations. One of them was the National Salvation Party (MSP), which placed itself toward the radical right on the political right-left spectrum (Sunar & Sayarı, 2004).

These parties and their precedents failed to ensure economic, social, and political stability in the country. High rates of unemployment, uncontrollable inflation, and recurrent economic crises radicalized large portions of the lower and middle classes. This situation resulted in the emergence of several extremist groups that were communist oriented (Sunar & Sayarı, 2004).

As a result of the emergence of these communist-oriented groups, there was a political rehabilitation of Islam as right-wing secular party leaders hoped to use Islam as a shield against their left-wing political rivals and also against the rise of communism. Turkey experienced a growth in religious activities, including the building of new mosques, the opening of religious schools, and the emergence of an Islamic press (Hooglund, 1996). This growth began a movement toward more private religious activities in different platforms, and Islam gained power and became visible in the social, economic, and political contexts of Turkey. This Islamist movement reflected itself in the context of higher education in the following way.

In the early 1980s, with the rise of the new Islamists explained earlier, some female university students began wearing veils and long coats either to demonstrate their loyalty to Islam or to make a political statement. In addition, the students veiled with the *türban,* which, as mentioned previously, tightly framed the head with the headscarf covering the neck and sometimes the shoulders too. The use of the *türban* was seen as a sign of a political ideology (Hooglund, 1996), and in response, the HEC forbade the wearing of the headscarf in postsecondary institutions (Hooglund, 1996).

Emerging issues. The headscarf becoming an issue on campuses dates back to 1967 when an unveiled student in a public university in Ankara decided to veil and thus with the decision of the university disciplinary committee ended up being expelled from the university because of her headscarf. Later on, in the 1970s, there were some covered students on campuses, and it is possible to see that universities tried to take some actions against their dress style. All these actions, however, were individual actions of the universities concerned; they were operating autonomously without following any policy that bound higher education (Yağcı, 2008).

This changed after the introduction of the headscarf ban policy by the HEC in the 1980s. In 1982, the HEC issued a dress code that asked its administrators, faculty, and students to wear modest clothes. The policy included a prohibition on covering one's hair in classes, explaining that the traditional and religious use of the headscarf had turned into a political and ideological tool as a result of *türban* wearing, an action that was against the secular nature of the country. The policy allowed the covering of the hair only when female Muslim students took classes in Qur'an studies (Hatiboğlu, 2000).

Numerous protests were conducted against this policy, so to improve the political atmosphere, the HEC revised the policy on May 10, 1984. The language of the revised policy was vague. It said that female students were required to uncover their hair but that they could use the headscarf in a modern *türban* way. This revised version of the policy led to many hot debates in the country. In spite of this revision, a medical student from Ege University was suspended for a month for attending classes with her headscarf. (Aksoy, 2005).

On December 24,1986, the HEC cancelled its 1984 decision and forbade the use of the *türban* in higher education institutions. Then in 1988, the HEC allowed the use of türban by adding an item to the "Student Rules and Regulations" which read as "The hair and the neck can be covered by the headscarf or türban for religious reasons". This item was cancelled by both the Council of State and the Constitutional Court in 1989. (Aksoy, 2005). In 1990, an item was added to the HEC Law which read that the style of dress was free as long as it complied with the laws currently in practice (*Yükseköğretim Kanunu*, n.d.). Here the reference to the law currently in practice is the decision of Constitutional Court against the use of türban in higher education institutions in 1989 (Aksoy, 2005). The debates and discussions around the issue of the headscarf ban continued.

On February 28, 1997, the military presented a memorandum to the government that resulted in the resignation of the government. In the extant literature, this intervention is referred to as a postmodern coup (Bacık & Aras, 2002; Dagi, 2004). This memorandum included a new program for the government to follow to protect the secular nature of the country. This program contained rules and regulations in several contexts, including education, with relation to several issues. One of these issues was the dress code (Bacık & Aras, 2002). After this, the HEC started to implement the headscarf ban policy more intensely and strictly than ever.

To sum up, as can be seen from the historical development of the policy, there are several arguments put forward by the secularists in favor of the existence of the headscarf ban policy. The ruling elite in the past argued that the headscarf ban policy entered the higher education arena with the intention of depoliticizing Turkish universities and furthering the stability of youths and the country (Hooglund, 1996). Another reason was to preserve the secular and modern nature of university campuses. Students were expected to appear modern, in line with the modern and secular nature of the country. The headscarf did not fit in with this appearance. Whatever the pro-ban arguments are, the outcomes of the policy in the context of higher education have been troublesome. First, because public and foundation universities are regulated in different ways, there have been discrepancies in how the ban is implemented in the public and foundation sectors. Foundation universities, regulated by special provisions, exercise the headscarf ban in various ways, such as restricting the use of headscarves in closed areas like classrooms or laboratories (Labi, 2006). On the other hand, public universities are under stricter control by the HEC, which makes them follow the headscarf ban policy more closely. This means that students who cover their hair are not allowed on campus at all (Labi, 2006). Second, the policy seems to be in conflict with the core value of equality and equity (including equal access to the higher education system).

In February 2008, in order to be responsive to the desires of the students who wanted to go to university in a veiled way, the ruling AKP, with the support of the opposition Nationalist Action Party (MHP), proposed some specific amendments in the Constitution that would eventually end the headscarf ban policy on campuses (Human Rights Watch, 2008). The parliament accepted these proposed changes, which were related to the issues of equality and the right to education, but would also automatically end the ban in the post-secondary education system. However, the opposition People Republic's Party (CHP) applied to the Constitutional Court to strike down these amendments and the Constitutional Court regarded the decision of the parliament as a violation of the principle of secularism enshrined in the Constitution and in June 2008 overruled these constitutional amendments proposed by the AKP . Hence, the headscarf ban policy remained in place (Human Rights Watch, 2008), and it still continues to be an issue of battle in the political and social arenas.

The headscarf ban policy has created tensions within the educational and political context of Turkey (Human Rights Watch, 2004). On the one hand, policymakers claim that the scarf is a symbol of extreme political Islam that threatens Turkey's secular nature and students who cover their hair are trying to make a political statement. On the other hand, female students with veils claim that they wear the scarf because of their religious beliefs. Students who refuse to comply with the ban report that because their access to higher education has been denied, their hopes for a future career have been terminated. Those who can afford it go abroad to study, but not all students have this option. What about students who choose to comply with the policy? How does the policy affect students who uncover their hair, the part-time unveilers, both on campus and in their private lives? What kinds of educational experiences do they go through on campuses? How does the act of uncovering affect their educational progress and identity as Turkish Muslim women? The study was undertaken to shed light on these questions.

All in all, this chapter has presented the political and social context of Turkey. It has shown that the macro-level drivers of the higher education headscarf ban policy are Turkish secularism, religion, democracy, gender, class, and identity. These drivers are sometimes in tension with one another, and one manifestation of these tensions is the headscarf ban policy in higher education.

This chapter also explored Turkish higher education and the ways in which some of its features are closely associated with the policy under study. These features are the secularization of the higher education system, the changes that occurred after 1980, the establishment of the HEC, and policymaking in the Turkish university. These features are the micro-level drivers of the headscarf ban on campuses. This section concluded with a discussion of the historical background of the headscarf ban and a discussion of emerging issues of the policy in the context of higher education.

Having discussed the background of the headscarf ban and the findings of some studies regarding its implementation and outcomes, I shall now present the conceptual framework I used to examine the educational and cultural experiences of part-time unveilers.

Conceptual Framework of the Study

To explore the educational and cultural experiences of part-time unveilers, I used variations and components of the following:

1. The policy-analysis framework (Downey, 1988).
2. The campus climate for diversity framework (Hurtado et al., 1999).
3. The student-involvement theory for higher education (Astin, 1984).
4. The model of multiple dimensions of identity (Jones & McEwen, 2000).

These frameworks were designed specifically for use in educational environments in the United States. Considering cultural differences, some parts of these frameworks may be inappropriate for the Turkish context. For the study I only chose the factors that were general and broad, because they were most relevant to Turkish-Islamic students' development. In addition, I conducted a pilot study in which I tested the relevance of the chosen components of the frameworks. Through the pilot study I was able to confirm the relevance of the components I had selected.

Downey (1988) developed his policy-analysis framework to analyze policies in the context of education. This is a comprehensive model that includes all the stages of policy-analysis, beginning with the initiation and continuing through the termination stage of a policy. To understand how part-time unveilers understood the policy, I employed one stage of Downey's framework: interpretation.

I used the interpretation stage to explore how part-time unveilers perceived the headscarf ban policy. The question I used to elicit their perceptions was: "What does the policy mean?" Here my intention was to illuminate understandings of part-time unveilers regarding what the headscarf ban policy meant to them. This component of the framework led me to formulate the following research question: How do part-time unveilers understand and decide to comply with the policy?

Hurtado et al. (1999) developed a framework to examine different elements of the campus climate that might affect the educational experiences of diverse students. In addition, Astin (1984) proposed a student-involvement theory based on the premise that the student who spends more time studying, devotes more time to campus activities, and interacts frequently with faculty and other peers is more intensely involved than other students, leading to more positive educational experiences and success. In my study, I was interested in the opportunities and challenges of part-time unveilers. Using selected parts of the frameworks of Hurtado et al. and Astin, I probed the following components as I explored the opportunities and challenges of part-time unveilers as a result of unveiling: (a) faculty-student interaction, (b) administrator-student interaction, (c) involvement in extracurricular activities, (d) motivation for studying, (e) activities on campus, (f) interaction with peers, (g) discrimination/prejudice against part-time unveilers in classrooms and/or on campus, and (h) overall success during undergraduate studies.

These probes guided me as I sought answers to the following research questions: What opportunities does unveiling bring to part-time unveilers on campus? What challenges are part-time unveilers faced with on campus and in their lives as a result of unveiling? How do part-time unveilers deal with these challenges? How do these challenges affect part-time unveilers' educational progress?

In studying the educational experiences of part-time unveilers, I was sensitive to the fact that the research and theory on which I was relying was developed in the United States, a different cultural context from Turkey.

Jones and McEwen (2000) proposed a conceptual model of multiple dimensions of identity. They explained that each individual has plural identities, such as class, religion, and race, with personal identity at the core. I used particular parts of Jones and McEwen's model to explore how complying with the headscarf ban affected the sense of identity of part-time unveilers: (a) citizenship identity as Turkish citizens, (b) religious identity as Muslims, and (c) gender identity as females. The responses to these dimensions of identity helped me address the following research question: How does complying with the policy affect part-time unveilers' sense of identity?

3

Part-Time Unveilers: Background Information and Selected Case Narratives

To help readers make better sense of the ways in which the higher education headscarf ban policy impacted the educational and cultural experiences of the part-time unveilers, I first want to familiarize readers with the identities, lives, and educational backgrounds of the part-time unveilers. I also make specific reference to the implementation of the policy. In the first part of the chapter, I give an overview portrait of the part-time unveilers to provide background information about who these women were. I explore their personality traits as young university students; discuss the kind of citizenship, religious, and gender identities they had as covered women; and pinpoint what higher education meant for them and their future careers by discussing their reasons for attending university and choosing the academic departments they were studying in at the university. In the second part of the chapter, I highlight the perceptions of the part-time unveilers about the ways in which the higher education headscarf ban policy was implemented in their institutions. I conclude the chapter with case narratives of five part-time unveilers to highlight the variety of life experiences among them.

Overview Portrait of the Part-Time Unveilers

Who were the Part-Time Unveilers?

I am a common type of student. Part-time unveilers appeared very similar to other students attending university. Many of them had a positive outlook on life and perceived themselves as hardworking, smart, and open to improvement. Suzan explained that she was clever and wanted to broaden her perspective:

> I am a common type of student. . . . I am a hardworking and clever person. I am very fragile too. I always feel sorry for people who are in need. I appreciate the good things people do for me. I cannot stand unfairness. I would like to improve myself in my religion and other subjects such as poetry and literature. I do not like to be passive. I prefer to show and prove myself. I want to become an important person in the future. There are many times when I think I am not good enough and make efforts to further improve myself.

Several part-time unveilers enjoyed engaging in social activities and used terms such as extrovert, outgoing, and sociable to describe themselves. They seemed to be like other energetic, vibrant young college students. Alara, for example, was a woman who liked to meet people and socialize with friends as often as possible:

> I am a woman who engages in dialogue with people quickly. I would talk to anybody without any problems. I always tell the truth and I do not hold grudges. I am an active person who likes to socialize. . . . I have good relations with my friends. They are important to me. I go to movies or dinner with them. I do not sit at home very often. I visit and explore new places with my friends from high school.

Similar to other undergraduates in their 20s on a university campus, the part-time unveilers presented themselves as having a wide array of positive and negative personality traits such as emotional, optimistic, stubborn, ambitious, depressed, anxious, relaxed, stress-free, responsible, self-sacrificing, and self-sufficient. Sevgi, for example, considered herself relaxed and happy: "I am somebody who likes her freedom with the spirit of a child. I am relaxed, happy, and satisfied. I usually make fun of life. I do not care about the mistakes of others. I smile and forget things that are done to me easily." On the other hand, Alara thought she was nervous and quick-tempered: "I am somebody who has responsibilities to Allah [God] and humanity. I am sometimes anxious and nervous. I am quick-tempered. Nobody knows how I am going to react. I am a little unbalanced. But I am self-sacrificing. But once I dislike someone, I dislike that person for the rest of my life." In addition, like some introvert undergraduate youths, there were a few part-time unveilers who had more reserved and quiet personalities, like Dilara. She explained: "I am a quiet and reserved person. I only become talkative and cheerful when I am with close friends."

All in all, the part-time unveilers who participated in the study appeared to be very similar to other young women who attend university. They seemed to be full of life and energy with lots of potential and hope for the future.

I am happy to be and be born a Turk. All part-time unveilers associated their citizenship identity with being a Turk. The majority of them closely related their Turkishness to their history and ancestors, which they took pride in. They also thought that this history of Turkey brought with it a rich culture. Selma felt great about being a Turk because of the accumulated history behind the Turkish identity, and Sevgi was happy to be Turkish with strong roots and a rich history and culture: "My Turkish identity is intertwined with our history. Turkishness means having roots. I am happy to be and be born a Turk. I am happy to be a Turk when I compare myself to other nationalities. We have a rich history and culture. I love my country, my city, and my home and would never want to live anywhere else."

In addition to the background and culture, half of the part-time unveilers also viewed Islam as an integral part of their Turkishness. Nurten believed that Islam had an important role in her Turkish identity: "Islam is a crucial part of the Turkishness. Social life is hand in hand with Turkishness and Muslimness in Turkey. There is a difference between a Muslim Arab and a Muslim Turk. Turks are polite and respectful people. I am happy to be Turkish."

Several part-time unveilers explained that they considered themselves to be hospitable and honest people and that these facets were a key part of their Turkish identity. They were attached to their families, customs, and traditions. They believed in the importance of their flag, of their national anthem, and of sacrificing themselves to save their country. Buket explained this as follows: "I love my Turkishness. I love my country. I love my national anthem and flag. I can do everything and anything for my country. I want to serve my country and my people. I love speaking Turkish and am happy living with people who speak the same language."

In sum, part-time unveilers seemed to predominantly associate their Turkish identity with their ancestors who lived in this land and left a legacy of rich cultural and religious traditions. In addition, they perceived the love of the Turkish flag and national anthem as another underlying characteristic of their Turkishness.

I am trying to be a good Muslim. All part-time unveilers associated their religious identity with Islam. For them, their Muslimness was closely related to following the tenets of Islam in life. Some perceived themselves as quite religious. Leyla thought she was fairly religious: "I am trying to live Islam as much as possible. I consider myself quite religious. . . . I love learning about Islam. I really like it." On the other hand, 19 part-time unveilers considered themselves as "modern" Muslims who lived in the modern world and did not consider themselves as religious as Muslims who devoted their lives to Islam. These modern Muslims believed that they were also well-educated, conscious, and good Muslims. Nurten distinguished herself from her parents as a conscious and knowledgeable Muslim: "I am a conscious Muslim who reads a lot about Islam. I read the interpretation and translation of the Qur'an. I also read many religious books. My parents are religious, but they have not read about Islam as much as I have. I am a more knowledgeable and conscious Muslim."

As part of their Muslim identity, part-time unveilers explained the different ways in which they followed their religion. Almost all of them reported to read and/or listen to the Qur'an, pray as many times as possible, fast during Ramadan, wear a headscarf, and lead a life of good conduct. They believed that in addition to the precepts of Islam, what the Qur'an wanted them to do was to have good morals and ethics. Thus, these part-time unveilers explained that they tried to respect family, help others, work hard, and avoid lying, stealing, and treating others badly; Sevim explored her understanding of Muslimness and the efforts she made to be a good Muslim:

> My religious identity is my Muslimness. I am trying to be a good Muslim. I am not an extreme Muslim. I have never been a radical. I am trying to find the middle way. I pray. I fast. I wear a headscarf. I am trying to be honest and helpful. I am trying to maintain good relationships with people. . . . I am trying not to talk behind people's back. I have a good relationship with my family. We try to have quality time together. This life is a test. I am trying to pass this test in the best possible way.

As part of their religious identity, all these women covered their hair in their private lives. Part-time unveilers discussed two specific reasons as to why they chose to wear a headscarf. Fourteen of them explained that they used the veil in order to obey the Qur'an and follow the tenets of Islam. (I refer to this form of veiling in the Tables A.V and B.IV as "voluntary"). Gamze explained that she decided to cover her hair to obey some of the Surahs, chapters of the Qur'an:

> Allah has commanded the use of the headscarf in the Qur'an. My faith in Allah motivates me to obey Allah's message and that is why I follow what Allah has commanded in the Qur'an. I cover my hair according to the Surah an-Nur verse 31 and Surah al-Ahzab verse 59. [See Appendix D for a translation of Surah an-Nur verse 31 and Surah al-Ahzab verse 59.] I believe in Islam. If this is not like this, then I am going to pay for it after I die. I cover my hair because of my belief system.

Fourteen women reported that they started to cover their hair first as a result of external circumstances such as the influence of family, friends, or school. Then they read about Islam and once they understood covering the hair was a wish of Allah, they continued wearing the headscarf. Sevgi, for example, started to cover her hair as a result of the influence of her parents. However, later she continued covering it as a result of religious readings she had done:

> My parents told me that I needed to cover my hair after I reached puberty. They explained to me the importance of the headcovering for them and for our religion. I was influenced by them and started to cover my hair. But then the importance of the headscarf was also taught at the Qur'an course. Then I started reading about Islam when I was attending the İmam Hatip school. I learned about the life of the wife of our Prophet. After starting to cover my hair as a result of parental influence, I am now covering my hair understanding properly—as a result of my religious readings and research— the reasons why I have to cover.

In sum, part-time unveilers seemed to associate their religious identity with Muslimness. Muslimness meant following the tenets of Islam in varying degrees from praying and fasting to helping the poor and needy. Part-time unveilers all covered their hair to signal their Muslim identity for religious, social, or family-related reasons.

My female identity is that I will work, become successful, and be economically independent. The gender identity of the part-time unveilers included femaleness, the lifestyle they led as women, their role as daughters in the family, and the ways in which they interacted (or did not) with males.

Part-time unveilers perceived their gender identity as females who had an important role in society. They reported that in some parts of Turkey, especially in rural, conservative, and uneducated areas, women, perceived as born to serve men, were of secondary importance and did not need to receive education or have a job. Being aware of these challenges and sometimes facing some of them in their own families, they argued that their identity as women was very different from images of traditional Turkish girls. They perceived themselves as future women and mothers who were modern, educated, and economically independent, helping society shape future generations. They believed in the importance of gender equality and wanted men and women to walk hand in hand in different arenas of society, including the work environment. Semra explained that she believed that, as a woman, she had various crucial roles to play:

> I am a little bit of a feminist I guess. I know that in some parts of our country, women are not seen as valuable. But my female identity is as such that I will work, become successful, and be economically independent. This way I will contribute to the economy. I am strong. I have to prove myself and

I will. Another important mission of mine is motherhood. I have to be sensitive and sensible while raising my children. I also want a marriage that is equal. I do not want male dominance. There are many roles and duties of women in society.

As daughters of their families, 24 part-time unveilers had very close relationships with their parents, whereas six were in constant conflict with their families. Yeliz explained her happy family life: "I have a great relationship with my parents. I am so grateful for that. I still sit on my father's lap. I adore him and I know that he adores me. We always chat together as a family. We also pray together in the morning and evening." On the other hand, Reyhan had some problems with her parents: "I am in conflict with my parents at all times. This is mainly because of religion. They want me to behave in the way they want. They did not want me to quit because of the ban. They do not want me to follow Islam strictly. I did not happen to be the daughter they wanted me to be."

In terms of social life, part-time unveilers led lives that excluded drinking alcohol and going to bars or discos since drinking alcohol and being in places where alcohol was served were prohibited according to their understanding of Islam. The majority of these women had active social lives without going to bars or discos and consuming alcohol. Some of the various activities of 27 part-time unveilers with active social lives included going out with their friends; watching movies; going to restaurants, coffee shops, the theater; playing backgammon, smoking, doing sports, attending concerts, joining clubs, listening to music, and watching TV with their family members. Nurten explained that she had a busy and satisfying social life with a diverse group of friends:

> I am part of the social life. . . . I have friends from high school and university. We go to the movies, do sports, go to the theater and cafes. We smoke. We play cards and backgammon. I am also a member of an Islamist club. This club intends to help people who are in need. I do not go to bars or discos. I do not drink alcohol. I have friends who drink. Sometimes they drink heavily and they call me to help them. In such instances I go to pick them up and help them. I also have friends who wear mini skirts, are socialists, and are atheists. We picnic together. We go to pop concerts all together.

On the other hand, three women had more limited activities compared with others. Buket, for example, had a conservative lifestyle due to her religious preferences:

> I do not have a TV in the house where I am staying. It is a principle of our [Islamist] house. There are a lot of terrible programs on TV that are not appropriate for us to watch. The same thing is also true for movies. I do not

go to movies either. I usually listen to the radio and read newspapers. I listen to music. I go to the theater. I do not have a very active social life.

Part-time unveilers had differing degrees of relationships with men. Twenty-four part-time unveilers had male friends, close or distant; they talked to them or socialized together within certain limits. A couple of them had boyfriends as well: "I have male and female friends. I am not very close to my male friends though. And I have a boyfriend" (Suzan). "I have great male friends. They understand me. We go to eat or watch movies together" (Semra).

Six part-time unveilers were stricter in their relationship with men due to religious reasons. They rarely talked to them and did not socialize or shake hands with them: "I do not have male friends. There were two guys who were in love with me, but I did not talk to them. I do not think there is such a thing as a male friend. My honor can be hurt if they try to take advantage of me. So I prefer not to talk to them" (Sevda). "I do not shake hands with men. I only salute them. Sometimes I talk to them, but just briefly" (Buket).

All in all, part-time unveilers seemed to be regular young women who were in their 20s, with a range of personalities, identities, and lifestyles. They appeared to be dynamic, active young women like other female undergraduate students attending higher education institutions. Their personality traits ranged from free-spirited and stress-free to highly strung and depressed. Their citizenship identity was mainly associated with Turkish history, dating back to the ancestors and its rich culture and traditions. Their Muslim identity seemed to have a dominant role in the way they lived their religion, led their lives, and had interactions with men. They were engaged in numerous social activities, to varying degrees, such as going to movies or dinner with friends. Many of them considered themselves to be conscientious and well-educated modern Muslims who tried to reconcile their Muslimness with the contemporary Turkish society. As with any other young person, they sometimes got on well with their parents and sometimes were in conflict with them. These part-time unveilers believed that they had an important role to play in society, valued their female identity, and considered themselves to be women who would shape future generations in Turkey.

What Was the Meaning of Higher Education for Part-Time Unveilers? Why Did They Choose the Discipline They Were Studying?

Here I highlight perceptions of part-time unveilers vis-à-vis their rationale for attending university and choosing the discipline they were studying.

I provide an overview of what higher education meant for them in general. In addition, I pinpoint some background information about the choices part-time unveilers made regarding the discipline they were studying due to the educational, social, and political contexts of Turkey.

Understanding the perceptions of the part-time unveilers about the role of higher education in Turkey and the reasons for their choices of academic disciplines was important for several reasons. First, it showed the benefits and importance of higher education for the future of the part-time unveilers. Second, it highlighted the ways in which they wanted to establish themselves as a new generation of covered women in society. Third, it provided background information as to why and how they chose to unveil to gain access to higher education as opposed to those who chose not to unveil or continue their studies as indicated in Chapter 1. Fourth, it made the portrait of the part-time unveilers more complete in terms of who they were, how they lived, and what they thought within the focus of this book. Fifth, it hinted at the role and status of post-secondary education in Turkey in the eyes of its citizens.

In this part, there are references to two different headscarf ban policies by these female students. One of them is the higher education headscarf ban policy, a policy that exists within the context of Turkish universities and that is the focus of this book, and the other is the general headscarf ban policy, as I call it here, mainly exercised in public institutions. This general headscarf ban policy in Turkey does not allow covered females to attend primary and secondary schools or work in public institutions in every sector unless they remove their headscarves.

Why higher education? Part-time unveilers discussed the importance of higher education for themselves in general and elaborated on their motives for going to a higher education institution. Their reasons were various and could be categorized as intrinsic or extrinsic reasons. Intrinsic reasons were more to do with themselves, their families, and their lives. Extrinsic reasons were related to the larger society surrounding them. In any case, either implicitly or explicitly, both the higher education headscarf ban policy and the general headscarf ban policy seemed to shape some of these reasons in one way or another. Furthermore, some women had only one clear goal to attend university, while others had multiple reasons, intrinsic and extrinsic.

Intrinsic reasons: The intrinsic reasons for part-time unveilers to attend university seemed to be parental motivation, self-motivation, and a desire to become a well-rounded person.

My parents motivated me: The first intrinsic reason seemed to be parental motivation. More than half of the part-time unveilers mentioned the supportive role of their families, regardless of their own level of education, to motivate them to attend higher education institutions. There were some part-time unveilers who were simply not ambitious enough for a university education. Their parents motivated them by highlighting the importance of higher education and the ways in which it would contribute to their lives in the long run: "I did not have enough motivation for university education; my parents motivated me by shaping my thinking about higher education and its importance in Turkey" (Sezen).

Some other women, such as Yeliz and Gamze, used parental motivation when the general headscarf ban policy in their high school years was a reason that discouraged them from continuing higher education. Parents of these students seemed to have played crucial roles in their lives when part-time unveilers felt helpless and wanted to quit. Gamze explained how her parents convinced her to continue school when she decided to drop out:

> In October 2000, when I was in the second year of high school, the headscarf ban policy started in high schools. In those days, in İmam Hatip schools, boys and girls were separated. One will either unveil or leave the school. First, I said OK, I will unveil. Then I thought I couldn't. I've been dismissed from the classroom. Everybody was crying. I said I would quit studying. I became unhappy in the place I was once most happy. My parents said I wouldn't be worth anything in their eyes. I unveiled and kept on going to school. I was successful at the university entry examination. Thanks to my parents' motivation, I am here in front of you today as an undergraduate.

My ambition paid off: The second intrinsic reason for attending university seemed to be self-motivation. Fourteen part-time unveilers explained that they were very ambitious throughout their secondary education and felt that they had to continue higher education to prove themselves— first as smart individuals and second as covered women. In addition, the existence of both the higher education and general headscarf ban policies seemed to have further self-motivated some part-time unveilers. Melek was an ambitious student who constantly motivated herself to be successful during her secondary education and continuing into higher education:

> I was very successful in science classes in high school. I knew I could do well in Health Sciences. I was very ambitious in the university entrance exam, and worked very hard. When I found out I was placed in Health Sciences, I realized that my ambition paid off since as a smart person and covered woman, I would be a university student.

You broaden your horizons and improve yourself: The third intrinsic reason why part-time unveilers went to university could be their desire to improve themselves. A couple of part-time unveilers reported that they wanted to go to university to become well-rounded persons and improve themselves. For some of them, this was the sole purpose of attending a higher education institution; for the rest, it was one of many reasons. From the way they elaborated on their reasons for attending university, it was clear that part-time unveilers attached different values to being well rounded and had different understandings of improving themselves, which also affected their immediate and/or long-term educational expectations from their campuses. Zeynep wanted to improve herself by attending university and becoming an expert in one area:

> There is no future for a person who does not go to university. Higher education makes you specialized in one area and you read so much in that area that you become an expert. Professors are trying to guide you on your way to becoming more and more knowledgeable about the particular subject matter you are studying.

Semra had a different view about improving herself. Her understanding of self-improvement specifically focused on reaching a level of sophistication where she could learn more about Islam and religious teachings:

> The reason why I wanted to go to university was to become cultured. By cultured, I mean becoming an intellectual and sophisticated person who would go to operas and theaters. After university, I hope to reach a level where I can understand the depth of philosophy. In addition, I also hope to appreciate the values of my ancestors more. As a result of becoming cultured, I hope to better understand how the people in the Ottoman Empire lived and what kind of intellectual and spiritual activitiesthey were engaged in. This will help me learn more about my own religion, Islam.

Bahar was going to university to improve herself and become part of the global society, where she could use technological devices:

> I am going to university to become part of the global society. We are living in the world of science and technology. We cannot fall behind. I cannot imagine myself without a mobile phone or a computer. The campus gives you the opportunity to use such devices. You interact with the global society; you interact with intellectuals, professors, and smart students. Your way of engaging in conversations with others in your environment changes substantially. You broaden your horizons and improve yourself.

Extrinsic reasons: In addition to intrinsic reasons, part-time unveilers pinpointed several extrinsic reasons for attending university. These included better job opportunities, their willingness to become fully integrated into the society, their ambition and their desire to switch to a higher social class, to earn respect, and to change the perceptions of secularists about Islamists.

The main reason why I wanted to attend a university was to get a better job. The first extrinsic reason for part-time unveilers to attend university seemed to be job opportunities. Fifteen part-time unveilers, such as Semra, Bahar, Leyla, Sevim, Beyza, and Sevda, reported that they started university because they believed that they would have better job opportunities after graduation. For eight part-time unveilers, this was the sole purpose of receiving higher education; for others it was one of the multiple goals they wanted to reach with a diploma. In any case, they all perceived higher education to be a key to a successful career, and subsequently, economic freedom. This was especially important since the job market was competitive and the general headscarf ban policy already restricted their job opportunities in public institutions. Sevda stated that the main reason why she attended college was to secure a good job after graduation:

> The main reason why I wanted to attend a university was to get a better job. As a covered woman, if you are a university graduate, you have many more options. . . . My mother did not go to university and has always had problems in finding a good job, plus she has financial difficulties. After graduation, I am hoping that I will not have such hurdles in life.

Sevim perceived higher education as a doorway to economic independence:

> Higher education is a way to economic freedom in a male-dominant society. My mother is economically independent thanks to the university she attended. But I know there are many women of her age who are dependent on the pocket money they receive from their husbands. I do not want to become like them. In the twenty-first century, one should be economically self-sufficient. That is why they need to go to university, and so do I.

Part-time unveilers who had attended or were attending two-year higher education institutions seemed to think that the number of years spent in a higher education institution also mattered with specific reference to job opportunities after graduation. They stated that job opportunities were even better and more lucrative for four-year higher education graduates as compared with two-year ones. Sevgi, for example, explained that she wanted to go to university to obtain a good job. After graduating from the two-year institution she was in, she realized that she would not be able to make as much career progress as she would like with an associate degree, which was one reason for her to continue her education. Mine, a student who was attending a two-year degree program, had a similar opinion about two-year institutions vis-à-vis career prospects:

> There is a big difference between a two-year graduate and a four-year graduate when you are in the job market. Four-year graduates are almost always better placed and find higher paying jobs. This is why I want to continue my education.... I am hoping to be able to transfer my credits into a four-year program and receive a bachelor's degree to make myself more competitive in the job market.

I can become a better citizen. The second motive for part-time unveilers to continue higher education appeared to be their desire to become active citizens in Turkish society. According to them, the higher education headscarf ban policy intended to make Islamists passive and to segregate them from society; they did not want this to happen. Part-time unveilers mentioned that one of the reasons they started university was to become fully integrated into the society in the future. For many part-time unveilers this integration meant contribution to the leadership and economic and social welfare of the country. Gamze explained the ways in which she could become a better citizen thanks to higher education:

> One other reason to attend a university is to learn how I can become a leader so that as an Islamist, I can contribute in governing the country in the future. People like me [part-time unveilers/Islamists] need their voices heard. Our voices have been suppressed as a result of the higher education headscarf ban policy on campuses. I can make my voice heard by means of higher education. Higher education is preparing me to help shape the future direction of Turkey. [It is because] higher education is a platform where one can learn social and national values in a more refined way. When I learn them better, I can then go out and teach them to others who do not know. I can also take part in activities, where I can apply things I have been taught. I can become a better citizen and take part in useful social activities such as helping the poor, marginalized, and oppressed.

On the other hand, for two part-time unveilers, full integration into the society meant contribution to the spiritual/religious development of society. One interesting observation was that both of these part-time unveilers appeared to have had intense involvement in the teachings of Islam through formal or informal Qur'an courses at some point in their lives. Alara shared her views in the following way:

> Allah commands that human beings receive education so that they can read and understand His teachings and teach them to those who do not have

education. This is the big difference between a student who is educated and one who is not. After I graduate, I will be able to become a more religiously responsible person, and help the Turkish Muslims realize their own responsibility as well.

I wanted to be part of the upper class. Another motivation for attending university appeared to be the desire of the part-time unveilers to climb up the social class ladder. A couple of part-time unveilers remarked that their primary reason to attend university was to change their social class. Implicit in these comments seemed to be the dissatisfaction of these part-time unveilers with regard to their current position on the social class ladder because of either their current socioeconomic, educational, or professional situation; the city they originally came from; or how they were viewed as females. For these women a higher social class meant better socioeconomic status, gender equality, urban life, and speaking a foreign language. They all perceived higher education as a vehicle that would provide them with some or all of these qualities to climb up the social ladder. Sevtap explained:

> University is a knife that divides people into two: educated and non-educated. In Turkey, if you are educated, you are automatically seen as somebody superior. If you are uneducated, you are considered a lower-class person. So, in broad terms university categorizes Turkish people as high-class and low-class people.... In addition, women do not always have the right to continue their education. They are usually seen as inferior to the men.... considered second-class citizens. I wanted to change that. I wanted to be part of the upper class. The best way to achieve that was to continue higher education.

You earn more respect. Another motive for part-time unveilers to receive university education appeared to be their desire for respect in society. Four part-time unveilers reported that higher education brought prestige. According to these part-time unveilers, this prestige brought some extra privileges in addition to climbing up the social and economic ladder. In their minds, the most important of these privileges was respect. Dilara wanted respect:

> Some of the older members of my community are not taken seriously when they speak. It is because they do not have a university degree. However, my community members listen to those with diplomas carefully and accept their suggestions. It seems to me that the difference between a good and bad suggestion is that it is a good suggestion or piece of advice if it comes from a university graduate, and a bad suggestion if it comes from a primary

school graduate. You earn more respect and have more listeners and follow-ers if you attend university. This is one of the reasons why I am pursuing an undergraduate education.

I wanted to change all these misconceptions. Finally, the part-time unveilers wanted to attend university to change the perceptions of secularists about Islamists, especially Islamist women. Four part-time unveilers explained that one other reason why they were so eager to have an undergraduate degree was to change the way secularists perceived cov-ered women. The part-time unveilers thought that secularists perceived them as backward and narrow-minded people who could only be clean-ers or housewives. Part-time unveilers wanted to change this stereotype by attending university. Leyla explained:

> Secularists think that covered women can only be cleaners. Covered women can only clean floors or windows. They are there to be ordered around. They want us to stay at home and give birth to children. They think that we are backward, primitive, and unintelligent people. I want to change all these misconceptions, which is another reason why I attend university.

Part-time unveilers expressed various clear motivations as to why they attended higher education institutions and wanted to receive undergrad-uate degrees. Both the general and higher education headscarf ban policies seemed to impact and shape some of the reasons why part-time unveilers attended university. Another issue that appeared clear from the intrinsic and extrinsic reasons just discussed was that part-time unveilers craved a fruitful and rewarding future in which they would become respected, active, and successful citizens in Turkish society and maximize their potential. They hoped that higher education was a means to this end.

Why their current discipline of study?: Part-time unveilers pointed to four different reasons for choosing the discipline they were then studying. These were consideration of the job market, number of part-time unveilers in the discipline, their exam scores, and a desire to study in the program.

I chose to study this discipline so that I can work with my father in his pri-vate business without any worries in the future: The first reason appeared to be consideration of potential job opportunities. Twelve part-time unveilers mentioned that their primary concern while listing their choices accord-ing to their scores after the university entrance exam was their restrictions and limitations in the job market. Thus, they wanted to make sure that they chose a discipline that provided covered women with relatively more job opportunities after graduation. Leyla, for example, initially wanted to become a lawyer. However, she later decided against it since it would be impossible for her to enter the court covered, or with a hat, due to the general headscarf ban policy, which prevented women from working with their headscarves (and in some cases with their hats) on. She was not sure whether she would be accepted to the court as a part-time unveiler even if she decided to expose her hair. Thus, she decided to focus on science since she thought there would be more job opportunities for her. Alara opted for a discipline that would enable her to work with her father in his private business even if she did not find a job after graduation:

> I might have chosen a different discipline than the present one, but I would have had to go through the trouble of looking for jobs in the competitive market, which is not always veil-friendly. I did not want to put myself under this type of stress. So I chose to study this discipline so that I can work with my father in his private business without any worries in the future.

I chose this program because I knew there would be many students like me: The accounts of 12 part-time unveilers indicated that another criterion for their choice of study was the number of part-time unveilers in a discipline. They wanted to make sure that there would be many other part-time unveilers in the program they chose, to be able to ensure some network and support structure. So they filled out the university lists accordingly. As Suzan stated: "I chose this program because I knew there would be many students like me [part-time unveilers]. I thought we could support one another. Some programs are more popular amongst the Islamists, such as teaching and nursing. So I opted for the popular ones."

I am in this program as a result of my university exam score: The third reason determining the choice of program was part-time unveilers' university exam scores. Ten part-time unveilers reported that their scores in the national university exam decided their placement. Yeliz explained her case in the following way:

> I am in this program by mere virtue of luck as a result of my university exam score. I did not know what the program entailed until I started studying it. Then I found out how issues of dress and worldviews played major roles in the job market of my area of specialization. The national university entrance system is not a good model to follow.

It is the only program I have wanted to study: The final reason for choosing their program seemed to be a lifelong desire to study in a particular program. Eight part-time unveilers reported that, all their lives, they wanted to study what they were studying then, and they were really happy there. Regardless of the various reasons why they wanted to study in these programs, they all mentioned that they had never considered being in a different department. Beyza explained that she had listed this program as her only choice of department: "I love what I am studying. It has been the only program I have wanted to study in during my secondary education."

To sum up, part-time unveilers seemed to study in the programs they were in for various reasons. Besides the genuine desire to be in the program, part-time unveilers seemed to be studying in the disciplines as a result of external forces that were beyond their control. In addition to national university exam scores, the general headscarf ban policy in public institutions with reference to job opportunities seemed to influence the choice part-time unveilers made while deciding which department to go to. This seemed to have a restraining effect on part-time unveilers and could cause anxiety and dissatisfaction in the long term if some part-time unveilers are not satisfied with their program and are concerned about job opportunities after graduation.

Implementation of the Policy

Even though I was not asking any specific question in relation to the implementation of the headscarf ban policy on the campuses, the accounts of the part-time unveilers revealed that the policy was implemented differently in different public institutions. Moreover, it appeared that there were differences in the way the ban was implemented across colleges or departments in the same university, sometimes being left to the discretion of the professors. Although it is important to understand that the implementation of the policy seemed to have an impact on the way part-time unveilers unveiled on campuses, the fact that the policy was implemented in various ways is also an important finding that might have implications for the Higher Education Council (HEC), policymakers, and campus administrators.

One point that needs to be addressed is that in Turkey there are single-campus and multi-campus universities. Multi-campus institutions are usually scattered across a city, and when part-time unveilers referred to a campus, they could be referring to one college or numerous colleges. In this book, I do not specify if a university is one-campus or multi-campus because, in certain cases, it may serve as an identifier. In addition, what was not clear from the accounts of the students was that when they referred to a campus or university, whether they were referring to the whole campus of the university or to their colleges; this posed a limitation in the conclusions drawn from the accounts of these women.

The voices of part-time unveilers highlighted the various ways in which universities implemented the headscarf ban on campuses. Yeliz, who was in the field of Applied Social Sciences at University of West, explained that hats and wigs were forbidden on her campus: "In my campus, hats and wigs are forbidden. This does not mean that there are not students using them, but if the security or administration realizes that you are wearing hats or wigs, they will confiscate them." Buket, a Health Sciences student at University of East, explained that in the case of her own campus, the use of hats was left to the discretion of the instructor in class: "We are allowed to enter the campus with a hat, but in class, it is up to the teacher. The teacher decides whether you can sit in class with a hat or a wig." In the cases of Bahar, in Language & Literature at University of North, and Melek, in Health Sciences at University of South, hats were banned on their campuses, but students were allowed to use wigs.

According to the part-time unveilers, there were some public universities that did not implement the ban on campus. Gamze reported:

> [X] University does not deal with the headscarf ban policy. They do not deal with such things. Professors and administrators are busy with teaching and research. They are concerned with student learning and development. They do not hunt their students to see who is wearing what. Of course, there are some professors who do not let students with headscarves or hats in class, but they are individual cases.

Furthermore, it seemed that universities varied in the way they made unveiling more or less "comfortable" or "easy" for their students by providing them (or not) with "unveiling" resources. As explained by Gamze, Bahar, Semra, and Sema, there was a fitting-room with a mirror at the entrance of the campus for a maximum of two people where students could unveil. On the other hand, Sevtap explained that when she first started university, there was no fitting room in her university, so she had to unveil in the street or at the entrance of an apartment block with people watching her.

So what emerged was that some universities seemed to allow students with their headscarves on in the campuses, whereas others did not. Hat wearing appeared to be left to the discretion of campuses, colleges, departments, or individual professors. Apparently, in some cases, wigs were not allowed either. The variety of the ways in which the ban was implemented in universities or departments seemed to have some impact on the decision the part-time unveilers made about the way they unveiled. With this contextual information about the implementation of the ban, I now move on to the narratives of five part-time unveilers regarding their educational and cultural experiences.

Different Educational and Cultural Experiences of Part-Time Unveilers

To make better sense of the findings that address each research question about the impact of the headscarf ban policy on the educational and cultural experiences of the part-time unveilers, in the following chapters, I give an overview of some of the different types of experiences part-time unveilers went through. Turkish society is quite complex, with numerous juxtapositions such as the modern and the traditional. Not only does the environment have contradictions, but so do individuals within themselves, and this fact is reflected in the data collected from the part-time unveilers. It is crucial to comprehend this complexity, and it is my hope that these case narratives will highlight the extent to which the lives of these part-time unveilers were complex. The five narratives are stories of part-time unveilers with varying degrees of positive and negative experiences as part-time unveilers.

These accounts are by no means a complete illustration of all the different experiences of these women and of the whole group of women who participated in the study. Each woman's story is unique and has its own particularities. The aspects of these stories simply show the range among the women respondents in regard to background, identity, understanding of the headscarf ban policy, policy negotiation process, and educational and cultural experiences.

I selected these five part-time unveilers because of certain distinct characteristics that existed in their lives. Elif was a returning student whose narrative depicts how she dropped out of the university as a result of her decision not to comply with the headscarf ban policy and how and why she decided to complete her education as an unveiled woman a couple of years later. Also, her campus life seemed to be toward the very negative end of the positive-negative spectrum in terms of educational and cultural experiences. Hale was a student who started to cover her hair after high school knowing in advance that she was going to uncover her hair while attending university. That is why unveiling was possibly not as challenging for her as somebody who started veiling at a very young age and that is why the headscarf ban policy did not seem to impact her in any particular way. Seda, on the other hand, was a woman who started to veil on and off in Grade six and permanently in Grade seven in response to her understanding of Islam. She had a very strategic and systematic way of negotiating the policy, where she first made a choice between education and veiling, two precepts of Islam, and then about her way of unveiling. Sema, the fourth part-time unveiler selected, had a distinct way of understanding the headscarf ban policy. Even though she did not support the ban, she thought it was necessary to implement it given the then political and social context of Turkey. Unveiling impacted her well-being rather negatively, causing anxiety and some other psychological problems. Burcu, an observant Muslim who started to cover in the sixth grade, seemed to have a relatively less challenging campus life with a nonthreatening campus environment. Complying with a policy that she considered an imposition, unveiling challenged her female identity and made her feel like a woman who was restricted in different ways.

Elif

Elif was a returning student. The headscarf ban policy seemed to have impacted her educational and cultural experiences rather negatively. Despite her strong personality, she seemed to struggle on campus and unveiling appeared to create problems for her. She appeared to have problematic relationships with administrators, faculty, and peers, and she felt restricted and unsafe on campus. Even though she was an activist during her undergraduate years before she dropped out of college due to the introduction of the headscarf ban policy on campus, the experience of unveiling appeared to have made her quite passive. Unveiling and the challenges she encountered on campus seemed to have impacted her personality and religious, citizenship, and gender identities negatively as well. She felt like a second-class citizen, a Muslim who had committed a sin, and a woman who was humiliated without her headscarf.

Elif was studying in Applied Social Sciences at University of South with an average GPA. She was 26. She was from a small city. Her father was a businessman and her mother was an illiterate housewife. Her father had a big influence on her and her sisters' religious education and beliefs. A headscarf was always encouraged in the house during her childhood. As such, she covered her hair voluntarily in Grade six as a result of her father's teachings about Islam. She was married and had a child. As a family, they lived in their own house and led a happy and comfortable life.

Elif considered herself to be an honest person and she valued her neighbors and avoided lying. As a Turkish citizen, she thought that paying her taxes properly was an important duty. As a Muslim, she wanted to be a very good Muslim, especially after September 11. She wanted to live according to her understanding of the tenets of Islam.

A mother. As a covered woman who was also a mother, Elif believed that life in Turkey was not easy:

> I am a mother. I have to sacrifice a lot especially in Turkey as a mother and as a woman. There are a lot of missions for a woman in this country. . . . Allah

protects the woman.... The woman is a symbol of purity and innocence. Our Prophet also gives a lot of importance to women. I read somewhere that those who have and raise three daughters go to heaven. The problem is that the society is problematic. There are problems of drugs, alcohol, men who want to use and abuse you, and sex. So for a woman, there are lots of dangers.

After February 1998: As a returning student who decided to use a hat as her style of unveiling, she had a very different background from other university students since she completed some parts of her education veiled until the headscarf ban. The ban made her experience events she never thought she would go through and caused her to be cut off from university due to her resistance to comply with the policy:

I was born abroad. I came to Turkey when I was six. I attended an İmam Hatip school during secondary education. I was the top student in class. After graduation, I came to [this city] to start [this program] at university. I enrolled with my headscarf on in 1996. I attended university with my headscarf on until 1998. After February 1998, the headscarf ban was implemented in our campus. We were first asked to remove our headscarves while our pictures were taken for student IDs. Campus administrators wanted everybody to have pictures unveiled. Then, they extended the ban and asked us to remove our headscarves on campus. Thirty-five thousand students walked to protest the ban. I was one of them. We talked to the government and members of parliament. Some of our professors supported us. In the third year, we had problems while registering for classes. During registration, we [veiled women] were brought to the persuasion rooms. [A persuasion room is a room where professors and administrators try to persuade a student to remove her headscarf.] In my persuasion room, there were professors from other departments. I was told: remove your headscarf; you will not be able to continue your education like this. I also heard that some veiled students were humiliated in those persuasion rooms, but I never experienced it. When I refused to unveil, the university did not enroll me. And on November 6, 1998, after the protests against the Higher Education Council and its issuing of the headscarf ban, we were completely cut off from the university. I wanted to go abroad, but I realized it was not going to be a wise decision. The reason was that if I went abroad, I would not be able to practice my profession back here in Turkey since for some professions [i.e., those that require licensure], studying abroad precludes graduates from practicing in Turkey and my profession-to-be is one of them. So I took my case to court, it lasted 70–80 days but I lost the case. Then I took my case to the European Court of Human Rights. It is still there. After being expelled from the university, I joined the seated protests in front of the university and in different parks around the campus. I also met with some business people and influential people with friends. Nothing changed. I gave up and started doing other things. I attended speed-reading seminars. I went to England to improve my English. I got married. I became involved in religious studies and activities. I never thought I would have such experiences when I started university. I never thought these things would or could happen to me.

Back to university: As a politically active woman who had fought against the ban in every capacity, Elif was determined not to remove her headscarf and give up her education. However, after quitting, even though she was involved in various activities, she realized that her goals in life were not going to be met through the private courses or seminars she attended:

> Despite the activities I joined, nothing seemed to satisfy me. I realized that I would not be able to become someone successful without the prestige or label the university brings. I did not want to take continuously; I also wanted to give. So I decided to go back to university.

Besides these goals, Elif also added what higher education meant to her and why it was important that she had a university degree in her life. She also explained why she was studying the program she was in then:

> I grew up in a small city. To stay in a small city meant to get married. Higher education was not the appropriate thing for girls, but my father wanted me to go to university. When my brothers did not go to university, my father wanted my sister and I go to university. He always said that a person who was educated would not do harmful things, but would be beneficial to himself/herself and others. My teachers in high school also motivated me a lot. They also had an influence while choosing the program I wanted to study. . . . I know that after I graduate I am going to volunteer to work in nonprofit organizations to help those who need me. I also want to do a master's degree, but I do not know if I will actually do it. It depends on my experiences here in my undergraduate degree. I want to learn what I am studying as perfectly as possible. I know that my higher education will do a lot in contributing to my future.

Her account showed that she was a woman who valued education, which was another reason why she perhaps wanted to go back and comply with the higher education headscarf ban.

The ban caused hostility: Despite her compliance with the headscarf ban policy, Elif thought it was unfair and made her feel like a second-class citizen. Elif also felt that the ban caused hostility between Islamists and secularists and became a barrier preventing her from continuing her undergraduate studies:

> The ban caused hostility. I did not become hostile toward the policymakers because my religion tells me to be patient. If the headscarf is wrong, if it is bad, if wearing it is a sin, then they should have taught that to us; they should have trained us. They should have educated us in that direction instead of dismissing us from university. We could not get the education we wanted because of the ban. Many became rebellious and anxious as a result of their experiences with the ban on campuses. I was 17 when I started university. I was 19 when I was dismissed. The policymakers saw me as their enemy when I was 19 and kicked me off the campus.

She thought that the headscarf ban policy was a political tool for those in power who did not want Islamists to take an active part in society. She felt as if she was not wanted in the country even though she stated that she loved her country. She perceived the ban as a policy that had restricted her actions and caused her to leave the campus and then come back as a woman with a hat, which was not her real identity. As mentioned earlier, even though she had negative impressions about the policy and had resisted it for a while, due to her goals in life and how much she valued higher education, she chose to negotiate the policy.

I left my past in the past. Elif chose the hat as her way of unveiling. Her family seemed to have enthusiastically supported her decision of unveiling and continuing her higher education. She believed that her return to campus was a new beginning for her and involved leaving her past behind:

> Going back to university was to put an end to the complex of inferiority, incompleteness, and embarrassment. I chose my own happiness over many other things. I am not in a vicious circle anymore. I have a bright future now. I left my past in the past.

Her explanation of how she negotiated the policy indicated some remarkable contradictions within herself when she said that in Islam there was no definite way to cover hair and she chose to wear a hat since it was a way of covering the hair, while she later indicated that she would put her headscarf back on immediately after she left campus to continue being a good Muslim. In addition, the way she negotiated the policy clearly shows some lessons learned from her first university experience and the time spent between the dismissal from university and the return to campus.

Since I came back I have not sat in the campus garden: Elif did not feel as involved as she once was in campus life:

When I returned to university in 2005, on the one hand I was very happy that I was back to my department, studies, and books. On the other hand, I was sad that I lost so many years. I have chosen the hat as my style of unveiling. With my hat on, metaphorically speaking, my head is never up. I now realize how free I was with my headscarf on. Since I came back I have not sat in the campus garden. Before I used to sit there with friends all the time. I used to get involved in protests. Once there was a leftist protest and I had joined that as well, but not anymore.

She seemed to experience anxiety and nervousness because she was not sure if her style of unveiling would create problems with some administrators or professors:

I am very nervous in the exams now. What are the assistants going to say? Are they going to ask me to take the hat off? . . . While registering for classes this time, I gave the student services a picture of mine that is a photomontage [adjusting the photo to make it look like the person is unveiled; in other words, the picture on Elif's ID had her real face with hair painted on]. When the security guards at the campus entrance see it, they are very surprised, but I did it on purpose to express my reaction. . . . So far, three professors would not accept me in their classes with my hat on. They wanted me to remove that as well. In one exam, one assistant called the professor after half an hour and the professor told me that I would not be able to take the exam with my hat on. It is as if some people do not want me to continue higher education no matter what I do. It is as if they are asking me what I am doing here. It is as if they are questioning me, "You were dismissed, you made a decision, why are you back now?" . . . I am really grateful if I can survive classes and exams. I am really sad, anxious, and fearful.

Elif believed that her unveiling brought her some opportunities and challenges. However, her perception seemed to be that the challenges of unveiling outweighed the opportunities. She thought that the only advantage of unveiling was that it helped her go back to university. Despite this opportunity, she appeared to face various personal challenges regarding her identity and educational and cultural experiences on campus. She had tensions with some administrators and faculty and was subjected to bad treatment and hostility in and out of class:

Some administrators look at me sarcastically all the time. I am always a bad person in their eyes. Female administrators are really bad. I have not had a bad experience with male administrators. When the exam results came out, my grades in one exam did not show up. I went to Student Affairs to see what was going on. The minute I entered the room, a lady came up to me and held my hat. She shouted at me and told me to take my hat off and obey the rules. I lied to her and told her that I take my hat off in class. She wanted to take it off, but I stopped her. It is obvious that I am a covered woman. So the hat becomes a problem. There are uncovered women who wear hats. For them the hat is not a problem. . . . During the exams, the class is divided into two. Two different professors monitor classes. In the class I took one exam, once the Department Chair, a female, came to class. Apparently there was a problem between her and the professor. The problem was that the class I took the exam in was full of returning students. The Chair wanted to give us a different exam. We did not know this. Our own professor, a male, came to class and gave his own questions. The Chair came immediately and changed the questions. Later I heard that the Chair complained about our professor to the Dean. When she was in class, I was scared that she was going to see me and ask me to leave the room or remove the hat. Thank God, it did not happen. Some friends told me not to leave the class. I was happy that they supported me in that way. . . . In addition to problems in class, campus has also become an intimidating environment for me. I try to be invisible. I go to class; I take exams and then leave. I am even too shy to buy [a sandwich]. I am scared that somebody will say something. When I first went for registration, Student Services gave me a lot of hassle. So I am constantly scared that somebody will say something or make things problematic for me.

This ban made me antisocial: Elif's goal was to graduate without any problems. So she seemed to try hard to become as invisible as possible to avoid attracting attention and conflict:

My aim is to graduate without any problems. This ban made me antisocial. Before there was a human rights organization on campus that I actively worked in. It does not exist anymore anyway, but even if it did, I would not work there. I was so active before. I was everywhere on campus. I used to attend political debates, speakers series, and all. Now I do not take part in any activities anymore. I just want to be as passive as possible not to attract attention. Of course because of all these reasons, I become very nervous while studying for an exam. I was not like that before. I am in a state of panic. I am worried that in the exam somebody will come up to and ask me to leave the room [because of my hat]. Thinking about this over and over again has a negative impact on my motivation for studying and general performance as well. . . . I think about these things instead of focusing on my studies.

Elif faced various challenges to continue her education despite the fact that she was happy to return to her studies. She felt unsafe both in the classroom and on campus. From her accounts, it was also possible to see that she constantly compared and contrasted her university experiences in the present to those she had in the past, where she seemed to be happy and active until the headscarf ban policy implementation. Elif also perceived some hostility from some of her professors and administrators. This contrasted with the welcoming attitude of her friends and classmates. Clearly, her so far unsuccessful fights against the headscarf ban policy and her compliance with the policy had tired her and made her passive on campus. Different from the time she first attended college in the late 1990s, she did not spend time on campus apart from attending classes and exams and was not involved in any activities anymore. She hardly ever went to the canteen in between classes or exams to buy something. She had become fearful and anxious on campus. Her motivation was negatively impacted due to her fears that she would be subjected to discrimination by professors and/or administrators.

The ban and this experience of complying with the policy will affect my career in the future: In addition to these challenges, the experience of unveiling had also impacted her decision about her career in the future:

> The ban and this experience of complying with the policy will affect my career in the future because I will not work in an environment where I am supposed to unveil. . . . So I will continue my career performing my job in private companies. I know I could be more successful in public institutions, but I have already accepted the situation, and since I will not unveil in the future, this is how I am going to perform my job after graduation. So unveiling made me realize that I do not want to continue my life unveiled even for my job. So I will have a job on a smaller scale and more "low-key," but I am OK with that.

Her accounts also revealed some of her own contradictions or inconsistencies. For example, on the one hand, she constantly felt scared that somebody would say something, and on the other hand, she was fearless enough to have a photomontage picture on her ID since all the pictures used on campuses, including ID pictures, had to be faces of students with hair unveiled. Her using a photomontage picture on her ID i might have created problems for her since administrators could object to this kind of a picture and/or perceive it as deception. The contrasts in her accounts showed how she had her own internal inconsistencies. This was also perhaps a battle in her personality. Her "silent protest" with her photomontage ID was a residue of her politically active and rebellious personality, which she was trying to reconcile with her new, emerging passive and asocial character.

I feel naked as a woman without my headscarf: In addition to the way the unveiling impacted her experiences on campus and her character, compliance with the policy seemed to have impacted her citizenship, religious, and gender identities as well:

> The ban affected my citizenship identity negatively. As a Muslim, I feel I am committing a sin. I am happy with my headscarf, but I am not allowed to wear it. I am acting against my belief system. I am acting against everything I believe in. I am doing something I do not believe in. This makes me wonder if Allah is going to forgive me because of this sin. I am fearful because of this. I pray really hard to be forgiven. I know that once I graduate, I will wear my headscarf at all times again. I am looking forward to my graduation to go back to days where I used to be a [full-time] veiler. As a woman, I feel humiliated. I am treated unfairly because of my headscarf. If I am not educated, I will not raise my children properly so next generations will be affected negatively. So women have to go to university, but many cannot. I could not for a while, and I can now but this time not in the way I want. I feel naked as a woman without my headscarf.

Considering Elif's accounts, the headscarf ban policy seemed to have impacted her rather negatively in various degrees at different times of her life, changing her from being quite an active student to a passive one. Her unpleasant experiences during her first time at university and her act of unveiling seemed to play crucial roles in her passiveness and the challenges she went through. Her identity possibly was impacted negatively as well, making her feel like a second-class citizen, a Muslim who had committed a sin, and a woman who was humiliated without her headscarf.

Hale

Hale seemed to have different experiences from Elif in the sense that the headscarf ban policy and her experience of unveiling did not seem to have impacted her educational and cultural experiences. Even though, like Elif, she thought the ban was a barrier for veiled women, complying with the policy did not seem to have an impact on the personality and the citizenship, religious, and gender identities of Hale (compare this with Elif, who was severely impacted). She appeared to have negotiated the headscarf ban policy easily and comfortably throughout her decision to unveil. She thought her undergraduate experiences were similar to the experiences of any other student on campus and believed that her choice of unveiling, exposure of the hair, made her campus life smoother as compared with that of those who wore a hat or used a wig.

Hale was born in a small city. She came from a large family with four siblings. Her parents only attended primary school, which made it difficult for them to find lucrative jobs. They always had financial problems. She was a first generation college student and the only child in the family attending university. Her mother was veiled in a traditional way—that is, her headscarf was tied under her chin with her neck showing. Her parents moved to a big city when she was very young and had a conservative, traditional, and simple life.

Hale was a cheerful and respectful girl who had a strong Muslim identity. She believed that as a Turk she was different from other Muslims in that she had many opportunities as a woman that she would not have in other Muslim countries. The only problem that affected her identity was the fact that her parents gave more importance to her brother because he was male. She felt constant pressure to prove herself.

In order to achieve her aims in life, during her last two years of high school, Hale knew she needed to attend a "dershane," a private test center that prepared students for the university entrance examination, which was very competitive. However, she could not go to a "dershane" since it was expensive and her parents could not afford it. She was unsuccessful at the university exam when she first took it. In the summer of high school graduation, she found out from her friends about a "dershane" that provided poor students with scholarships. The only condition to receive a scholarship as a student was to become more involved with Islam and its teachings. Having accepted this condition, she enrolled into the test center. Hale was given religious books to read and attended meetings that focused on the teachings of Islam. At the same time, she worked hard the whole year, retook the university entrance exam, and was successful. She and her parents were very happy. When she started university, she realized that she needed money to buy books and equipment necessary for her Health Sciences classes. Two of her friends had already dropped out of university because of this very reason (i.e., they could not afford the books and the equipment) in the first week of the academic year, and she did not want the same thing to happen to her. She consulted her friends and teachers from the dershane, asking for their help. She was offered monthly stipends to help her pay for her books and materials, on the condition that she would cover her hair. She accepted it, covered her hair, and had been veiled for five years since she started university. Even though she started veiling at a relatively older age and as a result of external circumstances, she came to appreciate it when she read more about Islam and attended the meetings organized by the Islamists. She thought that veiling had become a part of her life and identity she would not give up. She lived with her parents and exposed her hair on campus.

Two main reasons why Hale wanted to attend a higher education institution were to achieve better economic conditions and prestige in society.

One of the reasons why she chose the program she was studying was that the job opportunities were ample and lucrative.

Thanks to unveiling, I am receiving a higher education: As a woman who had experienced life both unveiled and veiled, Hale thought that the headscarf ban policy was in place not to bar the use of the headscarf per se, but to bar the opinions and lifestyles of Islamists. After starting to use the headscarf, she negotiated the ban by choosing to expose her hair while attending the campus because she did not have any other options. The only way for her to advance in society was to go to university, so when she covered her hair, she knew she was going to uncover it on campus. She stated that because she was always uncovered until she started university, unveiling was not as challenging for her as for someone who started veiling at the age of nine, for example. She thought exposing the hair was the best style of uncovering for her as she became like any other student and was therefore protected from possible prejudices she could have been subjected to on campus. That said, she had some challenges and felt like a hypocrite when she unveiled:

> Thanks to unveiling, I am receiving a higher education. I always wear casual clothes. Off campus, I wear my headscarf. On campus, I take it off. When I take it off, nobody judges me. I become neutralized. I become an ordinary person as a result of unveiling. Some high society and elite students change their attitudes toward me when they see me covered outside. Somebody who does not know me judges me when s/he sees me covered even though s/he does not know me. However, I am the same person. The headscarf has become a means to categorize women. So as one would categorize people as black, white, fat, slim, tall, short, you are also categorized as the covered woman. So with a headscarf, there is an immediate categorization. Unveiling stops you being categorized as covered and all the prejudices it brings. However, unveiling has some disadvantages for me as well. Unveiling is something I do not believe in. I have some extreme ideological beliefs. I believe that I am on the right track doing the right thing with getting the education I need. When I unveil, I feel hypocritical. I am doing something I do not believe in doing.

Similar to Elif's, Hale's accounts also contained some inconsistencies. She believed she was doing the right thing getting higher education, but at the same time, unveiling was something she did not believe in and it made her feel like a hypocrite.

I do not feel any negativity toward myself: Hale did not feel any negativity toward herself and explained that she had good relationships with administrators, faculty, and peers on campus:

My ID has a picture of me unveiled. I used to unveil in the restroom before. Previously I could enter the campus with my headscarf on and unveil in the restroom. Then the system changed. Now we have to unveil in front of the campus gate. As a student who exposes her hair, I do not feel any negativity toward myself. I am a very hardworking student. My relationship with my teachers is wonderful. They always support me and tell me that they are really proud of me. I am not really sure if they know I am covered. I do not know if their attitude would change if they knew I was covered. They can definitely tell I am different. But probably what they think is that I am poor. You know that in Turkey you can easily identify which socioeconomic class one belongs to looking at their clothes. So the perception is that most poor people are covered. So you can definitely tell I am poor, but not always tell if I am covered or not. I have great friends. We always exchange class notes. I do not socialize with many of my friends outside campus. Some of them are really rich. I would not be able to afford to socialize with them, but on campus we sit together in the canteen or garden. We go to the restaurant together. There were two or three excursions and I went with the group unveiled. My best friends are my study group friends. They know that I am veiled, and this is not a problem for them. Overall I am treated like any other student on campus.

Right now I do not have any problems: She felt that her type of unveiling, exposure of hair, brought some opportunities since it eased her educational and cultural experiences on campus:

When you expose your hair, it is very hard to tell if you are covered or not. You become like the uncovered. So as a student who exposes the hair, both the campus and classroom environments are welcoming. Right now I do not have any problems. I became used to it. I covered my hair suddenly. I was inexperienced and ignorant when I first veiled. I had some question marks and suspicions. Nothing was for definite. Now I am very knowledgeable and conscientious about what I am doing.

She only felt challenged during the holy month of Ramadan in terms of unveiling.

My worry is for the future: Her major concern, though, was about her future and the kind of challenges she needed to face for a better life and lucrative career:

I was only challenged during Ramadan. It was the exam period and I was fasting and praying. I never asked the permission of my professors to leave the class to go to pray or break my fast. I was concerned that they could be judgmental, you never know. But this is a small challenge. My worry is not for now; my worry is for the future. I want to pursue a doctoral degree in a different department where I would like to specialize. However, the professors there are prejudiced against those who cover their hair in their private lives. I know this for a fact since one of my friends who exposed her hair in that department quit when her professors found out that she was covered in her private life and gave her a really hard time that affected her performance, and eventually, grades. Besides that, another problem is socioeconomic. The department I want to specialize in is very small and a kind of a society. No one is allowed to be part of this society unless you have a good car, good education, and a highly privileged family. This is another big drawback for me. I do not have a family with strong socioeconomic status. So I do not know what to do when I graduate. I will either pursue another area of specialization and pursue a graduate degree or start work.

Hale's accounts indicated that when she exposed her hair she became just like any other female student on campus and was treated like the others. She perceived the classroom and campus as safe places, felt welcome in her department, and did not experience many challenges. She used the campus resources and tried to join extracurricular activities. Her only drawback in terms of socialization was her financial situation, which seemed to affect her perhaps more than unveiling. Her main challenge appeared to be related to her future plans: she thought that both her veiling and socioeconomic status would put her at a disadvantage.

Unveiling did not have an impact on my citizenship or gender identity: In addition to the ways in which exposing her hair impacted her life on campus, Hale also shared her perceptions about whether complying with the policy had an effect on her citizenship, gender, and religious identities:

Unveiling did not have an impact on my citizenship or gender identity. The only identity unveiling impacted is my Muslim identity. It was a difficult choice to make. First it was difficult to cover the hair. Then it was difficult to remove the headscarf. What affects me negatively is that I am removing the headscarf, so, doing something against the wishes of Allah. Wearing a headscarf becomes a habit after a while as well. So giving up that habit is challenging too. But it is only temporary. I will not unveil after graduation. I will keep wearing my headscarf after university. I will find a job where I can work covered. This probably means that I will have to work in a private institution, but it is OK by me. It is even better in a way since I will make more money.

Overall, even though she was opposed to the ban and thought that it was a barrier for people who chose to live their lives according to her understanding of the tenets of Islam, complying with the policy and unveiling did not seem to have had an impact on her educational and cultural experiences. She believed that her undergraduate experiences were the same as the experiences of any other student on campus and that her choice of unveiling had made her campus life smoother than would have been the case had she chosen to wear a hat or use a wig. Hale's personality did not seem to be impacted either. Other than the challenge of acting against Islam by removing the headscarf, unveiling did not seem to have influenced her citizenship, religion, and gender identities in the ways it had affected the identities of Elif.

Seda

Seda, who started veiling at a very young age, seemed not to have that many challenges even though she faced some problems from time to time as a wig user on campus. Although she chose to comply with the headscarf ban policy, she was opposed to it and thought that it categorized women in numerous ways. She appeared to have good relationships with many of her professors, administrators, and peers. However, different from Hale, she did not seem to spend much time on campus and was not involved in campus activities. The headscarf ban policy did not seem to have impacted her personality. Different from Elif and Hale, Seda was uncertain whether she would unveil after graduation when she was employed.

Seda was born and grew up in a big city; she came from a small family that valued education. Both her parents were professionals with advanced degrees. After the fifth grade, she wanted to imitate the veiled women around her such as her mother or sister. Thus, she started using the veil on and off in Grade six. In Grade seven, she decided to wear the headscarf permanently. Meanwhile, she read extensively about Islam and its teachings, including the life of the Prophet.

Seda was a girl who considered herself to be sometimes quiet, sometimes talkative. She liked to be social at times. She also liked to take a leadership role. As part of her identity, based on history, she was proud of being a Turkish citizen and a Muslim. She tried to follow the tenets of Islam as much as possible. She had strong ties with her family. As a woman, she believed in gender equality and wanted to be as good as men.

During her high school years, she exposed her hair since the wig was banned. The act of exposing the hair was challenging for her. When she started university, she chose to wear a wig on campus. Her family was supportive of her decision, especially her father, who encouraged her to pursue higher education. She did not have a high GPA. This was because the exams were really challenging for all the students. She stayed with her parents and enjoyed the program she was in even though it was not one of her first choices in the university exam.

Higher education is important for me: She valued higher education; thought everybody, especially covered women, should go to university; and believed in the importance of an undergraduate diploma. She stated that education was also one of the precepts of Allah:

> If I do not go to university, if you do not go to university, who is going to go? As women we need to go to university. Covered women need the diploma even more. In addition, higher education is important for me because my parents are well educated and it is necessary for me to have a bachelor's degree. This is what Allah wants us to do as well. Allah wants us to get education. There is a big difference between somebody who goes to university, and somebody who doesn't. The program I am studying was not my first choice in the university exam. But in the exam I got a score lower than I expected so I was only able to enter this program. I was a little disappointed first, but now I really like it. I am also specializing in another subject at the same time. My GPA is not high but I am in the top five. I do not know what I will do when I graduate. But I will definitely do something good. I know that university education will contribute positively to my education.

Because she valued education and considered it as one of the precepts of Islam, Seda felt that the headscarf ban policy made her choose between two precepts, restricting her freedom to live her religion in the way she wanted.

I decided not to uncover until I was asked to remove the headscarf: Although Seda did not approve of the headscarf ban policy, she chose to comply with the policy after negotiating it with herself and her family because she did not have any other options to advance herself and make her father happy. While deciding on the type of unveiling, she seemed to have weighed the pros and cons of all different types of unveiling before she chose to wear a wig. Nevertheless, she also decided to arrive on the registration day as a veiled woman:

> I went to university with my father on the day of registration. I was covered. I decided not to uncover until I was asked to remove the headscarf. I hoped that maybe they would let me in with my headscarf. Some universities do, you know. In the registration area I, and other covered girls like me were invited into a room. There were some professors who chatted with us. They asked us why we were covered and said that they would like to help us if we were covered by force. They also explained the rules and regulations. They wrote down our names and departments we were in. They said the university did not allow hat wearers.

I am comfortable with people in class: Even though she was the only part-time unveiler in her program, Seda seemed to have a good relationship with most of her classmates, professors, and administrators; initially, she had felt nervous about their reaction toward her wig:

> I am the only [part-time unveiler] in my program. I am also the only one who is socioeconomically comfortable and well traveled. I have always been in nice environments. I have been abroad. I am a social and outgoing person. There are not many students like me. In fact, I am perhaps the only one. But this is not a problem for me. I am comfortable with the people in class. They have respect for me. For example, I do not shake hands with boys; I do not touch boys. They know this and never try to touch me or shake hands with me. So there has never been a problem in class. I am usually an active student in class, but it also changes from class to class and from teacher to teacher. My core courses are small. In those classes, I am really active. In crowded classes, usually electives, students do not know each other. In those classes I am a little nervous because I do not know whether students or professors are against the wig. In those classes, I am a little passive initially to understand the atmosphere. I usually ask people in advance to find out which professor is or is not against us [part-time unveilers] so I choose my electives accordingly, but still I become nervous every time I take classes outside my program. With one exception, I have a good relationship with my teachers. I visit my advisor and other professors from time to time. I usually chat with them. Whenever I have questions, I go and ask them. I met with some of my professors outside campus. So they know I am a covered girl. I do not wear a long coat but I wear a turtleneck at all times so they probably understand on campus too. And the way they treat me has never changed. But there is this one professor who is against the covered women and wig wearers. I try to avoid that professor as much as possible. I am also lucky in terms of friends. My friends are respectful. They always wait for me to unveil and veil back. They always support and encourage me. I have male and female friends, but I am distant to guys. There are a couple of people in the program who do not talk to me because I am a covered woman. They are against Islamists. They never liked me. Thank God, they never argued with me or said anything bad. They just did not want to talk to me and they do not. So I do not talk to them either. Other than those students, I am friendly with everyone. I also have a good relationship with my Dean. On campus, people sometimes stare at me when I walk. Those looks do not matter to me because I do not recognize myself there anyway. I always try to dress appropriately when I go to university. I am trying to be proper. I do not wear jeans. I have things I represent. I represent the headscarf. So I think I have to be very appropriate at all times.

I spend as little time as possible on campus: Despite her good relationships with faculty and friends, she tried to spend as little time as possible on campus and did not seem to be fully involved in campus activities:

> In addition, I spend as little time as possible on campus. I do not study on campus. I chat with friends, drink tea, go to class, or leave. Sometimes I sit in the garden with friends. I do not take part in extracurricular activities either. It is mainly because I am very active off campus; so I do not have time for campus activities. I attended Spring Festival once. My father came to pick me up in the evening. But I never went to concerts or other activities. I do not need to attend them. My unveiling does not affect my motivation. But I know there are some students who are impacted negatively.

I would like to pursue an academic career, but I know it is very difficult: In addition to the ways in which unveiling did or did not affect her life on campus, Seda also shared her perceptions about whether unveiling impacted her identity with specific reference to her citizenship, religious, and gender identities. She indicated that unveiling upset her identity greatly. But more importantly for her, the experience of unveiling challenged her with regard to her decision about her future career:

> Unveiling made me realize the extent to which it is going to impact my choice about my career. Under normal circumstances, I would like to pursue an academic career, but I know it is very difficult. This requires me to continue unveiling. I can become an associate professor or even a full professor. I can become a successful academic but this means that I am not going to veil. So if I choose to continue veiling, the option of academia is out of the window. I am very indecisive. Everybody is your inspector on campus once you start your graduate study; I know that. Everybody will be watching and evaluating you. Even if I chose to unveil completely, my mother is veiled. Those who do not like me can use my mother's veil against me and prevent me from becoming a full professor. On the other hand, I want to continue veiling after undergraduate education as well. So I am very confused.

To sum up, Seda did not seem to have many challenges, even though, as a wig user, she faced some problems from time to time. However, although she appeared to be comfortable with her unveiling and had a good relationship with most of her classmates, professors, and administrators, she did not spend a lot of time on campus and was not involved in extracurricular activities. These aspects suggested that while she felt safe in her program, she might not have felt the same in the campus environment. No matter how much she wanted to stay and be involved in activities, she felt unable to do so because that would mean being uncovered for an even longer period of time. Her identity did not seem to be affected as a result of her compliance with the policy, however. Even though she was upset due to the subjection to the ban and faced some challenges, she felt she needed to fight and be successful. As compared with Elif and Hale, Seda seemed to be more indecisive about her future decision of unveiling. Her passion for an academic career, which required her to continue unveiling, seemed to make her struggle between her religious duty and career choice. This might have been the reason why she could not definitively say that she would continue veiling.

Sema

Sema was a part-time unveiler whose understanding of the headscarf ban policy was quite different from that of Elif, Hale, or Seda. Although she was against the introduction of the ban, she believed that its existence was the only option at the time due to the then political and social climate in Turkey. Even though she had negotiated the policy trouble-free, she felt challenged due to the act of unveiling. Her unveiling on campus and veiling off campus made her feel as if she was two different people, and this had a substantial, negative impact on her educational and cultural experiences. Her biggest challenge seemed to be her social life on campus, where she felt isolated, which caused her various psychological problems.

I covered my hair because of fear of Allah, because of religious reasons: Sema was born in a big city; she came from a conservative family. Her mother was veiled in the traditional way. She was in a public school and planning to cover her hair when the big earthquake in Turkey took place. Shaken by it, she decided to cover her hair because of fear of God. She had been covered for seven years. Sema was very patriotic and an observant Muslim who tried to follow the tenets of Islam as she understood them. She had good relationships with her parents and friends. She had a boyfriend, whom she really liked. In the future, she wanted to work in the corporate world:

> I love my country. I want it to become developed. I do not want it to be a developing one. I believe everybody loves their own country. For me, my country is the best. I also love my religion. I am trying my best to do good things and avoid bad ones. I covered my hair because of fear of Allah, because of religious reasons. The veil became a habit. I feel better and freer with my headscarf on. I feel as if something is missing without my headscarf. I believe intention is very important. The intention of veiling and unveiling is important. It is also important to be a good person, avoid gossip, and visit your relatives, because religion is not only composed of fasting and praying. I have a wonderful family. We have close relationships with one another. I always

talk to them intimately, share my problems, and chat for hours and hours. I also like going out with them. I feel terrible when I am away from them. As a woman, in Turkey, I know that women are mainly oppressed. Before, almost all women were housewives. This is changing slowly. Women have started becoming active in the corporate world. I disapprove of gender discrimination. My boyfriend treats me as an equal. I also talk to male friends. Of course, I always keep some distance.

I want to pursue an academic career, but the headscarf ban is always a barrier for me: Sema exposed her hair during her high school years and on the university campus. She was living with her parents while attending university. She had a high GPA. One of the reasons why she wanted to go to university was to become an important person in society. She liked her program and believed that it would broaden her horizons. She did not think that there was a bright future for her after graduation due to the headscarf ban policy, which would affect her job opportunities and career choices:

> I want to become something. . . . I want to prove myself. I also like what I am studying. I believe my program broadens horizons. I am attending university, but I do not think there is a bright future for me. I want to have a job. Actually I want to pursue an academic career, but the headscarf ban is always a barrier for me. So if I want to become a professor, I need to continue unveiling. I have not decided what to do yet. I want people to accept me covered, but it is not possible now. Maybe I will work in a private institution. Anyway, for now, I will try my best to get a good education and make myself somebody of importance in society.

Like Seda, Sema also appeared pessimistic regarding her desire to pursue an academic career at a university due to the headscarf ban. It was a ban that affected her present and future situation. She did not know whether she wanted to continue living her life as a part-time unveiler.

The headscarf ban shows that, in fact, there is restricted freedom of thought: Different from the views of Elif, Hale, and Seda, Sema thought that despite its restriction on her freedom, this was a ban that had to exist to prevent worse things from happening:

> The headscarf ban shows that in fact there is restricted freedom of thought. The ban is an attempt to create one type of person. There is no success at the end of the road as a result of this ban. The ban oppresses covered women and tries to eradicate their religious identity. I do not know if this can be considered as a success. On the other hand, let's analyze the reasons behind this ban. One famous politician said, "İmam Hatip schools are the backyards of our

political party. On campuses, professors will bow with respect in front of the covered students." If you say these things as a politician, you create tension, which is exactly what happened. Things were becoming very tense. Political games became too much to accept. The atmosphere was as if there was an attempt to make the country ruled by Islamic law. It had to be stopped. Somebody had to say stop and [the general headscarf ban, together with the higher education headscarf ban,] was a response to stop this political tension and conflict.

As much as she appeared to be against the headscarf ban policy, Sema thought that the ban was necessary at the time due to the political atmosphere. But she also realized that it had affected her whole education, and since high school, had forced her to make decisions about the way she dressed.

I am exposing my hair on campus: Sema decided to unveil to receive higher education and become an active citizen in society:

I am exposing my hair on campus because my aim is to receive education and become a useful citizen in society. Maybe I can change the situation; I can make some corrections. Why shouldn't I go to university? Why shouldn't I become a university student like others? I did not even consider other options such as going abroad. I always wanted to go to university in Turkey. After primary school, I really wanted to go to an İmam Hatip school. Another option was to go to a normal public school. I was going to unveil wherever I went. In the 1990s, İmam Hatip schools were also applying the headscarf ban policy. But as an İmam Hatip graduate, my university exam score was going to be reduced. This was not going to happen in the public school. So I chose to go to the normal public school. I have potential. I always thought I could change some things. But this is not going to happen. I am not going to be able to do anything. Maybe some other people will do some things. You know what, everybody wrote love poems into their diaries during high school years, I wrote why I was in the state I was in as a girl who had to unveil to go to school. I collected all the articles, news, and comics about the headscarf. I am not a politically active person. I am distant to all the political parties and politics. I do not know which political view is right. I do not want to be misused and abused by politics. This is why I do not want to become a member of a political group. I attended headscarf ban protests, but left in the middle. I always exposed my hair. I heard that in one of the verses, our Prophet said he did not like the wig. I do not know how much of it is true but I would still not choose the wig as my type of unveiling. It attracts a lot of attention. I go to university in a normal way and I do not think I attract attention. We have a fitting room at the entrance to the campus. We have a masjid [small praying area] in the garden. My parents did not react to my decision; they would never do that anyway. My friends also approved of my decision to unveil.

Even though Sema exposed her hair and the way she negotiated the policy seemed trouble-free and relatively easy, she felt challenged by the act of unveiling and veiling. She was unhappy because of the fact that she had to unveil. This impacted her educational experiences greatly. In class she tried to avoid attracting attention and to concentrate on her studies. Even though unveiling did not appear to impact her motivation for studying, it seemed that it had a negative impact on her social life on campus. Sema did not seem to experience any type of abuse, discrimination, or marginalization, but by choice, she had quite an isolated existence on campus. She felt that if she socialized, she would or could be subjected to harassment as a result of her being a part-time unveiler. In other words, the fact that she was a part-time unveiler made her antisocial and cut her off from campus activities. Even though she did not perceive this situation as impacting on her motivation to study or general success, it affected her ability to build social capital informally that she could benefit from in the future.

I feel worried and anxious even outside campus: In addition, Sema's unveiling experience affected her identity negatively in different ways:

> I feel worried and anxious even outside campus. This is why I have problems in initiating dialogue with new people I meet. Maybe I am scared of meeting new people and communicating with them. The person who is unveiled on campus is not me, but with new people, I feel as if they are going to ask me to unveil or something like that. So I feel as if I do not have any rights.... This creates anxiety and lack of confidence. I began to develop some lack of confidence in the government as well. Each political party has its own game and when they are the government, they do everything to stay in power. So with this ban in place, I feel as if things are going to get worse. Another impact of unveiling on my identity is [that I am making a] concession. Unveiling is a concession from my religious duties. I hope Allah does not punish me for that. Sometimes I wish I were a man; life would be so much easier I guess.

Even though Sema thought that the ban had to exist due to the then political context of Turkey, her accounts showed that she was quite challenged as a result of complying with the policy. Unveiling caused her anxiety, worry, and a lack of confidence in things she used to believe. In addition, she felt isolated and socially handicapped as a result of unveiling, which prevented her from building the social network she might need in the future.

Burcu

Burcu was a part-time unveiler who considered herself to be a devout Muslim. Despite the fact that she had relatively non-challenging educational and cultural experiences as a result of complying with the headscarf ban policy, her religious, and gender identities seemed to have been impacted in a negative way due to her unveiling. Her female identity appeared to be particularly challenged, as Burcu felt restrictions in various ways that impacted her feminine identity.

Burcu was born and grew up in a big city; she came from a large family, where her mother was veiled too. She wanted to go to school with her hair covered, so she chose the Anatolian İmam Hatip school. When she was there, the headscarf ban policy was not in force in İmam Hatip schools. Her mother thought that Grade six was early for her to veil, but she insisted on covering her hair. When the policy of points deduction of Imam Hatip graduates at the university exam was introduced, she was sent to a coeducational private school, where she uncovered her hair during her high school years.

I am trying to follow the tenets of Islam as much as possible: Burcu was a woman who flourished in environments where she felt comfortable. She considered herself to be a good listener and quite introvert by nature. However, she did not like loneliness. She was happy she was born in Turkey, a country that she considered to have a rich history and great traditions. As a result of all this she was proud of being Turkish. She also considered herself an observant Muslim and tried to follow the tenets of Islam, as she understood them, as much as possible:

> I am trying to follow the tenets of Islam as much as possible. There are many things that I cannot do. I know that. I am covering my hair because I know that it is a requirement. It is a wish of Allah. I know that this wish is written in Surah an-Nur in the Qur'an. This is my identity as a Muslim woman. My headscarf is a symbol that distinguishes me from a non-Muslim woman. I also pray and fast. I help those who are in need. I believe I actually represent certain values and virtues as a covered woman. That is why I am trying to be extra careful with the way I behave and treat others.

After her secondary education, for her bachelor's degree, Burcu moved away from her hometown to another city and started living with friends in a flat while attending university. She chose the hat as her primary style of unveiling. However, when professors did not let her wear a hat in class she switched to the wig. In the final semester of that year, she mostly used the hat. Her parents were supportive of her decision. She had always had good relationships with her parents and siblings. Burcu considered higher education to be a source of prestige and a way to independence, and she liked the subject she was studying. She believed that university education would contribute greatly to her life and career in the future.

The headscarf ban exists because of the prejudices of policymakers: In addition to handling many challenges related to living on her own for the first time, she was also challenged by the headscarf ban policy. She perceived the policy to be a product of the prejudices of policymakers, who were trying to prevent covered women from receiving higher education and playing an active role in society:

> Generally speaking, the headscarf ban exists because of the prejudices of policymakers. They want nobody to look different. They want everybody to be the same.... They are trying to prevent covered students from attending higher education institutions. The deduction of points for İmam Hatip schools, the higher education headscarf ban policy, they both exist to prevent us moving forward, to cut our progress and advancement. Policymakers try to direct us toward religious studies. They say you must only study religion, and become a teacher of religion, and nothing else. They do not want us to be active in different parts of society. So this is a policy imposed upon covered women by policymakers.

Because she considered the ban to be an imposition, Burcu believed that covered women needed to fight against it by complying with the policy, which was what she had decided to do. Another decision of hers was to wear a hat until she was asked to take it off. She felt veiled even when she was wearing the hat and she also knew that when people saw her with the hat on, they understood that she was a covered woman. This was exactly what she wanted people to believe.

I feel like a different person on campus: Burcu felt that her main challenges were to not get accustomed to unveiling, a plight that had befallen many of her part-time unveiling friends, and to deal with the fact that unveiling made her feel a little passive:

> By unveiling, I am doing something that is imposed upon me. I feel like a different person on campus. I feel as if I have lost my identity, I behave as if I am a different person. The challenge is that once unveiled, you can easily become used to unveiling, as many of my friends did. The hat constantly reminds me that I am a veiled woman. My relationship with professors changes from teacher to teacher. Only one of my professors would not accept me into class with my hat, so in that class I wore a wig, thus removing any tension. Many of my professors found out that I am a covered woman. Some professors do not care; others started treating me differently after they found out I am a covered woman. The professor I had tension with sometimes becomes sarcastic. When I do something good, she is surprised and says, "Did you really do this yourself? Does this thought really belong to you? Is it really your idea?" et cetera. She is prejudiced and gives me a hard time when I take her class. Other than this teacher, I do not have any problems with my professors. When I attend extracurricular activities outside campus, I always wear my headscarf. Professors let me wear my headscarf in such cases. So they know I am a covered woman. There are other hat wearers on campus as

well. My friends also know that I am covered. They have known it since the beginning. I have covered and uncovered friends. I also have friends whose religious ideas are different from mine. I also have friends who are covered in their private lives, but expose their hair on campus. There are some class-mates who chose to distance themselves from me after they realized I was a covered woman. But they were not close friends anyway. . . . I have some close girlfriends. I am always with them on campus. Our campus is not a politically active place. There are some students who support me, some who do not. But they do not bother me. I sometimes take part in extracurricu-lar activities. I go to concerts with my headscarf on, do group projects, and attend seminars and conferences. In class, I am a little shy. That is because I am not perfectly comfortable with myself. I cannot be active and prove myself in the way I want as a result of this ban. I feel a little passive in class as a result of wearing my hat or wig.

Burcu seemed to be handling her unveiling experience better than some of the other part-time unveilers. It also appeared that the nonthreatening campus environment contributed to her university life positively, making it easier and more tolerable for her.

Career is not going to be a problem in the future: Burcu did not seem to be concerned about her career in the future either:

Career is not going to be a problem in the future. I want to work in the private sector anyway. There might be some companies that will not want to hire me, but this is not a big deal. If the worst comes to the worst, I can start my own company. So there are many options for me.

I feel inferior as a woman: One of the main challenges facing Burcu was the impact of unveiling on her identity, especially female identity. She did not think unveiling affected her citizenship identity and she was not sure if her Muslim identity was affected in any way:

I find it hard to understand the relationship between secularism, which is the separation of the state and religion, and the ban, which is the involvement of the state into the religion. Unveiling does not affect my citizenship identity. As for my Muslim identity, I do not know. I am not sure if my Muslim iden-tity is impacted in any way by unveiling. I know that my female identity is hurt. I feel inferior as a woman. This is a ban for women, not men. Islamist men do not suffer, but women do. As a result of unveiling, I am being forced into something I do not want. This is a burden for me. I am doing some-thing in which I do not believe. I hope people get rid of their prejudices and understand what the headscarf really means for covered women. I hope women like me can be in an environment where they have the freedom to live their lives in the way they want.

So even though she was challenged by the existence of the ban and felt like a different person on campus, Burcu appeared to have relatively non-challenging educational and cultural experiences and the nonthreatening atmosphere of her campus had a positive contribution, making life on campus easier to handle. However, she believed that unveiling challenged her female identity and made her wonder about her role and status in society.

4

Understanding and Negotiating the Headscarf Ban Policy

Understanding the Policy

While demonstrating their understanding of the policy, the part-time unveilers formulated their answers around three different subthemes: part-time unveilers' perceptions of the reasons why the ban existed, part-time unveilers' perceptions of the long-term goal of the ban, and what the ban meant to the part-time unveilers.

Why Did the Higher Education Headscarf Ban Policy Exist?

Part-time unveilers believed there were four distinct reasons why the higher education headscarf ban policy existed. While expressing their ideas and opinions, some part-time unveilers referred to the political and/or social context of Turkey, whereas others restricted their responses to the Turkish higher education context. In addition to these reasons, one of the part-time unveilers stated that she did not know why the ban existed.

Power struggle between secularists and Islamists: Eight part-time unveilers believed that the reason why the ban existed was the political context of the country. They elaborated upon this to state that there was a power struggle between the secularists and the Islamists in Turkish politics. İpek explained this political tension between these two groups as follows:

> The headscarf was banned in higher education due to the power struggle between secularists and Islamists. Secularists have been the people in power for a long time in Turkish history. They have had control of the bureaucracy and the decision-making mechanisms. When they realized they were going to lose their power or give some of it away as a result of Islamists gaining

political power, they looked for ways in which they could prevent Islamists from gaining this power. The ban is one way of protecting their power. You need to understand that the headscarf is one of the visible faces of Islam, so it is a kind of symbol. As a response, Islamists used the ban as a provocative tool to mobilize the conservative people. This worsened the situation and the ban became more intensified.

Other part-time unveilers shared similar views, but also added a new dimension. They believed that some international political parties contributed to the power struggle between different groups in different ways, worsening the political situation in Turkey. Buket explained:

> In my opinion, some Western countries do not want Turkey to have peace. External powers provoke Turkish politicians in different ways creating a conflict between secularists and Islamists. It is Turkey that suffers as result of the power struggle between different political views. It is Turkey that suffers from the headscarf ban in higher education context.

The perceptions of these part-time unveilers seemed to hint at the intricacies lying behind the headscarf ban in terms of the national and international political contexts since the foundation of the Turkish Republic. One way to approach the perceptions of these part-time unveilers might be to conclude that the headscarf ban policy was a result of competition between secular and Islamist identities in Turkish politics. From this perspective, the accounts of the part-time unveilers highlighted that, when the political climate started to lean in favor of Islamists, secularists found ways in which to prevent this from happening so that they could continue to rule. One of these ways was through the banning of the headscarf in universities. Through this ban, (female) Islamists could be deterred from going to university, thus losing their chance of becoming future leaders of the country.

Another interpretation might be the issue of political Islam. Some part-time unveilers thought that the headscarf ban existed due to the instrumentalization of Islam by opposing parties for political purposes. Part-time unveilers even commented that Islam was used as an instrument in international politics as a way for Western countries to control the internal affairs of Turkey. So, from this perspective, it might even be possible to argue that the voices of the part-time unveilers suggested that the driving force behind all the existing political tensions was the politicization of religion, in this case, Islam. Following this argument, it was then natural to conclude that the real issue behind what part-time unveilers perceived as a political struggle between Islamists and secularists as a reason for the headscarf ban policy might in fact be the struggle of political Islam trying to establish itself in the Turkish political context.

Eliminate religious symbols: Six part-time unveilers stated that the reason why the headscarf ban policy existed was to help hide the religious identity of Turkey so as to make Turkey appear more modern. They highlighted that policymakers in different Turkish contexts tried to make sure that the visible face of Turkey looked as modern as possible by pushing the Islamic identity aside. Yeliz stated:

> Some of the ruling elite do not want to see people who look different. They see themselves as the symbol of modernity and want others to look like them. In order to achieve their goals, they apply bans that will eliminate religious symbols in different contexts in the country. Unfortunately, higher education is one such context. When the ruling elite wanted to implement the ban in higher education, the Higher Education Council members approved the decision as they are obviously alike in their thinking. So this way, both politicians and Higher Education Council members want to create one type of person in Turkey. This is the reason why the higher education headscarf ban policy exists.

Reyhan added:

> The reason why the higher education headscarf ban policy exists is to hide the Islamic identity on campuses. Interestingly enough, there is also a ban on tight trousers, extremely short skirts, beards, and mustaches; but none of these are applied. Only the headscarf ban is applied on campuses. It is because it is the most visible facet of Islam. This ban confuses professors. Some who do not support the ban still had to enforce it in order not to be in conflict with the administration. Those who support the ban keep asking me if I have a political reason to wear the headscarf. They always "hunt" for the covered female students. They forget their academic jobs, the fact that university is a mosaic and all that and "hunt" us in order to make us look modern and secular.

The accounts of these part-time unveilers suggested that they believed policymakers were using the ban as a way to "improve" the country, to help Turkey become a developed nation. The belief was that universities were the contemporary face of Turkey, and campuses with all students appearing in nonreligious looking clothing conveyed an image of modernity and advancement. What seemed to be an issue for part-time unveilers was that, on the one hand, policymakers wanted citizens to be contemporary and active, and on the other hand, they implemented bans that might dissuade students from attending higher education or cause them to leave Turkey and attend university in a different country. In this sense, part-time unveilers found that what the policymakers claimed to want was in conflict with what they did.

Preserve the secular nature of the campus: Two part-time unveilers believed that the reason why the headscarf ban existed was to ensure campuses preserved their secular nature. They highlighted that, since secularism is the separation of state and religion, one way to ensure secularism on campus was to remove all the symbols associated with Islam. They added that, this way, all students, free of their visible religious symbols, could receive an equal education without being subjected to any potential marginalization or discrimination due to political prejudices that students, professors, and administrators might hold. In this sense, these two part-time unveilers perceived that the ban might help their educational process, providing them an educational opportunity where students were treated equally since they all looked alike on campuses. As explained by Fatma:

> This is a fair policy. It is true that there are differences between Islamists and secularists. If the policy did not exist, there would be serious repercussions. Right now, it is true that my freedom is restricted and I look like someone else as a result of unveiling. But the policy helps everybody look similar. The policy prevents students from political or religious mobilization and oppression. It also helps eradicate biases. If I attend university with my headscarf on, men might compare me with other women. They might think I have higher morals and I am more innocent than others. So the ban helps us to separate the state and religion. We preserve the secular nature of the campus and the country.

Show students that government controls the higher education system and will not condone violence: Two part-time unveilers believed that the reason for the existence of the ban was to prevent the type of chaos and violence that existed before 1980 on campuses. This limitation on some students' freedom would deter students from violent activism. They stated that, before 1980, terror escalated in universities due to the fights between left-wing and right-wing students. So, according to these part-time unveilers, the headscarf ban could be used as one deterrent to inhibit thinking—that is, as a way of the government controlling thoughts and making individuals passive. This showed universities that the government was powerful enough to control higher education when necessary in order to prevent chaos. Reyhan explained:

> On the surface, the headscarf ban exists to prevent the Islamist students from expressing their thoughts and ideas freely on campus. If you are [part-time unveilers], you are never really relaxed. This prevents you from expressing your thoughts freely. You become passive. This is just on the surface. The real reason why the headscarf ban policy exists is actually to show students

that government controls the higher education system and will not condone violence. By oppressing one group, policymakers show they have the power to control students in different ways. They started with the covered women because at the time the headscarf was also seen as a political statement. So it gave policy administrators the opportunity to kill two birds with one stone and unfortunately covered women have become the victims of this situation.

According to this belief, the ban was not actually against the headscarf, but against all political ideologies and ideals that in any way challenged the status quo.

Part-time unveilers believed there were many different reasons why the headscarf ban policy existed. All these reasons seemed to derive from part-time unveilers' perceptions of a struggle between Islamists and secularists or political Islam trying to stabilize itself in Turkish politics or secularists trying to preserve their power in the political, social, and educational context of Turkey. These perceptions of part-time unveilers revealed how the headscarf ban policy seemed to be closely connected and intertwined with the issues of secularism, Islamist and secularist identities, class, gender, and religion (Islam) that existed in the country.

What Was the Long-Term Goal of the Policy?

One group of part-time unveilers thought that the long-term goal of the policy was to create one type of person. Another group perceived that the ban was in force to prevent covered women from having positions of power in society, economy, and politics by dissuading them from going to university.

One type of person: More than half of the part-time unveilers believed that the long-term goal of the policy was to create one type of person on campuses. Part-time unveilers stated they understood that "One type of person equalizes students and prevents problems that might arise due to socioeconomic, religious, or political differences" (Reyhan). They thought that this type of system was good in primary and secondary schools where students were not mature enough to understand, respect, and appreciate differences. However, part-time unveilers viewed higher education as an arena for mature students who came from diverse backgrounds. That said, some part-time unveilers, like Semra, thought that the policy was relatively successful:

> We used to wear long coats. Each year, with the influence of fashion, these coats became shorter and shorter. Fashion designers design more and more modern clothes, and we buy them. I think this is purposeful. The same is

true for headscarves as well. Years ago, headscarves were only big, square, and plain covering the shoulders. Then they became smaller, now they are colorful, even in the form of long scarves matching the color of the clothes. So with the influence of fashion, the headscarf has moved beyond its original purpose. Then came the headscarf ban on campus. First, you uncover your hair on campus. Then, you need to go out to buy something for five minutes. You do not want to cover your hair for five minutes, so go out uncovered. This goes on like this. Some students slowly start to go out uncovered, and then they get used to it. I think this is happening slowly. The number of those who will become uncovered completely might increase in five to ten years. I think the ban succeeds in its long-term target. Students gradually become used to looking uncovered. The ban contributes to the creation of one type of student, causing covered women to lose interest in religion and headscarves.

Sevim shared a similar view, but also emphasized the fact that the focus of the ban was to specifically change Muslim women on campuses who chose to cover their hair because woman had the power to change society. According to her:

The long-term target of the ban is to change the religious woman, interrupt her values and beliefs. The ban makes a covered woman question herself and her belief system. The aim is to change the moral system of those Muslim women who lead a conservative and religious life. This is a ban for women because they are more influential in society. It is women who bring up children, shape them, train them, and teach them values. So whether men accept or deny the argument, it is a fact that women are the fundamental parts of society. If you change women, you change the next generation. So when you comply with the ban, you become part of the system; there are some who do not change, but there are many who change. I know a lot of friends who started college covered, and graduated uncovered. This is an action to castrate religion and a religious lifestyle, particularly to castrate the visible face of Islam by trying to change covered women. And I know for sure that the ban partially achieves what it intends to achieve.

A couple of part-time unveilers took this point one step further and stated that the long-term goal of the policy was in fact to secularize Islamists in general. Two part-time unveilers explained that secularists perceived Islamists as non-secular people and wanted to secularize them by asking them to unveil themselves during their educational years, including university:

The ban is a psychological battle. Since there is a phobia of religiosity in Turkey, the long-term goal of the ban is to distance students, future citizens of Turkey, from Islam. In this way, it is hoped that [part-time unveilers] will become [full-time unveilers] and secularized after many years of uncovering the hair in schools or on campuses. I do not know how effective the ban is or will be in this sense, because it is true that there are some students who give up covering their hair as a result, but there are some who become more attached to their headscarves. So I do not know the extent to which the ban succeeds in this sense.

(Melek)

A similar issue that emerged earlier with reference to the relationship between modernity and Islam emerged here in the form of a relationship between secularism and Islam. The part-time unveilers perceived that secularists viewed Islamists as non-secular and so tried to secularize them using the ban as a means to this end. This seemed to suggest that there might be a lack of clear understanding as to how one would reconcile secularism and Islam in Turkey.

There were some other part-time unveilers who believed that the policy was not powerful enough to change them in the future:

I know the target of the policy is to create one type of woman in the future. This woman, regardless of her degree of religiosity, is the one who is uncovered and is wearing Western clothes. I am wearing a hat to look like others on campus. This makes me ashamed of myself, and I am sad that I have to remove my headscarf. So the headscarf ban policy reminds me of the value of my headscarf. The ban reminds me how important the headscarf is, and how I need to keep wearing it for the rest of my life.

(Selma)

Even though these women had similar perceptions about what the policy intended to achieve in the long run, they diverged in opinion in terms of whether the policy was successful or not. One interesting observation was that those who thought that the policy had achieved what it intended to achieve in the long run, in terms of causing covered women to lose interest in religion and headscarf, were mostly part-time unveilers who had chosen to expose their hair as a way of complying with the policy while attending higher education institutions. In the same way, those who thought that the policy was not or would not be successful were those who wore hats or wigs.

Prevent Islamists from becoming active participants in society: Eleven of the part-time unveilers believed the headscarf ban was a way to prevent covered women from becoming active contributors in society, the economy, and politics by dissuading them from gaining access to higher education. These part-time unveilers believed that secularists were prejudiced against covered women, and the ban, as an application of this prejudice, was in place to prevent Islamists from receiving higher education and becoming active citizens of the country. Sevgi stated: "The ban aims to prevent Islamists from becoming active participants in society since the perception is that a covered woman cannot contribute fully to the economy of the country." Yeliz elaborated on how the policy could prevent Islamist women from taking an active part in society in the long run:

> The aim of the policy is to hinder the success of Islamists. If you do not have an undergraduate degree, you cannot be influential in Turkish society. If you do not graduate from a university, it is very difficult to become somebody who has a say in critical matters concerning the economy, society, or politics. The ruling elite and the Higher Education Council members do not want conservative and religious people to become powerful in the country. The best and easiest way to achieve this goal is to prevent Islamists from attending higher education. They have not found an effective way for Islamist men yet, although they have a way to stop Islamist women by means of the headscarf ban policy. It is a critical barrier for women to decide what they want to become in the future. It is true that there are many covered students who stopped continuing their education because of the ban.

Mine added that in the past the education of many covered women had been interrupted as a result of the ban. According to her, these women lost the opportunity to have a say in society. She did not want to be one of them:

> The policy intends to dissuade covered women from attending higher education institutions. If I do not go, and you do not go, who is going to go, who is going to represent me? The policymakers are stubborn and they want to keep the ban. I am stubborn too. I am complying with the policy so that I can obtain access to higher education.

The accounts of part-time unveilers suggested that they perceived that the policy resulted in keeping numerous covered women from obtaining higher education. Part-time unveilers wanted to change this and continue their education by agreeing to comply with the policy.

In short, part-time unveilers considered two issues as the long-term goal of the policy. Considering their perceptions about the long-term target of the policy, the ban seemed to have achieved what it intended to achieve in some ways and did not in other ways. The question of what this meant for policymakers and administrators from the perspective of the headscarf ban policy seemed to be an issue that needed to be discussed and evaluated.

What Did the Policy Mean to the Part-Time Unveilers?

Half of the women believed the ban resulted in restriction of their free-dom and questioned the extent to which higher education institutions were democratic. For some women, the ban was related more to their psy-chological well-being, affecting their emotions and personalities. A couple of women saw the ban as a concession from their religious beliefs. There were also a few part-time unveilers who considered the ban as a signal that labeled them as the "other" or as a stimulator that made them ambitious.

A restriction of freedom on a free and democratic campus: Half of the women mentioned that the ban restricted their freedom since it did not allow them to be the way they liked. While expressing their feelings, these part-time unveilers spoke passionately about how they felt and were treated. Some women used strong and assertive words to explain what the ban meant for them. Others appeared more emotional with a softer tone while highlighting their points:

> The ban means a restriction of freedom on a free and democratic campus. The ban resulted in the removal of my rights. I cannot do what I want to do. Am I a woman with the plague? This is how I feel right now. The ban creates an environment where people might catch a disease as a result of communicating with covered women.
>
> (Buket)

Part-time unveilers appeared to struggle to understand the place of the ban in a democratic higher education system in which they believed they all had the right to freedom of religion and to use the headscarf as they wished. They seemed to perceive the ban to be a violation of their equal educational rights, which could be argued to contradict the core of the higher education system in Turkey (T.C. Yükseköğretim Kurulu, n.d. b).

A psychological battle: For eight women, the ban meant an impact on their emotions and personalities. Some part-time unveilers focused on the relationship between their psychological well-being and the policy, while others explored how the ban impacted their personalities at a young age. The women also made a distinction between how they initially felt when they complied with the policy and how their feelings had evolved over the years:

> What the ban initially meant to me was a psychological pressure and loss of confidence. The first day on campus, I felt tired and weak. But later on, I got used to uncovering. It is not a psychological pressure anymore, but it still has a huge impact on my confidence, and the way I carry myself on campus.
>
> (Melek)

Sezen had a different perspective:

> To me, the ban is a psychological battle. It always has been. I have been forced into a large struggle at a very young age. Subjected to such hurdles, I have become mature maybe more quickly than I should have. It has affected my psychology extremely negatively. After I was dismissed (from university), I went abroad, but felt fearful on campus. I thought somebody was going to come at any time and tell me to leave the campus. I had therapy abroad. Then I changed. When I returned home, I realized I was a grown up. I felt like a human being. Now I realize that all this issue of the headscarf ban is a test. This is how I see it now.

On the other hand, Selma explained:

> The ban means strengthening my character, solidifying it. I have learned how to fight injustices. I have come to see that there is always an alternative solution as long as I am strong. I know how to resist. I feel very strong. The ban taught me how I need to stand firm in the face of difficulties without falling down. It really made me brave and courageous. It gave me the energy to start a battle.

The part-time unveilers perceived the headscarf ban as an issue that had a negative impact on their psychological well-being in numerous ways. For those who perceived that their emotions had been affected negatively, it was possible to argue that the ban had a negative impact on their psychology. The issue seemed to become complex and not so clear when some part-time unveilers stated that the ban had some contribution in making their character stronger. It was possible to interpret their perception of the contribution of the ban on their character in two different ways. One perspective was that the ban had a stimulating effect on part-time unveilers that helped them develop solid identities. Another perspective might be that the ban had such a deteriorating impact on the part-time unveilers that those who managed to survive matured and grew stronger.

Concession from Islam: For four women, the ban meant a concession from their religious beliefs. Some women thought that their decision to uncover was a concession from Islam:

> The headscarf ban means a concession from Islam. I know it is a sin to remove my headscarf. I have to do it to continue my education. I hope Allah forgives me for this. I am sad because of this situation, but I think it is the policymakers who need to be sad for making my life miserable and causing me pain and sorrow.

(Fatma)

Yeliz saw the concession in a different way:

> In the Qur'an, there are some precepts that need to be followed. One is the precept of education, and the other is the precept of covering. I cannot do both. So, as a result of this policy, I make a concession from one precept to follow the other precept. This is what the policy means to me. I know people who should not have seen my hair did, but I believe that Allah will forgive me. I have only removed my headscarf, I have not changed my behavior. In addition, the intentions behind removing the headscarf are also important. I am only removing my headscarf to serve another cause. It is an unfortunate situation, but this is a fact I need to take into account.

Different from the rest of society: Three part-time unveilers considered the ban as a way of being labeled as the other. In their minds, the higher education headscarf ban policy was a marker that separated them from the rest of the campus population, labeling them as different from the majority:

> The headscarf ban policy means polarization to me. It is the reflection of [polarization] on campus. The headscarf ban policy labels you as someone different from the rest of society. The policy creates many groups that did not exist before. Now there are policy compliers, policy noncompliers, and people who are not concerned with the policy. So even within Islamists, the ban creates differentiation and otherness. Policy compliers and noncompliers have become polarized. So on campus I am a policy complier, not an uncovered woman. So in the minds of many uncovered women, I am the other, I guess.
>
> (Leyla)

Stimulator: Two part-time unveilers explained that they saw the ban as a motivator: "The ban is a motivator; it is like a whip that helps me move forward. It gives me ambition" (Gamze).

In short, these women perceived the ban as a policy that restricted their freedom and created otherness. Their perceptions also indicated that for part-time unveilers the ban led to a psychological battle and concession from religious beliefs. A few women considered the policy as a motivator.

Negotiating the Policy

Part-time unveilers formulated the ways in which they negotiated the policy around four subthemes. These were consideration of other options, reasons for compliance, reaction of others to their decision of unveiling, and reasons for the type of unveiling they had chosen.

Options

Many part-time unveilers explained that the first stage of the negotiation with the policy was to consider their options. A majority of part-time unveilers expressed their initial desire to continue their education abroad, but for various reasons they could not do so. A couple of part-time unveilers stated that they initially decided not to go to university as an option, but changed their mind due to parental pressure. In addition, some part-time unveilers did not consider any other options but to comply with the policy and go to university.

The first thing that comes to your mind is to leave: Seventeen part-time unveilers stated that they first considered the option of continuing their education abroad. They mentioned that going abroad was initially a logi-cal thing to do since Turkish higher education policymakers did not want them:

> If higher education policymakers do not want you, why should you stay? Of course, the first thing that comes to your mind is to leave. My reaction in those days was that if I were not wanted, then I would leave and not come back. I would not work here. I would not serve here. This is why I started looking at other options such as America, Russia, and Austria.
>
> (Sevtap)

Five part-time unveilers could not go abroad because their parents could not afford it. They looked for scholarships, but could not find any either: "I wanted to continue my education abroad, but I knew it was very expen-sive. My parents could never afford it. I looked for a scholarship, but could not find one" (Semra). For four part-time unveilers, going abroad was not possible because their parents, especially their father, did not give them permission to go. Two part-time unveilers stayed in Turkey when they real-ized that for some professions (i.e., those that require licensing), including their professions-to-be, studying abroad precluded them from practicing in Turkey. Two part-time unveilers went ahead and applied to universities abroad, but could not enter the programs they wanted. Two other part-time unveilers had permission to go abroad with the finances in place, but decided against it later on because they realized they were going to go through a lot of adaptation problems. They did not want to be on their own either. There were two other part-time unveilers, returning students, who went abroad, but came back, for personal reasons, without completing their studies:

> I went abroad after I stopped going to university in Turkey due to the headscarf ban policy. I quickly realized that it was not a good decision. First

of all, it was very expensive. I felt very lonely and I was scared. Even though I was able to attend university with my headscarf on, I returned home. I could no longer stay in a strange country, where I had no family or friends.

(Nurten)

I did not think about any other alternatives: Ten part-time unveilers stated that they did not consider other options. They did not want to go abroad. Not going to university was not an option for them either: "I did not think about any other alternatives. I always wanted to go to university in Turkey. Since my headscarf is not political, it was not difficult to come to the decision of complying with the policy. I had other problems after removing it, but the decision of compliance was not a problem for me" (Fatma).

Some students explained that they started university unveiled first and decided to veil during their undergraduate education. So after covering the hair, removing the headscarf was not a problem anyway. They never considered dropping out: "I started university unveiled. So unveiling after veiling was never a problem. I never considered any other options other than complying with the policy after I decided to cover my hair" (Dilara).

I did not want to continue university: Three part-time unveilers mentioned that they did consider the option of not going to university, but their parents pushed them toward compliance with the policy and attending university. Yeliz, for example, explained that she did not want to remove her headscarf during higher education. So the only option for her at the time was not to continue higher education: "I did not want to continue university because I did not want to unveil." However, the pressure from her parents forced her to revise her decision and continue her education.

To sum up, the majority of the part-time unveilers had considered other options such as going abroad or not continuing their education before they eventually decided to comply with the policy. When their first option appeared to not have worked, they then chose to comply with the policy. For many of these part-time unveilers, not going to university was never an option; they were all determined to continue higher education, but they did not know where. Some other part-time unveilers did not seem to have even considered other options. Compliance with the policy was the only choice they wanted to make. They had known what they were required to do to continue higher education in Turkey and were prepared to follow the "rules."

Reasons for Compliance

After highlighting other options they considered before complying with the policy, part-time unveilers moved on to explaining the rationale behind their compliance. One observation was that a majority of part-time unveilers who considered going abroad but could not, pointed out that they complied with the policy not because they did not have any other option. They provided some rationale for their compliance. The way they packaged their reasons for complying with the ban showed that these part-time unveilers might have seen not having any other option than compliance as a sign of helplessness or weakness, and thus they portrayed their compliance from a different perspective that appealed to them. Whatever the reason was, it appeared that these part-time unveilers had gone through a lot of internal battles and psychological challenges to rationalize and justify the compliance to themselves and others.

Part-time unveilers highlighted five distinct reasons why they decided to comply with the policy. Some of these reasons were directly linked to their concerns about their future, while others were related more to social justice and efforts to advance the place of covered women in society. There were a few who had other personal reasons. Returning students wanted to complete unfinished business.

To have a better life: Thirteen part-time unveilers mentioned that the reason why they complied with the ban was to have opportunities for a better future. This future included prestige and respect in society, becoming more conscientious about religion, and being educated, with lucrative job opportunities leading to economic freedom, among other benefits. Part-time unveilers believed that university would open doors in the future that would not be open otherwise. This seemed to be even more critical for those who came from smaller cities where opportunities for jobs and advancement were scarce. All of the 13 part-time unveilers passionately echoed one another and emphasized that the reason they chose to unveil was their belief in the instrumental role of higher education in helping them reach their ideals. Semra complied with the policy to gain better job opportunities and more appreciation for her religion:

> I have always wanted to go to university. Not to go to university was never an option. The university will prepare me for a brighter future. I will be able to have a better and more lucrative job. My status in society will increase. This is why I decided to comply with the policy and unveil against my wishes. If I did not, I would never be able to reach the ideals I have. Some women stop their education because they do not want to uncover their hair. If you do not obtain higher education, you do not become a doctor or a lawyer. In addition, without education, you will not fully comprehend your religion. You will just cover your hair for traditional purposes, without fully appreciating Islam. So to reach my ideals and become a truly religious person, I need higher education.

On the other hand, Bahar stated that her main reason for compliance was for economic independence:

> I do not want to become dependent on my husband. I want to earn my own money and have an income of my own. I also need to be able to raise my children in a responsible way. To achieve these goals of mine, I need a university education. If I did not comply with the policy, I would not be able to accomplish any of these goals. I want to have a good job; I want to be respected in society. I want to become a leader. University will help me reach these ideals of mine. This is why I uncover my hair even though I do not necessarily want to do it.

Leyla explained that even though she was not comfortable with the idea of unveiling, she did not regret her decision—in order to become the person she wanted to be in the future and to achieve her goals:

> I grew up in an environment where my family members always encouraged me to seek a university degree. So I have been conditioned since the beginning: I was going to attend university and there was no other way. This is how I was brought up. In addition, I have been a successful student.... I know that every day I give up the tenet of Islam [covering] and follow some other rules. I know there is no excuse. However, I do not regret my decision. Right now, I feel guilty, but still I think I have made a good decision. This decision is going to help me become the person I want to become in the future and reach my ideals. I am removing my headscarf to become a productive person. This is my aim. I want to do useful things for others, and perhaps contribute a little bit to a change in the process of the higher education system. Why shouldn't I go to university? I have dreams as all the other students do. I have the potential to realize my goals. I never wanted to give up my dreams and my future.

Beyza echoed a discomfort with the act of unveiling, but stated that she had to do it to have a better life and a say in society:

> I never thought it was OK for me to give up what I really wanted to do. The price of giving up is a lot higher.... University education is a must if you are planning a better life for yourself. You will have a say in society. You will have prestige. This is why I decided to comply with the policy. This is why I decided to remove my headscarf even though I know I am acting against the wishes of the Qur'an. I am hoping that Allah will forgive me. Intentions are important. I am not removing my headscarf for fun, but for an important cause due to a policy imposed on me. In order to have a better life, I am complying with the policy.

Part-time unveilers perceived university as a key that would open the door to a better life in the future. This was consistent with their reason to attend university explored in Chapter 3. Since they perceived higher education as a life-changing activity, it seemed that they compromised some of their religious practices to clear the road to university. The voices of the part-time unveilers showed that they perceive how hard it was for them to give up their headscarf, emotionally and morally. But their perceptions also indicated the value they attached to higher education and the sacrifices they were prepared to make to gain access to higher education even though the ban required them to act against the teachings of their religion.

To advance and prove ourselves. Seven part-time unveilers stated that the reason why they complied with the ban was because they wanted covered women to advance in society. They thought that if all covered women gave up on college education, then there would not be leaders who would relate to covered women and represent them in society. If all covered women chose to stay at home, then there would not be covered doctors, lawyers, teachers, et cetera Only through higher education, part-time unveilers believed, could covered women advance and find the place they really deserved in society.

Sevgi thought she needed to fight and complied with the policy in order not be isolated from society:

> Some of us [covered women] need to go to university. Some of us [covered women] need to develop and grow. I will put up with this ban for four years so that as a covered woman, I have a say in society. I want other covered women to attend higher education as well so that we [covered women] become part of the next generation of leaders. I cannot isolate myself from society. I need to fight. I cannot let the headscarf become a reason for isolation.

Sevda added that compliance was necessary for covered women to educate themselves and defend the rights of other covered women:

> If you quit as a covered woman, who is going to defend you? Who is going to support you? Who is going to defend your rights? Many of my friends quit. What are they doing now? They are at home, sewing, drinking tea, and watching television. I am a successful student who loves studying. If I did not go to university, I would never have a say in society. Now I can say "Here I am, I also exist, and I am part of society."

Alara explained that she decided to comply with the policy in order to be visible in Turkey:

> We [covered women] need to fight this ban. If covered women do not attend higher education, they will become invisible in society. They will never be able to advance themselves in the corporate world. I want covered women to become respectable doctors, lawyers, businesswomen and take part in the economy.

Gamze wished to become a role model for other covered women:

> It is crucial that a woman with a headscarf has an important place in society. To make this possible, I, as a covered woman, need to go to university. Whether you [covered women] want to go to university or not is irrelevant. You [covered women] must attend university to have an important place in society. We [covered women] need to advance and prove ourselves so that we can show the world that covered women have a place in society. In addition, if I advance in society, I can become a role model for other covered women. They can follow me. This way, other covered women who hesitate attending university can look at me and envy my advancement and success, and follow my footsteps. I can become a leader.

Focusing on more concrete reasons, having an important role in politics and the economy was the driving force for Hale to comply with the policy:

> I am uncovering my hair; I am complying with the headscarf ban policy. Why? I want covered women to advance in society. I want covered women to have important roles in politics and the economy. Also, when covered women advance, they can be in the position of administrators, or decision makers. They can have the power to change the policy. Those who support the policy will not change the policy. So as covered women, we need to become powerful enough to change the policy. To be able to do this, we need to attend higher education institutions and get the education necessary for advancement.

Part-time unveilers perceived that university was a vehicle for covered women to have power and an important place in society. It seemed that they perceived university as a savior that would help them take the place they deserved in Turkey. In addition, part-time unveilers appeared to believe that one way to change the ban might be for covered women to have a say, so that, as policymakers, they had the authority to propose change. In this sense, it looked as if these women viewed university as a means to become agents of change in the future, and they were willing to compromise their headscarf wearing so that other women did not have to go through the same experiences in the future.

To complete this unfinished business: Six part-time unveilers mentioned that the reason why they complied with the policy was to complete unfinished business. As mentioned earlier, these part-time unveilers, all returning students, echoed one another and explored the challenges they faced after they quit or were dismissed from the university because of their initial resistance to remove their headscarf in the 1990s when the ban started being applied strictly in their campuses. For these women, compliance with the policy meant a way to overcome the problems they faced in their lives after they left their education incomplete. Nurten realized after quitting university that the only way to fight the psychological problems and depression she had was to comply with the policy:

> I have been at home for two years. I was neither a high school graduate, nor a university graduate. I did not know what to call myself. I did not know who I was. I became depressed. I sought clinical help. I spent some time with counselors who tried to help me decide what I really wanted to do. Then I realized that I would never find myself if I did not finish this business [university]. The only way was to comply with the policy. I do not know if I matured or lost my energy to fight anymore. I do not know if I am a loser. I have changed.... I did not want to go back to my old university though. I did not want to see the friends and professors whom I had fights with because of the ban. I took the university exam again and started at the university I am in now.

Zeynep, on the other hand, felt some lack of wholeness and wanted to overcome it by complying with the policy and going back to school:

> When I first quit, my parents excluded me. Society excluded me. They looked at me as if I was useless and unsuccessful. They considered me a failure. I could not find my true place, neither at home nor in my neighborhood. I had to continuously explain myself, my reasons for quitting university, for not wanting to remove my headscarf. Some understood, others did not. I became very unhappy. I felt incomplete. Many of my friends who quit university at the same time I did, started going back, complying with the policy. I felt very alone. I felt as if my own people [covered women] cheated on me, leaving me on my own. Then I realized that one way to fight the policy is to comply with it to show policymakers that the ban was not going to work as a deterrent. So I went back to complete this unfinished business. My family is so happy.

Unlike other part-time unveilers, Sezen simply stated that she wanted to complete what she had earlier started by complying with the policy:

> I did not want to live with incomplete business. Since I stopped going to university, everybody looked at me with pity. They felt sorry for me. After

some time I also started feeling sorry for myself. Life goes on, people make choices, and you suffer, but nobody cares. I do not have great expectations; I just want to make sure that I finish what I started earlier. I do not want to look like somebody who is not capable of finishing things.

The perceptions of these part-time unveilers suggested that they had negotiated the policy in different ways. Even though their initial choice seemed to be to refuse to comply with the policy, circumstances caused them to renegotiate the ban and take a different approach on the basis of their challenges, experiences, and learning points.

They insisted that I complied with the policy: Three part-time unveilers mentioned that their reason for compliance was the pressure of family. They stated that they did not want to comply with the policy and decided not to continue with a university education after high school. The continuing pressure from their parents over the course of years during their secondary education made them reconsider their position with regard to the policy:

> I did not want to go to university, but my family never agreed with this decision. They kept pointing to the difference between my mother, a housewife, and my aunt who is a professional. They insisted that I complied with the policy. It is not that I did not want to go to university because I did not like school; I just did not want to unveil. You unveil in high school, but it is different. High school is a small and homogenous environment. You are not mature yet. University is different. There are all sorts of students from different backgrounds. I did not want to unveil in that environment.
>
> (Yeliz)

These three part-time unveilers differed from other part-time unveilers, such as Sezen, who mentioned that she simply was not motivated to go to university because she was not interested in education, independent of the existence of the ban. These women, on the other hand, seemed to appreciate the value of education, but were initially reluctant to continue higher education due to the headscarf ban policy. So the parental support or pressure appeared to have helped them negotiate the policy in a way they were originally not going to do.

Compliance was my only option: One woman stated that her reason for compliance with the policy was that compliance was the only option at the time. She mentioned that she did not have any other alternative to follow. She had the option of Open University as well, but she did not think Open University was equal to attending a university on campus. So she had to reluctantly complied with the policy. Apparently, she searched for some other options for her education, but thought that compliance with the policy was the best option for her.

All in all, part-time unveilers presented various reasons as to why they complied with the policy. Their perceptions indicated that they appeared to have weighed the pros and cons of the compliance before they finalized their decision. The voices of these women highlighted that they perceived that the policy forced them to make a decision where they had to compromise in one way or another. In the case of these part-time unveilers, clearly university outweighed their religious preferences, and in order to achieve their goals they had to make a decision mostly against their wishes. It is important to note that there is a parallelism between part-time unveilers reasons for compliance with the ban and the role of higher education in their eyes and the meaning they attach to it as explored in Chapter 3.

The Reaction of Others to the Decision of Unveiling

The strong support for compliance with the policy usually came from parents. The reactions of friends and people outside the family varied, ranging from supporting the decision to being totally against it. One interesting observation was that, in some cases, people in general supported the idea of compliance with the policy, but criticized the type of unveiling part-time unveilers chose for themselves. On the basis of the ways part-time unveilers formulated their answers, the reaction of others to their decision to unveil can be categorized as follows: total support from family and friends, lack of support from friends and others, and lack of support for the type of unveiling.

My family members and friends supported me: Almost two-third of the part-time unveilers reported that their family and friends supported their decision to comply with the policy. Feelings and type of support varied from family to family. It was also apparent that, in the case of returning students, parents supported and welcomed the decision of part-time unveilers more enthusiastically. Some parents supported the decision of their daughters more; others, less strongly. Berna had family support for her decision of compliance with the policy:

> There was no negative reaction from my parents. They totally supported my decision. They have always respected my decisions anyway. My friends supported my decision as well. Probably because they also made the same decision when it was time for them to go to university.

Mine received similar parental support and stated that she did not face any negative reaction from her parents, other family members, or friends since

"Due to the headscarf ban policy, unveiling is normal and expected [if one wants] to go to university." Sevda explained that her parents were happy as well that she was uncovering her hair to go to university. They were happy that she was going to become educated and have a bright future. Fatma explained that her parents too supported her decision, but they advised her to continue behaving in the way a veiled woman would, despite her unveiling on campus:

> My parents did not react negatively; they were very supportive of my decision. The only thing they wanted me to do was to restrain myself from inappropriate behavior. They wanted me to continue being the girl they knew and were proud of. They told me to continue preserving my integrity and honor. My family members and friends supported me as well. I was not criticized for my decision because I have always supported those who removed their headscarves to continue higher education. I never said I was not going to remove the headscarf. I am not trying to prove a point wearing the headscarf. There are millions of covered and uncovered people. The headscarf does not eradicate the wickedness.

The parents of returning students, compared with other parents, showed greater enthusiasm when their daughters decided to comply with the policy. İpek, for example, expressed the joy and enthusiasm of her parents:

> My father has always wanted me to finish university. When I told my parents I decided to comply with the policy they were enthusiastic and so happy that they nearly cried. They bought me presents. My father told me that he was proud of my decision. My mother cooked all the food I liked for a week. They tried to do everything I wanted. I never saw them this happy and proud. I was happy too.

Alara, on the other hand, stated that she had the support of her family too, but she was not sure if this support was given willingly or reluctantly:

> My parents said nothing when they heard my decision. I unveiled during my secondary education anyway. During my secondary education, my father was against the idea of my unveiling. When I was attending a girls-only school, he said that if the school became mixed, I would go to another school. The school then became mixed. I told my mother, who informed my father. He did not force me to change my school. He got used to the idea. He had to. They knew I wanted to go to school. They also knew I did not want to wear a wig. Thus, there was never an argument. Willingly or reluctantly, they accepted my decision. My friends and other people did not say anything. They could not; they did not have the right to say anything. If my parents let me do what I wanted to do, then others did not have a right to

comment on the decision. I decided to expose my hair. Again, my parents did not react. I do not know what I would do if they forced me to wear a hat. I think I would still expose my hair, but there would be some arguments. Thank God, everything went smoothly.

The lack of support for my type of unveiling: Seven part-time unveilers explained that despite the support of their family and friends vis-à-vis compliance with the policy, there was a lack of support from family and/or friends for the decision they made with regard to the type of unveiling on campus. As explained by Bahar, who chose expose the hair as her style of unveiling, her friends objected to her decision and suggested that she use a wig:

> I received no negative reactions concerning my decision of compliance with the policy. I would have received negative reactions had I said I was not going to remove my headscarf. Everybody in my family is educated. Education is very important in my family; my husband is a university graduate too. The problem was the lack of support for my type of unveiling. When I decided to wear a hat on campus, some friends said that I should wear a wig instead. Some other friends insisted that I did not expose the hair. They all gave me instances from their own experiences on campus or in other institutions, and tried to convince me why I should wear a hat or use a wig, but not expose the hair instead. I did not listen to any of them.

Suzan, who wore a hat and exposed her hair when necessary, shared a similar experience where she was subjected to the negative reactions of her friends as a result of the type of unveiling she chose:

> My parents supported my decision of complying with the policy, but were not entirely happy that I was going to wear a hat. They did not want me to attract attention on campus, and thought a hat would be a way of doing so. My parents told me that I should expose my hair to make life easier for myself. I always wear turtleneck jumpers. My parents do not approve of them either. They do not see them as necessary. But those jumpers and hats help me deal with my feelings of guilt for removing my headscarf. I am struggling with my own emotions in my private life due to the double life I am leading. So these jumpers and the hat help me ease this struggle a little bit, giving me a sense of being covered to a certain extent.

Sevim, who chose to wear a wig, had also faced some negative reactions for the type of unveiling she had chosen for herself:

> My friends and some of my family members are against the way I am unveiling. They think the wig attracts a lot of attention and looks very artificial. Some friends think that I should expose my hair for my own comfort on

campus. However, a wig is not like unveiling. You remove the headscarf, but cover your hair with something else. So you do not expose your hair in any case. This is why I have chosen the wig in the first place.

Beyza, who exposed her hair on campus, stated that she also did not receive support for the way she chose to unveil:

> My parents told me to do whatever I had to do to continue my education. I chose to expose my hair. My friends and some family members reacted badly. They wanted me to wear a wig or a hat. Maybe they thought if I exposed my hair on campus today, I would get used to it and end up unveiling off campus as well. When I received such reactions, I asked myself if I should wear a hat. I debated between a hat and exposure of the hair for a while. I was angry with myself because I did not know which one was a better way to unveil. I did not know which one was less sinful. I also thought about which one I would be able to handle. I chose the exposure of my hair. Had I chosen the hat, the struggle I would go through would be bigger, and I would pay a bigger price. The most important thing is that in the way I unveil now, I feel comfortable and normal on campus.

Many friends and family members asked me if it was worth it: Four part-time unveilers mentioned that they had partial support for their decision to comply with the policy. As highlighted by Gamze:

> When I decided to comply with the policy, many friends and family members asked me if it was worth it. They said things like the following: "Why do you want to comply with the policy? Clearly policymakers do not want you on campus. How can you act against your religion? Is it worth committing a sin? Your complying with the policy is not going to make a difference to the situation of covered women. You are just one person, so why be the one who commits the sin? It is not right." I was initially influenced by these comments. I hesitated and did not know what to do. I thought maybe my decision was not the right one. My parents helped me understand that compliance with the policy was in fact the best decision for my future.

My parents reluctantly supported me: Two part-time unveilers explained that their parents had supported their compliance with the policy a little reluctantly and had faced some challenges as a result of seeing their daughters unveiled. In the case of Yeliz, it was her father who felt more challenged:

> The decision was up to me. I decided to comply with the policy and my parents reluctantly supported me. However, my father has never been to campus since I started university. He tells me that he does not want to see me the way

I am on campus. He is sorry that I have to go through this experience to gain access to education in my own country.

In the case of Sema, both parents did not like seeing her unveiled, despite the support they give her for her education:

My parents supported me, I think reluctantly, when I decided to comply with the policy and unveil. My friends supported me as well. They all wanted me to unveil and get the education I need for the future. My parents came to campus a couple of times. When they saw me in an unveiled way in the crowd, they told me they felt weird and sorry. They say that they constantly pray to Allah for forgiveness because of my unveiling. My mother keeps telling me that once the class is over, I should leave the campus immediately and cover my hair.

As can be seen, part-time unveilers perceived the support of family and friends as playing an important role in their lives in terms of carrying out their decision of compliance with the policy. Part-time unveilers felt that a majority of parents seemed to have supported their daughters' decision even though it might not always have been easy for them to accept. Lack of support for the decision of compliance with the policy or the type of unveiling chosen seemed to cause some part-time unveilers to second-guess their decision for a short while. It was apparent that the headscarf ban policy impacted not only part-time unveilers but indirectly also impacted their parents and friends in different ways.

Why Did the Part-time Unveilers Unveil the Way They Did?

For the part-time unveilers, another phase of the negotiation of the policy was to decide on the type of unveiling. This decision was as complex as the decision of whether to comply with the policy or not. Some part-time unveilers explained that they tried one type of unveiling for a couple of days, but did not feel comfortable, so they switched to another type. There were three apparent reasons as to why the part-time unveilers unveiled the way they did. Besides the apparent reasons, part-time unveilers mentioned other motives and incidents that influenced their mode of unveiling. Part-time unveilers, while highlighting their reasons for the type of unveiling they preferred, usually compared and contrasted all types of unveiling and showed vehement objection to the types of unveiling they did not choose. One interesting observation was that besides the side motives and incidents mentioned, the fundamental responses of the part-time unveilers in each of the three categories was defined by type of unveiling. So in the first category, the responses consisted of the opinions of all those who exposed their hair; in the second one, of all hat wearers; and in the last one, of wig users.

To avoid attention: Sixteen part-time unveilers stated that the reason why they unveiled the way they did was to avoid exclusion and attention. This reason belonged to those who chose to expose their hair as their style of unveiling. They felt that they blended in, looking exactly like the "other." While explaining what they meant by avoidance of exclusion and attention, part-time unveilers also highlighted their opinions about wigs and hats. Beyza stated that she did not want to become excluded by wearing a hat:

> The policy categorizes women into two: covered and uncovered. The hat and wig bring other subcategories within the category of being covered. You are excluded once through the policy. I did not want to be excluded twice by wearing a hat or using a wig. They attract a lot of attention. Policymakers do not like me with my headscarf on, and I do not like myself with a hat on. So I decided to expose my hair.

Mine explained that she chose to expose her hair to avoid exclusion and added the supportive perspective of her father as well.

Melek shared a similar feeling about exposure of hair:

> I did not want to attract attention. I wanted to start with one type of unveiling and graduate that way. Wearing a wig means being psychologically covered. Once you remove the headscarf, all types of unveiling are sins. So since I was committing a sin, I at least wanted to be as comfortable as possible on campus. . . . The hat . . . is not allowed in our department and also in the future there is a possibility that the wig will become banned as well.

Melek's voice highlighted another issue: How was the policy implemented in different higher education institutions? There were a couple of other part-time unveilers who considered the implementation of the ban in their universities while explaining their position regarding the type of unveiling they chose. In the case of Bahar, for example, the hat was banned in her department:

> The hat is banned in my department. The wig is a psychological relief. It is a feeling of hiding your own hair under someone else's hair. It is not a solution. Girls are using it to feel relieved. But they attract a lot of attention. I do not want that. I am trying to avoid attention as much as possible so that people will leave me alone.

Sevda explained that even when and where you exposed your hair made a difference in terms of attracting or avoiding attention:

> When I expose my hair before getting on the minibus, I do not become the source of attention. I blend in and nobody bothers me; I am left alone. For example, when you are on the minibus entering the campus still with your headscarf on, the security guards stop the minibus at the entrance. They enter and ask you to remove the headscarf. Occasionally, some male students who are opposed to the ban swear at the security guards and arguments start. Sometimes, the minibus drivers shout at you, asking you to remove the headscarf before you enter the campus. When you remove your headscarf in the minibus, others look at you in such a sly way that you know they are making fun of you. A friend of mine has started exposing her hair before leaving the house, because she says she could not take the minibus experience anymore.

The voice of this part-time unveiler revealed that in certain circumstances she needed to consider not only which type of unveiling was best for her, but also when to unveil the hair in order to avoid further problems or complications.

Leyla argued that students used hats or wigs to make a statement or become a target, and brought a different understanding of attention avoidance:

> The wig users and hat wearers make a statement. By drawing attention to themselves, they are saying, "we are here." They become a target or maybe they want to make themselves targets. Maybe it is their way of fighting against the policy. In my opinion, when you expose your hair, you become the injured party. With a wig or hat, it is not as if you are subjected to any unjust treatment. When you do not attract attention and others find out about your situation later, they feel sorry for you. When you attract attention, they exclude you and do not like you straight away.

It is the closest to the headscarf: Eleven part-time unveilers explained that the reason why they unveiled the way they did was because their type of unveiling was the closest to the headscarf. Their type of unveiling reminded them of their headscarf. Part-time unveilers also thought that this way they were trying to avoid becoming accustomed to being uncovered. This reason and rationalization belonged to part-time unveilers who wore a hat. Eleven hat wearers shared their reasoning and also compared and contrasted their type of unveiling with other types. Merve explained: "The hat is the closest to the headscarf. The wig is the same as exposing the hair: complete surrender! I do not think these are the appropriate ways to comply with the policy." İpek echoed this and added that the hat covered her hair and neck like a headscarf: "I am wearing a hat that covers my hair and neck. I also tie my hat under my chin. So it is like a headscarf. It is the closest to the headscarf." Sevgi compared and contrasted the use of a wig and a hat and exposing the hair and explained that she chose the hat since it reminded her of the headscarf:

> When you expose your hair, there is a danger of getting used to it. In addition, it is a complete surrender. You look like the others who do not cover their hair. My little sister, for example, exposes her hair on campus. My big sister never went to college and got married. At some point, I considered exposing my hair, but could not. I have been covering my hair since Grade six. I covered my hair at a young age so it was very difficult for me to expose it.... A wig looks funny. So I went with the hat. The hat reminds me of my headscarf. It reminds me of the fact that I am a woman with a headscarf.

Suzan felt covered with her hat. Her account also showed how some of her professors did not allow her to enter classes with the hat on, in which case she exposed her hair:

> I knew I was going to make a concession. I wanted this concession to be minimal. I did not want to concede totally. A wig is like exposing the hair. In addition, it looks ridiculous. The hat is another version of the headscarf, especially if you wear it with a scarf or a turtleneck sweater. You are still covered. This way I constantly remind myself that I am a covered woman. Some teachers do not let me into their class wearing my hat. In those cases, I expose my hair.

A way of making a statement: Three part-time unveilers, wig users, indicated that the reason why they unveiled the way they did was to make a statement and attract attention. They mentioned that one of the main reasons was because the wig attracted attention and conveyed the message that the woman who wore it was a covered woman. As explained by Berna: "A wig is a way of making a statement. It is my way of expressing myself. I did not want my hair to be seen. People look at me and know immediately that I am a covered woman." In addition to making a statement, Sevim added that the use of a wig was a psychological relief and a way of telling people that she was in fact a covered woman:

> I am using a wig because it is a way of making a statement. It is a way of telling policymakers that I am complying with the policy without doing what you really want me to do. In addition, the wig is a heavy thing. So I know that it is there. Other people also know that I am a woman with a headscarf

when they see my wig. So I do not have a headscarf, but I do not show my hair either. It is a psychological relief as well. I wear my wig and I wear a turtleneck jumper at all times.

To sum up, participants seemed to have rationalized the way they unveiled from different perspectives. While explaining their points and highlighting their perspectives, they also seemed to hint at their opinions about other types of unveiling women had chosen for themselves as a way to comply with the policy. Another interesting issue that emerged from the data as a result of part-time unveilers describing the reasons why they unveiled the way they did was the implementation of the policy in different institutions. Whether directly related or not, the participants seemed to have taken into consideration the way their campus, department, or teachers implemented the policy.

All in all, part-time unveilers seemed to have systematically negotiated the higher education headscarf ban policy. They had made or had to make various choices after evaluating their situation. The negotiation of the policy included consideration of other possible options, reasons for compliance, dealing with reactions of family and others, and their decision for the way they unveiled. The accounts of the part-time unveilers indicated that this negotiation process was complex and difficult at times. It looked as if it required part-time unveilers to come up with a lot of reasoning and rationalization, for their own peace of mind, for the decisions they had made about the policy negotiation. They had to justify their decision to themselves. Challenges they faced, such as a lack of support from others regarding their decision or type of unveiling, seemed to have caused some of them to second-guess the decisions they made. Their reasons why they unveiled the way they did also highlighted their rationalization about their type of unveiling and constant internal debate. While trying to show how their decisions were best for them, they also explained why other types of unveiling did not suit them.

5

Impact of the Policy on Part-Time Unveilers' Campus Experiences

This chapter explores the perceptions of the part-time unveilers about advantages/opportunities and disadvantages/challenges unveiling brought to them on campus. It first discusses the overall impact of unveiling in terms of the opportunities it provided, and then focuses on particular aspects of the opportunities in regard to daily life on campus. Specifically, the chapter discusses the part-time unveilers' relationships with faculty, peers, and administration; the way they were treated on campus and in class; and their involvement in campus activities and extracurricular activities. Later, the chapter considers the overall impact of unveiling in terms of challenges that arose and the strategies that these women employed to deal with these challenges. The chapter concludes by unpacking the ways in which these challenges affected students' educational progress.[1]

Advantages/Opportunities Unveiling Brought to Part-Time Unveilers on Campus

This section highlights the perceptions of part-time unveilers with regard to opportunities or advantages the act of unveiling brought to them on campus. Students formulated their answers in both general and more specific ways. When they explained their views in a general way, they approached the opportunities/advantages of unveiling on campus holistically. Later, they moved on to the specifics of what they perceived as opportunities or advantages in terms of faculty-student relationship, campus environment, et cetera. This section is divided into two, so general opportunities are presented first, followed by the specific categories.

Overall Impact of Unveiling in Terms of Advantages/Opportunities

Part-time unveilers formulated their responses around three subthemes. Four participants did not think unveiling had any general advantages. The remaining 26 students explained that unveiling provided them with an opportunity to attend (or reattend in the case of returning participants) higher education. Using it as an umbrella opportunity, 26 part-time unveilers expanded their views on the general opportunities of unveiling.

My unveiling opened the door to academic and cultural opportunities of campuses: Twelve part-time unveilers highlighted that unveiling opened the door to the academic and cultural opportunities in the higher education system. Selma explained that unveiling gave her the opportunity to attend college where she could improve herself:

> Thanks to unveiling, I am academically [and culturally] well equipped. I am improving myself and learning a lot of things [on campus]. Thanks to unveiling, I will be able to broaden my horizons and take part in different environments. Education has a lot of advantages and brings a lot of things to people.... My unveiling opened the door to academic and cultural opportunities of campuses.

A way of protecting yourself in the world of prejudices: Seven part-time unveilers mentioned that unveiling protected them against prejudices. They perceived that uncovered people or people who considered themselves modern or secularists were biased or prejudiced against covered women and/or Islamists. So unveiling was a way to hide their identity. Beyza explained that unveiling helped her receive unbiased treatment from people she had newly met and gave her a chance to show others that she was like them:

> Someone who does not know I am covered in my private life approaches me in a less prejudiced way. It shows me how unbiased people can be. It shows them that I am a human being too. When people later on find out that I am covered, sometimes they do not know how to behave. I do not get angry or upset because it is difficult for people to be out of the box, to act against everything they have learned.

Fatma added that unveiling protected her against prejudices by making her look like an uncovered woman: "Unveiling makes you one of them. You become like the other. So the other approaches you in a neutral way. Your unveiling is a way of protecting yourself in the world of prejudices." Sevda stressed the importance of unveiling in terms of the way it stops marginalization: "Unveiling stops marginalization to some extent. I feel as if people who are uncovered look at me without any prejudices. They approach me in a way they may not have if they knew I was covered."

One interesting observation about these seven part-time unveilers was that they were all women who chose to expose their hair as their type of unveiling. The fact that no hat wearers or wig users perceived their type of unveiling as a way to protect themselves from prejudices made the researcher question if this specific perceived opportunity was dependent on the type of unveiling.

Unveiling helped me become part of a community: Two part-time unveilers who were returning students explained that unveiling helped them become part of a community. These part-time unveilers felt that they lost their sense of belonging to a community after they quit higher education as a result of initially refusing to comply with the policy. Unveiling seemed to contribute to their regaining their identity in society. Reyhan explained that unveiling made her become part of the academic community she lost but missed a lot: "Unveiling helped me become part of a community, a culture that I really liked and longed for. My psychological condition got better. I became part of the higher education community. Now I have a say in class and on campus to some extent."

Unveiling does not have opportunities or advantages for me. Four part-time unveilers thought that unveiling did not bring any opportunities or advantages to them. According to them, their hats or wigs or clothes revealed who they really were, so unveiling did not really neutralize them or make them look uncovered. They believed that the real opportunity would be to attend higher education institutions with their headscarves on. Burcu highlighted that unveiling would not have any opportunities or advantages since higher education should be a natural educational right whether one was veiled or unveiled:

Unveiling does not have opportunities or advantages for me. Higher education is or should be my educational right anyway. People understand that I am a veiled woman because of my hat and clothes I wear. So I think the real opportunity for me and people like me, would be the ability to attend campuses in the way we are, that is, with our headscarves on.

All in all, generally speaking, under the circumstances of the existing higher education policy, part-time unveilers perceived their act of unveiling as an opportunity that provided them with knowledge, technology, culture, diversity, and a sense of belonging. In addition to these general comments about the opportunities or advantages that unveiling brought to them, participants also mentioned specific points in their campus life with regard to opportunities of unveiling. These specific points included perceptions of the part-time unveilers about their relationships with their faculty, friends, and administrators; their treatment on campus and in class; their involvement in extracurricular activities; and their activities on campus.

Opportunities/Advantages of Unveiling Pertaining to Daily Life on Campus

Not every student discussed each of the specific points in detail. Part-time unveilers emphasized what they saw relevant to their campus and university life, and elaborated on issues that seemed more important to them.

Relationship with faculty: Thirteen part-time unveilers discussed two specific opportunities or advantages that unveiling brought with regard to their relationship with faculty. One of them was that unveiling protected them from being academically discriminated against by some of their professors. The other was the support and encouragement they received from some of their professors as a result of their unveiling. So, unveiling had a protective role and played a supportive role in the relationship part-time unveilers had with their professors.

My unveiling protects me against discrimination and marginalization: Seven part-time unveilers explained that in their departments there were different types of professors. There were some who were against the headscarf and some who were not or just indifferent. In the case of some of those who were against the headscarf, data reveal that part-time unveilers perceived professors discriminated against students who wore headscarves in their private lives by grading their papers with some prejudices and giving them lower marks, which affected student motivation and success. According to the perceptions of the part-time unveilers, this type of professor seemed to treat covered women differently in class. Part-time unveilers explained that before such professors, unveiling was a shield that masked their identity, especially in a big and crowded class, and protected them from being academically disadvantaged. Zeynep summarized how she thought she might be treated differently if some of her professors knew she was a covered woman: "I feel that some of my professors would treat me differently if they knew I was a woman with a headscarf. My exposing the hair protects me from this."

Some part-time unveilers explained that not every type of unveiling helped. Their perception was that professors might be against the hat or wig, and if they realized that students were using wigs, they might embarrass them in class . Gamze, for example, highlighted this point as follows: "I hear that if a teacher is against the wig, s/he asks the student to remove it in front of the whole class. This is quite embarrassing for that student." Sevda agreed and added that " . . . Students with wigs are scared and always try to hide themselves in the crowd in class." These perceptions of the participants indicated that, in their cases, wigs created problems and exposure of hair and/or hats protected them from discrimination. On the other hand, there were also some other cases where wigs protected students from discrimination. Seda, a wig user, explained that her wig protected her from academic discrimination that could impact negatively on her success:

> I did not want to attract the attention of my professors in class and create an environment that would negatively affect my success. So I decided to be what my professors wanted me to be. My unveiling makes me look the way some professors want their students to look. So my unveiling protects me against discrimination and marginalization.

Accounts of these participants showed that they perceived unveiling as a way to protect themselves from being discriminated against academically. One observation was that six of seven participants who discussed this specific point were those who exposed their hair, which raised the question of whether or not exposing the hair might be protecting participants better than wigs or hats.

Some of them were really supportive, which encouraged me a lot: A second point six part-time unveilers mentioned as an opportunity of unveiling was the support and encouragement they received from some of their professors. Part-time unveilers explained that when some professors realized that they were part-time unveilers wearing a headscarf in their private lives, they supported them for unveiling to gain access to higher education and encouraged them to get through the process despite the challenges that might appear. Yeliz appreciated the support of some of her professors and thought that had it not been for their encouragement, she might have dropped out. Sezen, a returning part-time unveiler, also appreciated the support of some of her professors for her unveiling and the encouragement for her academic success:

> Now that I am back at school, some of my professors have invited me to their offices to talk about my decision and future plans. Some of them were really supportive, which encouraged me a lot. They told me that they were there whenever I needed them and would try to make sure that I graduate from university. They congratulated me on my decision of unveiling. They wanted me to go and see them whenever I need academic or personal help

with regard to coursework or challenges that might appear along the way during my education. They gave me encouragement saying that as a returning student, I am mature so I need to be a role model to other students by studying hard. They also said that they were sure I would be very successful and graduate as one of the top students. They said they would be there beside me whenever I needed them. To know this keeps me going.

All in all, the perceptions of these part-time unveilers indicated that many part-time unveilers seemed to appreciate the support they received from some of their professors, and the encouragement kept them motivated, giving them the strength to fight against potential challenges on campus. In addition, these part-time unveilers perceived unveiling as an opportunity to conceal their covered identity in cases where professors were prejudiced against women with headscarves. In a way, unveiling, and perhaps more so exposing the hair, protected them against perceived biases and discrimination that could create academic disadvantages for them.

Relationship with peers: Eighteen part-time unveilers explained that one advantage unveiling brought to their relationship with peers on campus was the opportunity to mingle with uncovered women while overcoming the prejudices of other students.

I met a wide array of people with different lifestyles: According to ten part-time unveilers, unveiling made it easier for them to become friendly with other students and they viewed this as a chance to introduce themselves and get to know people they might not otherwise. Gamze explained that unveiling helped her socialize with the uncovered, who she might not have otherwise met at all. Alara echoed this by stating that she had friends from all backgrounds: "Now I have friends who are more diverse. Unveiling helped me meet students from different backgrounds . . ." Sevgi responded similarly, noting that unveiling helped her grow and develop: "Unveiling contributed to my growth and development. I met a wide array of people with different lifestyles. My circle of friends has changed. It is more diverse now." Sevtap shared her own experience as a woman who used a hat and wig and explained how her unveiling helped her make friends on campus and gave her the opportunity to introduce the world of Islamists:

My wig and hat helped me look alike. Even though you could tell it was a wig, it still helped me look uncovered and approach students. Once my classmates started to get to know me, we became really good friends. I am not any different to them with my everyday clothes on in an unveiled way. I do not wear a long coat either. I have a conservative but modern way of dressing. So all these things helped me to make friends. I was able to get to know others and they had the chance to get to know me. For many friends, I am their first covered friend. Also for me they are my first proper uncovered friends. So I had the opportunity to explain the viewpoints of Islamists and learn the worldview of the uncovered.

Five of ten participants also added that, in one way, unveiling helped the covered to approach the other by overcoming, if not eliminating, the prejudices of other students, but in another way, it provided an opportunity for the uncovered to get to know the covered, leaving the prejudices behind.

Gamze explained how unveiling helped her overcome her own worries about making friends by initially eliminating the possible prejudices of her friends against the covered. She also added how some of her friends might not have approached her had they known she was covered in the first place due to their own biases against the Islamists:

> When I first entered university, I had some worries. Would I be able to make friends? Would classmates be prejudiced? With my unveiling, peers first did not realize I was a covered woman. They approached me and we started building friendships. I listened to them and they listened to me. After a while, when we got to know each other better, I told them I was a covered woman. Apparently some of them had already suspected it because of my clothes and way of talking and behaving. They told me that it did not matter to them since my ideas were more important for them. One friend confessed that she might not have approached me had she known I was a covered woman. She told me that she did not really like the Islamists and she was biased and prejudiced against them. She saw this as a learning point and realized that she shied away from making friends with covered women until that time. So even though all my friends are uncovered, they have respect for me and I have respect for them.

One interesting observation about eight out of ten of these part-time unveilers was that they were all women who chose to expose their hair as their type of unveiling. The fact that the majority of part-time unveilers socialized with others by looking like them might raise the question of whether or not this meant that when part-time unveilers exposed their hair, they looked more like the "others" and built better social relationships as opposed to hat wearers and/or wig users.

The accounts of these part-time unveilers showed that they perceive that unveiling might be an opportunity for some secularists and Islamists to meet and create platforms where they could learn from and understand each other. It seemed that in the case of these part-time unveilers, unveiling had helped them and their uncovered friends appreciate and respect one another by means of shared experiences during their friendship.

Relationship with administration: Thirteen part-time unveilers discussed the advantage of being unveiled in terms of their relationship with their administrators. They mentioned that unveiling prevented any potential problems that might exist between the administration and part-time unveilers.

I also try my best to unveil in the way my administrators want: Thirteen part-time unveilers elaborated on the ways in which the act of unveiling protected them against any conflict that might otherwise have arisen. Berna explained that, for administrators, unveiling meant complying with the policy, so, in following the university procedures, "Unveiling is a symbol of complying with the policy. In addition, it means I am obeying the rules. I also try my best to unveil in the way my administrators want. So my unveiling prevents conflict." Nurten responded similarly, noting that as a returning student who resisted the policy, her unveiling signaled her compliance with the university rules in the eyes of the administration: "When the headscarf ban policy started years ago, I had a lot of problems with the administration because I resisted the policy. Now as a returning student, I am obeying the policy. So my unveiling is a sign of submission in the eyes of the administration." Buket stated that even though she did not have much contact with them, she obeyed the rules and avoided making the administrators angry, thanks to her unveiling:

> I do not often get to meet with the administration. Once administrators were against the wig, and decided not to accept students with wigs. Wig wearers were going to be punished, but some professors objected to this and saved these students. So this experience of others showed me that I needed to obey them in order to graduate. I unveil in the way they want. I never do anything that would make them angry. I know that if I make them angry, they will try their best to dismiss me. So I am doing everything they want. My unveiling helps me with that.

Berna added a different point by highlighting how her unveiling helped her avoid the problems and made the administration select her for off-campus activities to represent the university:

> The administration is against women with headscarves. So I am trying my best to follow all the unveiling rules the university has, to avoid problems that may affect my studies. But interestingly, the university administration usually assigns me as part of the team when there is a need for representatives to represent the university outside campus. I always go to these outside places with my headscarf on. It is really weird. Maybe they choose me because they think that I can represent the university well. Or maybe it is their way of praising me for complying with the policy and unveiling on campus. I do not know.

Treatment on campus: Twelve participants discussed their perceptions about the benefits of unveiling with regard to the way they were treated on campus. They formulated their responses around the issue of how unveiling helped them be treated equally without discrimination on campus in general.

Thanks to my unveiling, I am no different from any other student on campus: Twelve participants explained the ways in which they perceived they received equal treatment without biases, prejudices, or discrimination as a result of unveiling. They perceived that uncovered people or people who considered themselves modern or secularists were biased or prejudiced against covered women and/or Islamists. Unveiling was a way to hide the identity of the part-time unveilers and receive equal treatment on campus. Beyza explained that unveiling helped her receive unbiased treatment from people she had newly met and gave her a chance to show others that she was like them:

> Someone who does not know I am covered in my private life approaches me in a less prejudiced way. It shows me how unbiased people can be. And it shows them that I am a human being too. When people later on find out that I am covered, sometimes they do not know how to behave. I do not get angry or upset because it is difficult for people to be out of the box, to act against everything they have learned. . . . I do not receive any looks since I am unveiled. Years ago, when there was no headscarf ban policy in Imam Hatip schools, I attended school with my headscarf on. In those days, I realized that people categorize others. I was not treated the same way an uncovered girl was treated. They were more careful and distant while communicating with me. They maybe thought that I would not understand where they were coming from since we were not speaking the same language.

Fatma added that unveiling protected her against prejudices by making her look like an uncovered woman. Sevda stressed the importance of unveiling in terms of the way it stopped marginalization. Dilara echoed, "Thanks to my unveiling, I am no different from any other student on campus. So I am not treated any differently. I have never felt different on campus." Alara added that those who later found out that she was covered had respect for her. Reyhan, a returning student, compared and contrasted her treatment with the treatment she had received on campus years ago, before she quit:

> When the ban started in our university, nobody knew how to treat one another. They thought we were there to cause problems. I was badly treated on campus in the final years of my university life before dropping out. Ten years on, I can see that things have changed. People have learned to listen to one another on campus. Uncovered women and we [part-time unveilers]

socialize. Before it was all conflict, argument, and problems. Things seem to have calmed down. Islamists do not fight anymore. We have become passive. Others have learned to listen to us and try to understand who we are. Those years were a transition period. Before, I heard that if you wore a wig or hat on campus, people would make fun of you. They would insult you. You would not be able to walk on campus. This does not happen anymore. That type of treatment has lessened a lot in my case. Despite a couple of unpleasant instances, I am not treated as badly as I was treated when I resisted unveiling. People have learned and I have learned and my unveiling is helping me to receive better treatment on campus.

Treatment in class: Twelve part-time unveilers explained the opportunities from unveiling in terms of treatment in class. All of them mentioned that the treatment varied from class to class and from professor to professor. Part-time unveilers reported that they felt more comfortable in bigger classes, where they had the opportunity to blend in without attracting much attention, or in classes where they knew everyone. This seemed to be more of a case for hat wearers and wig users than for those who exposed their hair. For all 12 part-time unveilers, unveiling helped them blend in in class.

My unveiling helps me blend in and be treated like any other student in class: Twelve part-time unveilers explained the ways in which they felt they blended in and were included in class as a result of their unveiling. Leyla explained that she felt comfortable and respected in class, and illustrated her election as class representative to prove her point:

> I have close friends and acquaintances in class. Everybody treats me equally and with respect, thanks to my unveiling. I am not even sure if the acquaintances in class realize that I am a covered woman. I do not think they even care. My unveiling helps me blend in and be treated like any other student in class. One proof of this is the fact that I was chosen as class representative this year. I think I have succeeded in explaining myself. I think I have introduced myself in a neutral way. My aim is not to impose ideas, but find the middle ground, not to create groups, but unite the whole class. That is why I think the class has voted for me. I am not sure if the same thing would have happened if I had my headscarf on.

Berna stated that she felt included in class:

> I am an active student who always sits in front and participates in discussions. So I always attract attention, but my unveiling has helped me not to attract any negative attention. I have good relations with my professors. Of course, there are exceptions, but in general, my classmates do not seem to consider me to be ... different from them. I think they have come to accept

me as one of them. When there are differences in opinions, we discuss them and try to sort the problems out. I am part of the class. I never feel excluded.

Activities on campus: Eight part-time unveilers mentioned that the only advantage unveiling had with regard to activities on campus was that it opened doors to activities that would be unavailable to them otherwise. Some part-time unveilers perceived themselves as more outgoing and social, trying to do as many activities as possible on campus, as opposed to some of the other part-time unveilers who took part in the study. A couple of women emphasized that they tried to maximize their time on campus by staying as long as possible on campus every day in order to benefit from the opportunities of the academic environment as much as they could.

My hat gives me the advantage of doing activities on campus: Eight part-time unveilers described their beliefs about how unveiling opened doors to activities on campus that they might not have had access to had they been veiled. Sevtap explained that unveiling helped her use the campus effectively. Buket had different activities on campus and explained: "My hat gives me the advantage of doing activities on campus. I go to the library, use the computer lab, attend classes, and have lunch in the cafeteria with my friends. . . . I sit on the benches with friends." Sevgi explained that she took advantage of the opportunity of being on campus, thanks to her unveiling, and used this chance in the best possible way by maximizing her time on campus: "Since unveiling gives me the right to be on campus, I am trying to take advantage of this opportunity. I am trying to spend as much time as possible on campus. I visit the Student Affairs department a lot. I applied to work in the Computer Lab, but have not heard from them yet."

The collective voice of these students seemed to indicate that some part-time unveilers believed that they were at peace with themselves as part-time unveilers and wanted to benefit from all the activities their higher education institutions offered them.

Involvement in extracurricular activities: A few part-time unveilers discussed the advantages of unveiling with regard to their involvement in extracurricular activities that took place on or off campus. Six part-time unveilers viewed unveiling as a way to take part in extracurricular activities. Four of these six part-time unveilers considered themselves quite active with regard to taking part in such activities and believed that their involvement helped them to stay connected with the academic world. One or two of them mentioned that they also tried to encourage their friends to become involved in various activities.

I try to benefit from all other extracurricular activities: Six part-time unveilers explained that unveiling helped them take part in various extracurricular activities on and off campus.

Semra described the kind of extracurricular activities on campus and thought that she might have received some harassment had she done them with her headscarf on. These activities helped her stay connected with the campus and her friends. Sevgi described her extracurricular activities and stressed that unveiling was a key that opened doors to them on and off campus:

> I try to take part in all the activities, except Spring Festival, because people become drunk and try to flirt with one another. I attend competitions, conferences, talks, and panels on and off campus. I go to watch movies and plays. I have joined some social clubs. The only ones I never attend are those that require one to wear short sleeves or mini-skirts. I never join those clubs, and probably I would not be welcome there anyway. I try to benefit from all other extracurricular activities. Unveiling is a key that allows me to have access to all these activities.

It seemed that these part-time unveilers perceived unveiling to be a key to different activities and tried to take full advantage of the opportunities that unveiling and campus life provided them with, in order to stay connected with their higher education institution. Their perceptions indicated that they tried to maximize their time spent on campus to have an active higher education life and benefit from all the opportunities their universities offered and to become as involved as possible, socially and culturally, besides their educational experiences.

In short, part-time unveilers explored their numerous perceptions about the advantages/opportunities of unveiling in terms of their relationships with faculty, administrators, and peers; the way they were treated on campus and in class; and their activities and extracurricular activities on and off campus.

All in all, this section has dealt with the opportunities or advantages of unveiling from the perspective of part-time unveilers. Part-time unveilers perceived unveiling as a passport to attend university and a shield that might protect them against prejudices and discrimination. Some participants perceived some specific advantages or opportunities of unveiling on campus, such as enhancing their campus activities or motivation for studying. Thus, whether these women complied with the policy reluctantly or not, they tried to take full advantage of some specific opportunities to become as involved in the higher education experience as possible. Even though part-time unveilers highlighted opportunities from unveiling, they also stressed the challenges or disadvantages that unveiling had brought to their lives on campus. Their accounts highlighting opportunities on the one hand and challenges on the other could be perceived as inconsistencies, internal conflicts, or juxtapositions that they were going through on campus.

Disadvantages/Challenges Part-Time Unveilers Faced on Campus and in Their Lives as a Result of Unveiling

This section highlights the perceptions of part-time unveilers with regard to the challenges they faced on campus and in their lives as a result of unveiling. Part-time unveilers first discussed their challenges as a result of unveiling in general terms and then elaborated on some specific points. These specific points included the disadvantages or challenges of unveiling with regard to the relationships of these women with faculty, peers, and administration; their treatment on campus and in class; and their activities and extracurricular activities.

Overall Impact of Unveiling in Terms of Disadvantages/Challenges

Part-time unveilers discussed various points with regard to the general disadvantages or challenges of unveiling. They usually formulated their responses around the issues of the psychological challenges of unveiling and the emotional distress they faced. Some part-time unveilers mentioned more than one point as a challenge. Nine subthemes were identified, including one where part-time unveilers mentioned that they did not experience any challenge and elaborated on their reasons. These subthemes are explained in detail.

Unveiling made me realize the problems that are waiting for me in the future: Twenty-six participants mentioned concerns about their future career as a challenge of complying with the policy. As women who had complied with the policy and experienced unveiling, some of them realized that to continue unveiling in a work environment was not a temporary situation, as opposed to four years of undergraduate education. However, they realized that they needed to continue unveiling in order to achieve their primary goals. Sixteen part-time unveilers wanted to pursue an academic career on campuses and 12 part-time unveilers wished to work in state institutions, both of which would require them to continue removing their headscarves. Unveiling made them realize that they would not be able to follow careers or work in companies they would like to unless they covered their hair, and they felt challenged that they had to make such an important decision about the rest of their lives. Sevtap, for example, did not want to work in a private company, but she did not know how to tackle the issue of unveiling. She was challenged with the question of whether or not her compliance with the higher education policy meant that she would unveil for the rest of her life:

> Unveiling made me realize the problems that are waiting for me in the future. I will have struggled as an unveiled woman for four years when I graduate. Probably, I will be emotionally very tired at the end. I want to work in a state institution, but if I continue unveiling, my psychology state might deteriorate. So if I want to remain veiled, I have to work in a private company, which is not what I want. I do not know how to handle the experience of unveiling anymore. I do not know if I should unveil and work in a state institution or veil and work in a private company. Complying with the policy challenges me with the kind of decision I need to make. If you do not comply at all, there is no problem, you know. . . . Once you comply, then you start questioning whether you will continue complying or not.

Semra was challenged by the fact that her unveiling made her understand how the academic world really worked, because she wanted to become an academic and thought she would not have the opportunity to advance even if she unveiled:

> I want to pursue an academic career, but I know that this is not going to be possible. First, I have to continue unveiling. I am not sure if this is what I want after going through the experience of unveiling. For the sake of argument, let's say, I will unveil. Other professors will eventually find out that you are a [part-time unveiler], which is more or less what is happening to many of us. Once they know you are in fact a covered woman, they will not let you advance. So you will be stuck at some point. I do not know what to do.

One challenge of unveiling for me is the psychological problems I have to go through: Sixteen part-time unveilers highlighted the psychological problems they had or had to go through as a challenge or disadvantage of unveiling. These psychological problems included depression, nervousness, anxiety, and feelings of guilt, often caused by the conflict in their act of unveiling, which was against their values and belief systems. Their psychology seemed to be negatively affected by the fear that they were making a concession from their religion and making a compromise by unveiling and did not know how far it would go, which created some sort of identity crisis. Emotional problems seemed to be exacerbated by the fact that they had these experiences at such a young age when other people of the same age group did not have to go through such hard moments. İpek explained that she felt angry and frustrated as a result of unveiling:

One challenge of unveiling for me is the psychological problems I have to go through. You have a way of expressing yourself. I am expressing myself and trying to live my religion with my headscarf on and through other religious activities. All of a sudden, there is this policy in front of me. I make a choice of complying with the policy. For this choice, I compromise my beliefs and preferences. This causes frustration and anger. There are times when I want to scream and rebel, but cannot.

Buket expressed similar feelings and added that she had experienced depression and anxiety: "I do not think I will ever want to go back to university after graduation. I do not know where I belong. I do not know why policymakers do not understand me. Things I have gone through have been really difficult for an adolescent, for a girl at this young age." Alara stated that unveiling made her stressed and nervous: "Unveiling has negatively affected my psychology. My behavior has changed negatively. It first created distress and made me very nervous. Then I got used to it. It is a concession. I keep asking myself why I am in this situation." Sevda perceived unveiling as a sin and knowing this impacted her psychology negatively. She explained: "Unveiling is a sin. I know that. Veiling is an obligation of a Muslim woman. We are unveiling for a materialistic thing. I do not know why they want us to unveil. Allah will punish us for this sin. Knowing this and still unveiling caused some psychological problems and made me very nervous and anxious."

While these part-time unveilers perceived they still experienced emotional and psychological problems, others who also suffered from these problems perceived that they had started overcoming some of them. Gamze, for example, stated that she cried a lot and suffered from obsession and depression in her first year of college, but had started overcoming some of her problems:

I have started overcoming some of the negative feelings. This experience of unveiling caused me depression. I was not going to follow my religious beliefs anymore. To know this made me an obsessive, depressed, and introvert person. I closed my doors to people. People are asking me if I am unveiling. Do not ask me this question. You know that I am unveiling. I am tired of repeating the sentence that I am unveiling. Why do people keep reminding me by asking over and over again? My first two years have been like this. Youngsters who are at the same age as me are having fun and enjoying their youth outside while I am suffering and going through all these psychological problems because of the ban and unveiling. This is something hard to accept and overcome. I have overcome it to some extent and I think I am stronger now.

Why am I being subjected to this discrimination?: Sixteen part-time unveilers mentioned that a challenge of unveiling was that they felt like second-class citizens and were subjected to discrimination from either policymakers, who had issued the headscarf ban policy, or secularists. They felt as if Turkish women were being categorized into two polarized groups: covered and non-covered. They perceived that secularists did not approve of covered people and thought they were lower class and needed to become uncovered to receive their (secularists') approval. Dilara explained how, by unveiling, she was made to feel that she belonged to a different category: "The reason why there is the headscarf ban policy is to categorize students, women, and people in general into two distinct groups: the modern and the backward. So the policy tells us that we belong to the backward. By unveiling, it is as if I accept that there are categories and groups in society. It is as if I am seeking approval of the modern."

On top of these feelings, they perceived themselves as hypocrites living a lie as a result of unveiling. So, in a way, the part-time unveilers perceived their unveiling on campus as trying to be turned into a "first-class" citizen. Their existence as an unveiled and "first class" citizen on campus appeared hypocritical to them. Suzan explained she considered herself different on campus and did not understand why she was subjected to the discrimination of the policymakers:

> I am not the same person when unveiled. I am different on campus. I am different at home. Why am I being subjected to this discrimination? I do not want to go to the fitting room on campus. I want to go directly to my class, but I am not allowed to. When my friends see me covered outside, I am very happy. This is the real me. I want them to see me covered all the time. I do not want them to see me unveiled, but it is not possible.

Buket responded similarly, noting that she was treated as a second-class citizen: "I am not sure how I am being treated. This is like a second-class citizenship." Reyhan had similar views and this was why campus life was hard for her: "This is discrimination and I do not feel as if I belong to my university. I think unveiling makes me live as if I am another person and my being that way on campus is hard."

There is something about my outfit that tells everyone that I am a covered woman outside campus: Fourteen part-time unveilers mentioned that the fact that they removed their headscarf did not necessarily mean that they became unveiled. They drew attention to the difference between looking unveiled and being unveiled. They perceived that their challenge was that they removed their headscarf to look like others, but they had come to realize that their efforts did not always pay off. No matter how hard they tried, their clothes or behavior gave their identity away when people started spending time with them. They became frustrated because their unveiling did not protect their Islamist identity in the way they had hoped. So despite removing the headscarf, their perception was that they still remained veiled women in the eyes of many people on campus. Sezen explained her challenge with regard to her dress and how she was always perceived as a covered woman even though she removed her headscarf:

> As a result of removing my headscarf, I thought my problems would come to an end. You soon realize that your covered identity is part of who you are. I cannot wear tight jeans or mini-skirts. Clearly there is something about my outfit that tells everyone that I am a covered woman outside campus. No matter how hard I try to change that, I cannot. It is a challenge because it makes me vulnerable to potential discrimination and marginalization.

On the other hand, Selma was usually challenged in the way in which she behaved and treated others:

> I do not play cards. I do not gamble. I do not drink alcohol. I do not walk with guys arm in arm. I am usually distant with them and try not to become too close with a specific man. This puts me at a disadvantage immediately among the modern circle of friends. They first think I am very conservative, but later on start suspecting that I am covered and so on. So removing the headscarf does not become the solution you once hoped it would be.

You become an introvert: As mentioned in earlier sections, even though for six to eight part-time unveilers unveiling was an opportunity to socialize and open doors to extracurricular activities, for another ten women, unveiling meant just the opposite, making them quieter and passive and leading to them becoming asocial. Reyhan explained that, in general, unveiling made students introvert:

> University students are usually young and dynamic people who support their ideologies enthusiastically. . . . If you are a covered woman, your belief system and ideology are shaped up accordingly. When unveiled, you are out of your system and start living like someone else. This affects your social life. You become an introvert. You have less people to socialize with. I can be unveiled, but this does not necessarily mean that I have the mentality of an unveiled woman. This makes you asocial. The number of people you become friendly with on campus decreases.

Alara explained that unveiling had made her shy and stressed in class and among friends, causing her to become an introvert: "I have become asocial as a result of unveiling. Since I am not comfortable with my unveiling, I try to remain invisible. This puts some barriers between me and my friends, distancing me from having a social life."

I have developed a phobia: Six students mentioned that they had developed feelings of paranoia. The reason why they became paranoid seems to be the thought that they could be dismissed from class or campus for one reason or another. This was mainly because of experiences they had in the past and were not sure if these experiences could happen again. One point to mention is that the part-time unveilers who felt that way were the ones who were hat wearers or wig users and mostly returning students. Clearly, these students did not feel safe on campuses, and İpek was worried that she would be asked to remove her hat or leave the classroom or campus:

> I have never felt as comfortable as I did when I was attending college with my headscarf on. I have developed a phobia about being asked to leave the class or campus, or being asked to remove my hat. I have also developed a paranoia of being warned. Every time there is an administrator or faculty approaching me, I feel as if they are going to warn me about something in the way they did in the past.

I wish we had a changing room: Five part-time unveilers perceived that one of their challenges of unveiling was the actual act of unveiling in the street or on public transport before entering campus, due to a lack of a fitting room. Nurten explained that she had to unveil on public transport until she bought a car: "I wish we had a changing room like some other departments do. I had to remove my headscarf in the minibus while everybody was watching me, until I bought a car, in order not to embarrass myself any further in front of others. Unveiling while others are looking at you is a big challenge."

Unveiling created groups within the covered women: Three women stated that unveiling led to different types of unveiling creating some sort of categorization within the community of the veiled women. Part-time unveilers explained that there was some sort of hostility and distancing created among the covered women according to their type of unveiling on campus. Sevgi stated that she received negative reactions and even exclusion from other part-time unveilers who exposed their hair because she chose to use a wig:

> First I started with a wig. Uncovered students made fun of me. Even some of my professors made fun of me and told me I looked weird. I was really upset. What really made me more upset was the reaction of other veiled women who chose to expose their hair as their type of unveiling. They did not want to come and talk to me because they thought that if they did talk to me, this

would or might give away who they really were. So their shying away from me was a real disappointment. Unveiling created groups within the covered women.

No challenges or disadvantages during higher education: Two women pointed out that there were no challenges or disadvantages for them on campus because they were already challenged during their secondary education as a result of unveiling. In a way, they said that they knew they were going to remove their headscarf to go to university and they were used to it anyway.

To sum up, the accounts of participants showed part-time unveilers had concerns about their future career and experienced psychological problems, feelings of discrimination and paranoia, becoming asocial, and a creation of categories within a group of veiled women as the general challenges of unveiling. There were a couple of part-time unveilers who did not perceive themselves as being challenged by the unveiling in general. Having laid out the general challenges, participants shared their perceptions about specific challenges or disadvantages of unveiling. These specific points included perceptions of the part-time unveilers about their relationships with their faculty, friends, and administrators; their treatment on campus and in class; their involvement in extracurricular activities; their activities on campus; motivation for studying; and overall success during undergraduate studies.

Challenges of Unveiling Pertaining to Daily Life on Campus

This section highlights the perceptions of part-time unveilers with regard to their specific challenges or disadvantages as a result of unveiling. Some participants mentioned one point while others discussed several.

Relationship with faculty: Fifteen women perceived four main challenges or disadvantages of unveiling in terms of their relationship with faculty. Some of their challenges were more related to their type of unveiling rather than purely unveiling. In addition, the most important point they mentioned was that their challenges did not include all their professors, but specific faculty members who had some sensitivity about either types of unveiling or being uncovered in general.

One challenge of unveiling in the way I do is the remarks of some of my professors: Six part-time unveilers mentioned discouraging and negative comments of some faculty in class as a result of their unveiling. They explained that they were subjected to some ongoing disturbing remarks by a couple of professors, mostly female rather than male, during their studies. These remarks usually seemed to be in the form of disapproval about the hat or wig participants had chosen to use in class. Sevtap explained how she felt challenged by some of her teachers because of her wig:

> One challenge of unveiling in the way I do is the remarks of some of my professors. One female teacher who is against the wig told me not to wear the wig because she thought I was playing games with her, trying to deceive her and making political statements. According to her, by wearing a wig, I was making it obvious that I was a headscarf wearer. In her mind, my wig was a political symbol.

Dilara also added that some professors told them in class that wigs looked very artificial and ugly. Merve experienced the same challenge because of her hat.

When professors consider you to be an unveiled woman, they treat you that way: Five part-time unveilers perceived that one other challenge they had as a result of unveiling was that professors treated them as uncovered people and assigned them work they were not comfortable doing because of their belief systems. Suzan summarized the situation succinctly:

> When professors consider you to be an unveiled woman, they treat you that way. They give you a pat on your shoulder; want to kiss you on the cheeks during special occasions, et cetera. These are not very comfortable situations for a covered woman. In addition, they invite their class to an event or a gathering. So you have to go but, again unveiled, even though it is not a campus activity. If you go, you find yourself in an uncomfortable situation because the event may take place in the evening or there might be alcohol. So you either continue unveiling outside campus, or attend such events with your headscarf on and run the risk of turning your professor against you if he or she is prejudiced against covered women. If you choose not to go, you have to make excuses. I do not want to lie or come up with excuses. If you miss one time, it is OK, but if you do not go to any of the activities, that affects your success in class and the teacher becomes suspicious as well.

This is why I missed many of his classes unfortunately: Another challenge three women perceived that they faced as a result of unveiling was that they skipped a lot of classes, especially if their professors did not approve of their type of unveiling and wanted them to expose their hair to continue classes. In other words, when participants realized that their professors were going to give them a hard time in class or send them out of class, they avoided attending as many classes as possible. This did not seem to create problems for students, since attendance was usually not taken, and students exchanged class notes later on. İpek, for example, did not want to expose her hair when one of her professors did not approve of her type of unveiling and asked her to expose her hair. She did not want to do that, so chose to leave the class for that day hoping that next time the teacher would not notice her: "I have a lot of problems with one of my professors as a result of the way I unveil. He does not want me to sit in his class with my hat on. So I try my best to be invisible, but it is not always possible. This is why I missed many of his classes unfortunately and was not very successful during the final exams."

When she had one-to-one sessions with students, I just tried to be brief and quick: One final point that three women highlighted was the lack of dialogue with faculty as a result of unveiling. Since these women were trying to hide their covered identity, they tried to have minimum conversation with some of the faculty, especially those who were against the headscarf, in and outside class. They tried their best not to see faculty members. Their aim was to be invisible so that they did not say or do anything that might give away who they really were. Mine highlighted how she was trying to minimize the dialogue with faculty to protect her identity:

> There is one female teacher who is against covered women. So I was very quiet in her class, always sat at the back, and did not participate in many of the discussions. When she had one-to-one sessions with students, I just tried to be brief and quick. Whenever she asked me personal questions, I kept my answers short. Some uncovered friends told me that she was a really nice and talkative person. Apparently, they enjoyed chatting with her and learned a lot from her mentorship, but not me. If I ever saw her in the street outside campus, I crossed the street and changed direction. I kept my dialogue to a minimum so that I could protect my identity and pass the course without any problems.

Relationship with peers: Fourteen part-time unveilers formulated their perceptions around three main challenges of unveiling with regard to their relationship with peers.

They did not want to make friends with me: Eight part-time unveilers focused on the challenges that they faced on their way to establishing friendships as a result of unveiling. Reyhan had some challenging experiences while making friends on campus because of her type of unveiling. Other part-time unveilers did not know how to treat her as an unveiled woman with a hat because they thought that her friendship could give away their Islamist identity:

> Some [part-time unveilers] are against those who wear hats. This created communication problems when I first returned to campus. They did not want to make friends with me because they did not want their identities to be exposed. Later on, I met other people and became friends with them.

Alara highlighted a different challenge in terms of building relationships with peers as a result of unveiling. Her challenge concerned friends who did not initially realize that she was a covered woman. She started making friends and then when they met outside, they realized she was a covered woman and some of them stopped talking to her. She felt as if on the one hand she had deceived them and on the other hand had wasted all her time and energy building friendships with people who judged her physical appearance.

Peers can sometimes be harsh to us: Three women perceived hostility from peers as a challenge due to unveiling. This hostility from peers included verbal abuse and harassment, including harsh comments about their unveiling that saddened part-time unveilers, deeply and negatively influencing their relationship with these peers. Gamze made a comment about this issue in a very general way without going into details: "Peers can sometimes be harsh to us. You know what? They can be really critical about the way we unveil or get dressed or behave. It is not always easy to digest all this."

People, friends, everybody is watching us: Three part-time unveilers perceived that they were constantly under scrutiny from their friends. They explained that they could not become very close to friends because those who knew they were veiled watched them constantly to see if they were behaving properly, as a covered woman should behave. İpek indicated that "there is ongoing checking on part-time unveilers. People, friends, everybody is watching us to see whether we make mistakes or not. Why? I do not get this."

Relationship with administration: Five part-time unveilers mentioned the main challenge they perceived with the administration was the bad treatment from administrators, especially female ones, as a result of their type of unveiling.

She was rude: Five women explored their perceptions about the ways in which they received bad treatment as a result of unveiling. İpek had a bad experience with her new Dean, when she was called into a classroom by one of her professors, who wanted to dismiss her from class because of the way she was unveiled:

> The professor told me that she did not want to see me with a hat on in class and left the room, to apparently call the Dean. When the Dean entered the room with the teacher she looked at me and in front of everybody told me that she had enough of people like me. She was rude. She also said that she did not understand why I did not simply expose my hair and why I made my life difficult. She loudly asked me to leave the class immediately.

Treatment on campus: Fourteen part-time unveilers highlighted two main challenges about the treatment on campus as a result of their unveiling and mostly because of their type of unveiling.

They are looking at me cynically: One point that 11 part-time unveilers mentioned was the cynical looks or staring of others on campus. They usually came from students they did not know and the frequency and intensity of these looks varied from college to college on campus as well. İpek was disturbed and felt uneasy when others watched her on campus. Sevim was also subjected to constant staring and felt somewhat threatened by those looks, especially when she was on her own:

> I do not walk on campus when I am on my own. . . . When I have friends with me, I am here and there on campus. I do not feel comfortable in the campus environment. The way people look at me disturbs me greatly. They are looking at me cynically and as if I am somebody from Mars, as if I am somebody with a different body shape. This really upsets me and I feel threatened. I am trying to avoid these looks, but it is not always possible.

Berna complained about the initial reaction of others when they saw her with her wig: "When others meet me for the first time, they open their eyes wide with surprise on seeing my wig. First I was disgusted by these reactions and also ashamed of myself and how I looked, but I am used to it now." Sevtap also suffered from the same problem because of her wig. She dealt with the situation better and tried to ignore other people's reactions. At some point, her friends told her to take the wig off, but she insisted on wearing it because she felt more comfortable with it despite the harassing looks: "When I enter the campus, people look at me in a weird way. They look at my wig and start laughing. They make fun of me and how I look, I know. . . . This is a little disturbing, but not much because there are many other students with wigs on campus. I am not the only one."

It looks really funny, do you know that?: Another challenge for part-time unveilers was the verbal abuse. Three part-time unveilers shared some instances where they were subjected to verbal harassment by other students they did not know. Even though participants stated that these instances did not take place often, when they happened, they were powerful enough to hurt them. İpek shared her experiences about verbal harassment that happened twice, once in the canteen and once in class:

> One day, I was sitting in the canteen on my own drinking tea and eating a sandwich. A guy was sitting at the next table and all of a sudden he called me and asked me if I was cold. I did not understand what he meant initially.

Then he said: "It is really hot in here but you must be really cold since you are wearing that thing on your head." ... Another day, a student I do not know in a big class came up to me all of a sudden and asked me if I had a health problem. When I said I did not and asked her why she was asking me, she said: "I was trying to understand why you were wearing that weird thing. It looks really funny, do you know that?"

Treatment in class: Nine students mentioned two main challenges of unveiling with regard to treatment in class.

An Islamist male classmate came up to me and criticized me for wearing trousers: In addition to the scrutiny from their friends, as mentioned earlier, one similar challenge five part-time unveilers mentioned was that their Islamist male classmates, regardless of whether they were friends or not, criticized their behavior in class. Part-time unveilers perceived that these male classmates considered themselves as Islamist brothers and felt the need to watch and protect their sisters. Fatma shared one of her experiences that happened to her a couple of times in class and explained how she was criticized by one of the Islamist male classmates whom she hardly even knew:

> I do not usually wear trousers. One day, I did. Next day, an Islamist male classmate came up to me and criticized me for wearing trousers. He is not even my friend. I hardly even know him. He said that my behavior was inappropriate and that because I was unveiled did not necessarily mean that I was going to change everything completely. I was shocked. ... When you are veiled and wear trousers, you do not attract attention. When you are unveiled, and wear trousers and put on makeup, or hug a male friend, it is perceived as if you are changing as a result of removing your headscarf. So Islamist male classmates especially watch you at all times. I find unveiling a big challenge as a result of the way we are treated in class by Islamist male classmates.

People talked a lot behind my back: Another challenge four part-time unveilers mentioned was the perceived distance and gossip of some classmates in class. Even though this gossip only took place occasionally, it was enough to challenge part-time unveilers, especially at the beginning of their undergraduate studies. Yeliz explained the type of gossip she heard in class, which disturbed her, especially in the first year of her undergraduate degree:

> I heard that people were making fun of the way I looked and dressed. I was wearing a turtleneck at all times. ... Since I was not very comfortable with my unveiling, I was really shy and did not want to talk to people in the first

year. People talked a lot behind my back. Their perception of me was cold, distant, capricious, and fake [part-time unveiler].

This type of gossip caused some friction among friends in class as well. Because they perceived Yeliz as a distant person looking different, they ignored her initially:

At the beginning of the first year, my classmates did not talk to me very much. They usually ignored me because I looked different. They involved themselves in activities, but never invited me. Unveiling made me belong nowhere and I ended up being ignored in class. This changed as time passed.

Activities on campus: The main disadvantage of unveiling that 14 participants mentioned was the restriction on doing activities on campus as a result of unveiling.

I do not do anything a university student would normally do: Fourteen participants perceived that unveiling restricted them from doing activities. Since these part-time unveilers did not feel comfortable when unveiled, they spent as little time on campus as possible, leaving university as quickly as possible when their work was done. For some part-time unveilers, this was more of a problem during the first year of their studies and they became more comfortable afterward; for others, the problem existed. Reyhan did not want to spend a lot of time on campus because she felt ugly with her hat and clothes: "I do not take part in activities. Those who do not know me look at me in a weird way with my hat and turtleneck. One day I had to go to the library, but the assistant there [treated me really badly], so since that day I have not been back. I do not go to the computer lab or student union either.... So basically I do not do anything a university student would normally do."

Involvement in extracurricular activities: The reason why part-time unveilers perceived unveiling as a disadvantage in terms of involvement in extracurricular activities was the same as the reason for activities on campus.

I do not attend extracurricular activities: Eighteen part-time unveilers mentioned that the disadvantage of unveiling in terms of participating in extracurricular activities was that they did not want to take part in them because they did not want to be unveiled any longer than they should be. They believed that even though these extracurricular activities should be part of their university life, they preferred not to take part in them because, as they were university activities, they had to attend unveiled. Part-time unveilers reported that they chose not to unveil unless it was really necessary, such as attending classes or exams. They thought they were missing an important part of their higher education experience, but still believed that this was a compromise they needed to make. They stated that they would normally attend most of the extracurricular activities, except the ones where alcohol was served, if they were allowed to participate as covered women.

Dilara stated that she could not attend many of the activities because she did not want to unveil more than she had to: "I am not going to the picnic. I am not attending introduction meetings at the beginning of the year to meet the newcomers. I am not going anywhere with the rest of my class because I do not want to unveil for these activities." Sevda explained that she only wanted to unveil for class purposes: "I do not attend extracurricular activities. I do not want to remove my headscarf apart from class time."

In short, part-time unveilers perceived various challenges of unveiling in regard to their relationship with faculty, administrators, and peers; the way they were treated on campus and in class; and their activities and extracurricular activities on and outside campus.

All in all, this section presented the perceptions of part-time unveilers with regard to the numerous challenges they faced on campus and in their life as a result of complying with the policy. Having elaborated on the perceived challenges of the part-time unveilers that ranged from psychological problems to restriction on involvement in activities and extracurricular activities on and off campus, I will now elaborate on the ways in which these women dealt with these challenges.

How Did Part-Time Unveilers Deal with These Challenges

Despite their challenges during their higher education years, part-time unveilers seemed to find ways in which they could deal with their challenges. They reported that there were six main strategies that they used to ease the hurdles and manage the disadvantages that unveiling created. Some part-time unveilers followed one strategy, whereas others had two or three.

I Try to be More Religious

The first strategy that 23 part-time unveilers mentioned that they used as a way to deal with their challenges was more devotion to religion. Since they gave up on following one tenet of Islam partially and temporarily, wearing the headscarf, they wanted to compensate for that by trying to follow the religious teachings of Islam more closely. Melek, for example, focused on trying to be a better Muslim every day and did whatever she could to achieve her goal:

> The strategy I have to deal with challenges of unveiling is I am trying to nourish my religious feelings by other things than the headscarf. I read the Qur'an more and talk to Allah more frequently. I donate money, pray more often, and try to be a better person in general so that Allah forgives me for removing my headscarf. I wear really conservative clothes, lead a modest life, fast, and pray five times a day. I often read teachings of Islam. I listen to religious songs. I am trying to devote more time and energy to be a well-rounded and better Muslim. I try to be more religious. . . . I guess overall I am trying to be a better Muslim in many other ways.

In addition to talking to Allah and trying to be a good Muslim, Sevtap also believed in spiritual growth and helped the poor:

> I am dealing with the challenges of unveiling by sticking to my religion more. I have improved myself religiously over the years. I believe that no matter how terrible the situation is, there is always a light at the end of the tunnel. For me unveiling has been like this. The headscarf ban policy made me unveil against my wishes and religious beliefs, but unveiling strengthened my religious identity. I am a better Muslim now. I look for peace in the spiritual world. I smile to everyone thanks to my religious and spiritual growth. I have opened lots of new doors for myself, thanks to my smile. I respect people, and try to help the poor. I give presents and money to those who are in need. This way, I am rejuvenating my religiosity.

One of My Strategies to Deal with Challenges Is to Choose My Electives Strategically

The second strategy that 18 part-time unveilers used to deal with challenges was the careful selection of courses beside their required courses. While choosing their electives, they tried to make sure that the professors who taught the courses were not those who were against the headscarf or wigs or hats. They usually found out the information about professors from part-time unveilers who already took those courses. Reyhan, for example, chose the electives according to teachers whom she perceived treated students with hats equally in class:

> One of my strategies to deal with challenges is to choose my electives strategically. It does not matter which elective I am taking really. What matters is how I am going to be treated in class and whether or not my performance will be evaluated fairly. I am so grateful for students who give me advice on

that. They have been very helpful so far. They give me great tips so I know which course to take and which one not to take. That is really a great strategy for me to deal with the challenges.

I Had a Haircut

The third strategy five women used was a change in their appearance. Yeliz explained what she had changed in herself physically to feel better about herself as a part-time unveiler:

> I had a haircut, thinking that less hair will be exposed. I hate short hair, but I really had a very short hair cut. I will continue having short hair until the end of my studies. That was my first reaction to unveiling. I avoided jewelry. I avoided everything that would attract attention. I have not worn any necklaces, earrings, or rings for a long time. I did not do anything that would make me look different. By being very simple and modest, I was hoping that nobody would notice me, that nobody would see me uncovered. It is a psychological strategy I have developed for myself.

Nurten also changed her look, but in a different way:

> I started wearing baggy clothes and baggy trousers as a way to deal with unveiling. Since unveiling was something different, I wanted to look different as well. If I looked totally different, I thought I could convince myself that I was not really me, but somebody different who was unveiled. So I wore really big clothes that hid my body. I wore colorful fashionable bandanas with really flashy earrings. I am usually simple, but this time I wanted to look different.

My Strategy to Deal with the Challenges Is to Learn More

A fourth strategy that three part-time unveilers employed was that they convinced themselves that this was not something that they could control and it was not up to them. So instead of being upset about things that were beyond their control, they chose to make the best of what they could control, that is, receive the best of their education. Bahar dealt with her challenges by trying to learn as much as she could to make good use of her time on campus:

> My strategy to deal with the challenges is to learn more. I continuously learn new things. I read and learn. This is how I overcome problems. I learn about everything at university. I learn about history, art, literature, and different

people. This is a great joy to me. At least all this new information makes me excited and I am getting the best education possible, so making good use of the university education keeps me going.

My Strategy Is to Express Myself Continuously

Another strategy that two students used was talking about themselves and the ban to other students so that they had an opportunity to release their emotions, share their challenges, and express their true Islamist identities. They also hoped that this way other students could understand how the ban impacted the lives of part-time unveilers. Berna explained that she tried to communicate her challenges as well as her worldviews as a covered woman to other students:

> My strategy is to express myself continuously. Since I wear a wig, it is easy for students to realize that I am a covered woman. It is also a way of expressing myself. I keep telling my friends who I really am. I tell them my challenges. It is a way of relieving my stress. It is my goal to explain who a covered woman is and how similar we all are. I also explain in my own way how the ban has impacted on me. I talk about the ban. I keep discussing the policy from various perspectives. I engage students in intellectual debates about Islamists, the headscarf ban policy, and Islamist identities.

I am Using Humor to Deal with My Challenges

One participant, Sevim, mentioned that her strategy was to use humor:

> I am using humor to deal with my challenges. This helps me to overcome the difficulties and erase the scars unveiling may have left. When students look at me in a way they are trying to understand whether what I am wearing is my real hair or wig, I start laughing and say "Hey, you are new on campus I guess, you will get used to me." And then I continue laughing when I see them puzzled.

In addition to these six strategies, Nurten said that she bought a car as a strategy to deal with the physical act of unveiling. She did not want to continue unveiling and veiling outside her campus or in the minibus in front of other people, so she finally purchased a vehicle that meant she could remove her headscarf in private.

All in all, part-time unveilers shared their ways of dealing with the challenges of unveiling. Some women employed one, while others had multiple strategies. These strategies were varied and creative, and appeared to impact educational, personal, or social aspects of the lives of part-time unveilers. Clearly, their perception was that the ultimate aim for them was to survive their undergraduate years and minimize the challenges by trying different ways of dealing with them.

The Ways in Which These Challenges Affected the Educational Progress of the Part-Time Unveilers

Part-time unveilers explored their perceptions about the ways in which their challenges affected their educational progress. They particularly focused on how their perceived difficulties and problems, discussed earlier, impacted their motivation for studying and general success. Twenty part-time unveilers believed that the challenges negatively impacted their motivation for studying and general success, leading to lack of motivation and a disconnection from academia, while seven part-time unveilers believed that the difficulties had a positive effect on their studies, making participants more ambitious and determined to complete their studies. For some students, even though their motivation was negatively affected, they tried hard to ensure that their general success was not negatively affected.

Unveiling Affected My Motivation and General Success a Lot in a Very Negative Way in the First Year

Fifteen students stated that unveiling was a challenge to their motivation. Suzan explained how her motivation decreased as a result of unveiling: "Unveiling decreases my motivation for studying. I do not think I fully benefit from my undergraduate education. I just hope that these four years pass quickly and I graduate." For Sevgi, who had an average GPA, unveiling was more of a challenge in her first year: "Unveiling affected my motivation and general success a lot in a very negative way in the first year. I did not even want to go to university. Then I became more ambitious. . . . After the first year, I was more motivated and relaxed." In addition, Reyhan, who had a low GPA, worried about her hat while studying for an exam and wondered if there would be a problem in class, which affected her motivation negatively. Fatma, who had a high GPA, felt that her success was compromised from unveiling since she was psychologically weak and tired from fighting her emotions:

> My motivation is really badly affected including my success. My psychology is bad. I do not feel comfortable. Since my real identity is not there, I am not performing as well as I should. So there is no success. I am in a constant war.

I keep thinking about myself and unveiling. I am looking at my books, but not with pleasure and full concentration. I am studying because I have to. My mind is not peaceful. I keep questioning things.

Buket, with an average GPA, focused more on her lack of motivation and concentration in class as a result of unveiling that impacted the quality of her general success:

University is for classes and education, but there is a barrier for covered women. . . . So you face a barrier even before you come to school. You start your higher education with a low morale. You are held down. So you cannot concentrate on your studies in class. The teacher talks, but you are more concerned with your look and what others think of you. . . . This creates a lack of adaptation, motivation, and concentration. This creates a decrease in motivation for studying.

This Creates a Gap between the Academic World and Myself

Five part-time unveilers highlighted that as a result of unveiling they wanted to spend as little time as possible on campus, creating a break from academia and higher education that negatively affected their motivation. Beyza, who had a high GPA, explained that she spent little time on campus and this made her less involved and thus less motivated to study:

I prefer going to campus as little as possible. The day I go to campus, I try my best to do everything I have to do. I am using the campus very economically. I do not want to spend more time than I should. I do not spend as much time as I should with my advisor and professors to fully benefit from all the academic opportunities the university provides. This creates a gap between the academic world and myself. I cannot breathe enough academic air to inspire me and to motivate. Motivation for studying is all in the air of a university campus. However, unfortunately I am not getting that.

Unveiling Has Motivated Me So Much That You Would Not Believe

Five students mentioned that their unveiling had a direct positive impact on their GPAs. They perceived unveiling as a positive reinforcement for their motivation for studying. They highlighted that unveiling against their wishes had made them ambitious and they had to have high GPAs because they wanted to become very successful as a response to the higher education headscarf ban policy. Sevim, with an average GPA, explained that she became very ambitious to be successful thanks to her experience of unveiling:

> Unveiling has motivated me so much that you would not believe. It made me very ambitious, actually more ambitious than I am. I study at all times. I am going to graduate from this university and will fight against the higher education headscarf ban policy in a powerful way with my diploma. I do not want others to go through the experiences and challenges I have gone through. I want others to have the option to make choices.

Yeliz, with a high GPA, added that her aim was to receive grades no lower than 85 out of 100 in all the exams as a result of her motivation for success due to complying with the policy:

> Unveiling has had a positive impact on my motivation for studying and general success. I am studying very hard to make what I am compromising worthwhile. I am trying my best not to get any grades lower than 85 out of 100. Even though I am not super-ambitious about my career, unveiling made me extremely ambitious about my education and general success on campus.

Unveiling Made Me Determined to Graduate From University

Two part-time unveilers mentioned that unveiling affected their motivation indirectly, since they became determined to complete their studies and graduate from university no matter what challenges they faced. Sevda explained how she might have dropped out if she did not experience the act of unveiling:

> Unveiling made me determined to graduate from university. Had it not been for unveiling, I might have even dropped out. Who knows? So to graduate I need to study. So unveiling did not impact my motivation for studying directly, but it did impact it indirectly since I need to study to graduate. Thus I am studying as much as I can in order to graduate.

In short, on the one hand, some students perceived that the challenges of unveiling seemed to push them toward studying and becoming more successful. Their success appeared to be a way for participants to prove themselves and make their unveiling worth pursuing for their future. On the other hand, the perception of others was that the challenges of unveiling led to lack of motivation for their studies.

One interesting observation was that it seemed as if there was no correlation between student GPA and the ways in which participants perceived unveiling challenged or impacted them. Participants who felt unmotivated or spent time on campus without having a close working relationship with advisors and/or professors or without being involved in many activities or extracurricular activities had high, average, or low GPAs. The same was true for participants who perceived that they felt ambitious and motivated as a result of the challenges of unveiling. Students who perceived themselves as determined to be very successful had high or average GPAs. In addition, as indicated in Appendix B, almost half of the participants seemed to be doing well and had high GPAs. Eleven participants had average GPAs and only two participants had low GPAs. All these might indicate that, regardless of the challenges or impact of unveiling, participants appeared to be self-motivated.

To sum up, part-time unveilers perceived four different ways in which the challenges of unveiling affected their educational progress. The hurdles they went through seemed to, on the one hand, create disconnection from the academia and lack of motivation, and on the other, make them more ambitious and determined to complete their studies.

This chapter presented the perceptions of the part-time unveilers concerning the opportunities and challenges unveiling brought to them on campus. It also explored the strategies they used to deal with their challenges and unpacked the ways in which the challenges affected their educational progress. The following chapter presents participants' perceptions of the impact of the policy on their sense of identity.

6

Impact of the Policy on Part-Time Unveilers' Sense of Identity

In this chapter I present the perceptions of the part-time unveilers about the ways in which unveiling had impacted their sense of identity. Specifically, this chapter analyzes the students' perceptions of the impact of complying with the headscarf ban on their identities as Turkish citizens, Muslims, and females.[1]

How Did Complying with the Policy Affect the Identities of Part-Time Unveilers?

Part-time unveilers explored their perceptions of how unveiling impacted their plural self-identities: citizenship identity, religious identity, and gender identity. In terms of their identity as Turkish citizens, part-time unveilers mostly highlighted the ways in which unveiling had an impact on their citizenry and citizenship rights that existed both in society and in state institutions, including higher education institutions. In terms of their identity as Muslims, the perceptions mostly revolved around Islam and the teachings of Islam in relation to unveiling. Finally, part-time unveilers unpacked the effects of unveiling in terms of how unveiling impacted them as women in both their private and social lives.

How Did Complying with the Policy Impact the Identities of Part-Time Unveilers as Citizens of Turkey?

Policymakers are limiting me and my rights: One-third of the part-time unveilers mentioned limitation as an impact of unveiling on their citizenship identity. They stressed that they felt as if they were not free citizens and their freedom was at risk as a result of the headscarf ban policy that required them to unveil to attend university. Fatma explained that the fact that she could not enter higher education campuses dressed the way she wanted made her feel that she was restricted as a citizen.

> This ban is limiting me. Policymakers are limiting me and my rights. This is really sad and disturbing. Why am I being restricted? Why can another female student enter the university in the way she wants and I cannot. Why are some of us restricted and some others are not? What does this mean in the eyes of the policymakers? Are we not all free citizens? I think we are, but what about this ban, this imposition on some of us?

Gamze approached the issue from the perspective of job opportunities and explained how restricted she was when it came to finding a job.

> As a result of the headscarf ban we also become restricted when we apply for jobs. Some companies do not want women to work while wearing their headscarves. They insist that you unveil. Probably, they think we are unveiling at university so we can continue unveiling at work as well. So all of a sudden, there is an extension of the ban, even in the private sector. This is really restricting because it is not as if, ok, I will unveil for a couple of years and then I will work with my headscarf on. It is very vague, and you do not know where you can apply to and where you cannot. And which company will take you and which will not. As a graduate student, you should be thinking about the suitability of the place for you, but with the ban outside campuses, you should first think about which company would take you with or without your headscarf. I call this a limitation.

Every time I go somewhere new, I wonder if people there are going to ask me to remove my headscarf: Some part-time unveilers stated that another impact of unveiling on their citizenship identity was that they were not at ease in the streets, while entering state institutions, and while meeting new people. Semra felt uneasy when she was in front of the campus and wondered what other people thought about her. Nurten felt fearful in public places, wondering if she would be asked to remove her headscarf:

> I am fearful when I enter the public buildings.... I am trying not to go to state institutions unless I have to, but it is not always possible.... I feel as if somebody is going to come and ask me to leave the building unless I remove my headscarf. I want to do whatever I have to do in government buildings and leave quickly. When there are long queues, I do not wait. I leave and come back some other time. I prefer the early mornings.

Sevgi stated that she had become suspicious of other people's intentions in general, so meeting new people was not very easy for her:

> Unveiling made me become suspicious of others. Every time I meet some-body new, I cannot stop wondering if he or she is against the headscarf. Every time I go somewhere new, I wonder if people there are going to ask me to remove my headscarf. I am uncomfortable, troubled, and sad because of the way unveiling affects my citizenship identity this way. I feel as if I have become a person who suspects everyone.

Yeliz was uncomfortable with the idea of not being able to visit places in the way she wanted, even on special occasions, and was alert about being asked to remove her headscarf:

> Last year, I attended a graduation ceremony of a relative. I felt so restless. It was a different institution. There were other women with headscarves. But I still felt uncomfortable. I felt as if everybody knew me and was looking at me. It felt as if someone will come and ask me to remove my headscarf. I sat there with all these ideas in my head. I could not enjoy the ceremony properly because of how I felt both as an ordinary citizen and as a student on that specific campus.

The ban makes me feel as if I am not wanted in society: More than half of the part-time unveilers mentioned that unveiling made them feel as if they were regarded differently and were not the most desirable citizens in society. Alara stated:

> The ban makes me feel as if I am not wanted in society. It is a strange feeling. I am wondering if I am a second-class person in society. This problem is a problem of the whole country. This problem will not come to an end. Under-standings need to change. My cousin, years ago, went to university with her headscarf on. I cannot now. For more than ten years, this problem has not changed. What is this big issue about the headscarf, I do not understand. We have bigger issues to deal with. I want to feel that I am a desirable citizen in society. But right now, because of the ban I do not know . . .

A couple of part-time unveilers perceived the ban as a signal that women with headscarves were not the most desirable students on campuses in the context of higher education. Beyza questioned the way she was judged by policymakers as a citizen and also as a student, as a result of being subjected to the ban:

> I have realized that the system in not fair. I have started to question the ways in which the system treats me as a citizen in this country . . . . I am a good

and desirable citizen if I follow the policies of the policymakers; otherwise I am a problem citizen. I keep asking myself if I am not a good citizen and why I am not wanted in society. Why is it that policymakers do not want or like me? What have I done wrong? . . . The fact that people who do not know you see you as a threat and put your higher education rights at risk is a complicated matter. The higher education system threatens my rights of access to campuses. . . . All these questions make me question how policymakers view me.

Fatma concurred and added some more details about the issue:

I am not wanted with my headscarf on campus. So as a student, I am classified as different whether I am veiled or unveiled. Either way, I am different. Also when I am outside of my campus, I am still different. When I want to visit another university, for example, I cannot. And also, in the streets at the entrance of my campus, when people look at me, I sometimes wonder what they think about me. Maybe they feel sorry for me, maybe not. But for sure, they know I am different. What does this mean? Does it mean I am not equal to other students on campus? What does it mean to be equal on campus? . . . What signal are higher education policymakers sending to the academic community through this ban? I know it is a difficult question to answer.

As a society, we are losing some of our cultural values: One woman, Sezen, said that the impact of unveiling on her citizenship identity was the loss of cultural values:

As Turkish people, our citizenship identities were associated with various traditions, including the headscarf, conservative and modest lifestyle, celebrating the religious holidays, respect for the elderly, and the concept of neighborhood. Unveiling makes me realize that as a society we are losing some of our cultural values to look like Westerners or to become Westernized. This is how unveiling is impacting my citizenship identity.

As a citizen I have become more involved in politics: Some part-time unveilers indicated that as a result of the ban, their citizenship identity became more politicized and they were more involved in politics to defend their rights and eliminate the ban. Gamze, for example, thought that in general those who were subjected to the ban were more politically involved in society:

When I think of unveiling in terms of how it affects my citizenship identity, I find myself more politicized. While unveiling, I keep thinking about the meaning of politics. As a citizen I have become more involved in politics. I keep thinking about the ban and the act of veiling and unveiling in relation to politics. I started to read a lot about politics, especially how the ban is being politicized. I never thought my headscarf would be a subject of politics, but it has become so making me politicized as well. This is one of the ways how the ban has affected my citizenship.

No impact: Finally, a couple of part-time unveilers stated that unveiling did not have an impact on their citizenship identity. Two of these women briefly said that they did not think unveiling impacted their identity as citizens, while Melek stressed that the reason why she thought there was no impact was because it was a man-made policy and decision and could change at any time in the future. She did not attribute the decision or unveiling to herself as a citizen, and that is why she did not think that unveiling had an effect on her citizenship identity.

In short, part-time unveilers explored different ways in which complying with the policy impacted (or did not impact) their identities as citizens. Their perceptions ranged from feelings of not being the most desirable citizens in society to negative feelings for policymakers in relation to the headscarf ban policy. For some women, unveiling did not appear to have had an impact on their citizenship identity.

How Did Complying with the Policy Impact the Identities of Part-Time Unveilers as Muslims?

Part-time unveilers expressed their perceptions about how complying with the policy had impacted their religious identity. All part-time unveilers mentioned the ways in which the headscarf ban affected their Muslimness, framing the issue from the point of Islam and its requirements to become a good Muslim.

Did I now give up some of my Muslimness?: Some part-time unveilers highlighted that as a result of unveiling they felt as if they had given up some of their Muslimness. By giving up some of their religiosity, they meant that a hole was created in their Muslim identity that was either repairable or not. What they really questioned was whether they were becoming less religious as a result of unveiling, since after a while they felt that unveiling did not hurt them as much as it hurt the first time they removed the headscarf. Fatma, for example, thought that by the act of unveiling she had made the choice of giving up some of her religious identity and wondered if, as time went by, it was distancing her from her religion:

OK, now that I have unveiled, the question is what that means. Did I now give up some of my Muslimness? Am I not religious anymore? The headscarf is or was a part of me, but it is not anymore. How is this going to affect me in the long run?. I am really scared that I will not be a Muslim anymore in the way I was before. All these feelings really make me wonder about my relationship with my religion. I hope this unveiling will not weaken my belief system. This is all I want. University life is long and after a while unveiling becomes normal. But, of course, what is next? This is the question one needs to answer and think about. Not easy....

This is the new identity of some of us: This emerged as another theme a few part-time unveilers highlighted. In this new identity, some values became more important as compared with the past, including the headscarf and the intentions of one's actions. Bahar, for example, thought that some part-time unveilers became more attached to their headscarf and their religious values as a result of the ban and the act of unveiling.

> Speaking generally, it is true that some women give up veiling and decide to continue their lives unveiled. This is their choice. But on the other hand, some of us become more attached to our headscarves. Think about it: all this discussion is about my headscarf. How would you feel? Wouldn't you think: wow, this headscarf of mine must be really important; I should stick to it. I am wearing something really precious, like a diamond. Seriously, some women have become more religious than ever and they have realized or been made to realize how important the headscarf is. And, of course, when something is this important, you become more attached to it. Some of us have become more religious. This is the new identity of some of us.

This is a big dilemma for me: Challenging feelings as a result of acting against Islam were part of this theme half of the part-time unveilers highlighted. Part-time unveilers explained that in their understanding, veiling was one of the precepts of the Qur'an, as mentioned in various verses of the holy book (Appendix D), and complying with the policy, thus unveiling, was to act against the Qur'an and its teachings. According to their perceptions, acting against religion, which was an attempt that might destabilize the Muslim identity, created conflicts, dilemmas, fears, and negative feelings that made part-time unveilers question the strength of their religiosity.

Seda felt as if she was committing a sin by unveiling. This made her fearful and wonder if Allah would forgive her for the sin that she committed reluctantly: "I am acting against religion. Unveiling is committing a sin. I do not know if Allah is going to forgive me because of this sin. ...I am really scared that Allah is not going to forgive me. Sometimes I cry because of this. This is a big sacrifice." Yeliz stated that unveiling had negative impacts on her Muslim identity, creating negative feelings toward the material world and making her live with dilemmas: "My Muslim identity tells me not to uncover. My [material world] identity forces me to uncover. If Allah says not to uncover, then why are we even discussing the issue? This is a dilemma for me. If Allah asks us to wear a headscarf, this means that unveiling has bad effects. Unveiling is acting against the word of Allah; it is acting against the verse of the Qur'an."

I am afraid this concession might lead to other concessions: The fourth theme was the fear that making a concession from Muslimness would lead to other concessions. A couple of part-time unveilers explained that unveiling was a concession impacting their Muslim identity and they feared that concession would lead to other concessions:

> What is unveiling? Concession. I am making a concession by unveiling. I do not want to unveil, but I have to unveil. This is not my decision. But after a while, you get used to it. And then what? Today there is a ban about this, what if there is another ban on campus? Am I going to make another concession? Probably I will. Because I will think like this: I have already made one and I am in the middle of my studies, so I do not want to quit; I can make another one. The same thing might happen when you work as well. They may ask you for some concessions, and you might say "OK, I will make them." So I am afraid this concession might lead to other concessions. The challenge is the decision of making the first one. Once you make one, it is always easy to make another one. You get used to it. This is true, isn't it?
>
> (Seda)

I do not want to unveil after graduation: Another way unveiling impacted the Muslim identity of part-time unveilers was their decision of veiling versus unveiling in the future. Almost two-third of the part-time unveilers mentioned that, having experienced unveiling, they became more attached to their headscarf and appreciated the value of their religion and the act of veiling more. Thus, they decided that they would continue veiling after graduation even if they faced challenges in terms of career options or places to work.

> I will have unveiled for years when I finish university. So I do not want to unveil after graduation. I have many other options. I think I will find a job in a private company. I know that some private companies do not always hire covered women. So I know that the headscarf might be a barrier. But I have connections. Or maybe I will start my own company. The only thing I want is to continue my life according to my beliefs. I want to reflect my belief system via my clothing and lifestyle. And I do not think this is going to prevent me from having a career.
>
> (Sevgi)

Twelve part-time unveilers, on the other hand, were either hesitant about continuing to veil, especially in the work environment (nine part-time unveilers), or had decided to uncover for good or at least while working (three part-time unveilers). They considered this decision as a product of their unveiling experience. They reported that since they knew the consequences of not unveiling, and their opportunity to attend higher education as a result of compliance with the policy, they had either decided to remove the headscarf after graduation or were at least considering it as an option for the sake of better job opportunities. Alara, for example, was more decisive and knew that she would have to unveil in the work environment to find a good job and thrive:

> I wish I did not have to unveil. I know that I will have to unveil in the work environment after university. In the places I would like to work covered people are not accepted. So I have to unveil. I do not know how this is going to impact my Muslim identity. I have a quota; until that quota is full, I will work unveiled because I want my economic independence. I am ambitious and want to achieve things. So I know I have to unveil. I know that unveiling [reluctantly] is a bad thing. It has affected and will continue affecting my Muslim identity, but I have to do this. This is actually how unveiling on campus impacted my Muslim identity. It taught me to replace one bad thing, which is unveiling [reluctantly], with other things that are good. So this is what I am trying to do, and this is what I am going to do in the future as well.

Semra, on the other hand, thought that she might unveil completely, depending on future circumstances: "I want an academic career. Unveiling on campus may not be enough. Academia will not let you advance if you are a [part-time unveiler]. Knowing this I might have to unveil for good. I do not know yet. Time and circumstances will tell. Maybe things will change, maybe the policy will change, and I will not have to unveil reluctantly."

This is why it is not seriously disturbing my Muslim identity: Finally, two part-time unveilers who were hat wearers mentioned that unveiling did not have a strong impact on their Muslim identity since the hat represented the headscarf in their eyes: "The way I unveil, my hat that covers my neck and ears, is very similar to my headscarf. This is why it is not seriously disturbing my Muslim identity" (İpek).

All in all, part-time unveilers perceived numerous ways in which unveiling impacted (or did not impact) their religious identity. One common theme that seemed to emerge for many of the part-time unveilers was a close relationship between the headscarf and the tenets of Islam and how unveiling was in fact an act against their Muslim identity. Considering the fact that covering seemed to be perceived as an important component of their Muslim identity, another emerging issue was the impact of unveiling on part-time unveilers' decisions whether to continue veiling despite the career challenges they might encounter or unveil at least in the work environment.

How Did Complying with the Policy Impact the Female Identities of Part-Time Unveilers

Part-time unveilers expressed the ways in which they perceived unveiling impacted their female identity. They elaborated their views from a perspective of a woman, shared their feelings and experiences about being unveiled, and questioned the role and status of a woman in a male-dominated society. Their perception was that the headscarf ban policy was a product of men, leading to gender discrimination on and off campuses.

If you are a man, you have privileges: Eight part-time unveilers mentioned that they felt as if men and women were not equal and women were discriminated against. Semra explained how the ban was discriminating against the women on campuses:

> There are two main issues here. Who created this ban? Men. Who are suffering from it? Women. Men are discriminating against women. And also, men and women wake up in the morning, get dressed, and go to university. Women need to veil and unveil, are challenged on campus, whereas men continue their lives. Nothing changes for them. Life is easy for them. If you are a man, you have privileges. I wish I were born a man. As a woman, I feel challenged in society anyway. On top of it, this ban made me feel as a woman I am inferior to man. This is gender discrimination. Big time. This is why all women should get together to eliminate this ban.

Ezgi tried to understand the message unveiling sent to women in general in Turkey:

> The way unveiling affects my gender identity is that I am trying to understand what it means to be a woman in this society. Unveiling makes me wonder if I am seen as inferior since this is a ban that is directly targeted at women. It is not a ban for all Islamists. It is a ban for covered women. What kind of implications does this have for Turkish women in general? Is there gender discrimination?

I feel as if I am pushed backward: A couple of participants felt pushed to the back row in society as a woman, as a result of unveiling. Semra, for example, compared her female identity with men in general and stated that unveiling made her feel as if she was beneath them:

> Life has become difficult as a result of unveiling and veiling back again throughout the day. I wish I were a man. As a woman, I feel as if I am pushed backward, behind the man. Men say, "Women cannot do this; women cannot do that." However, a woman can do everything in a society. Women should walk hand in hand with men, not behind them. But unveiling makes me feel as if I am walking behind them in society.

I became angry with all the women who supported my unveiling: Another theme that Selma focused on was that unveiling made her angry with the women who did not support her and who supported the ban: "As a result of unveiling, I became angry with all the women who support my unveiling. I am angry with all these women who support the ban. They wear what they want; they look nice and beautiful. I cannot. So I am really upset with those women who do what they want to do and do not let me do what I want to do."

Another woman who is not me: Another theme some part-time unveilers highlighted was that unveiling made them feel that their gender identity was not fully expressed. Meltem indicated that unveiling was an attempt to change at least her visible identity as a woman:

> This is who I am as a woman. Unveiling makes me another woman who is not me. I feel different; it is not the same me anymore. The way I look as a woman, the way I carry myself as a woman, they are all different. Unveiling is an attempt to change my gender identity... or at least an attempt to change what is visible to others as a woman. There is not one type of woman in the world. There are veiled, unveiled, short, tall... We are not all size [eight]!

I feel as if I am naked: Three part-time unveilers mentioned that they realized the importance of being a covered woman as a result of unveiling. Merve, for example, associated her unveiling with feelings of nakedness: "I feel as if everybody is looking at me on campus because I feel as if I am naked."

I do not enjoy looking in the mirror: Another way unveiling impacted a couple of the part-time unveilers was that while unveiled, mostly because of their way of unveiling, part-time unveilers felt ugly. Reyhan, for example, indicated:

> Do you know how I look when I unveil? Pretty ugly. When I unveil, I look really ugly.

I do not enjoy looking in the mirror. Who would? Think about a woman who is forced to change her appearance in a way that is against her wishes. How would that woman like it? How would that woman take it? I believe she would not be particularly pleased with the way she looked. This is how I feel I look unveiled and I believe this is what others think about me as well.

There is a decrease in confidence: Some part-time unveilers mentioned that unveiling made them lose some of their confidence. Reyhan explained how she had lost some confidence as a result of unveiling: "Unveiling affects me negatively as a woman. There are lots of conflicts in me. I keep asking myself if I am doing the right thing. I used to be a woman who had confidence. Now I have lost my confidence. Or at least there is a decrease in confidence. However, as a woman I need my confidence to survive in the society." Beyza also felt a lack of confidence when she removed her headscarf, but her thoughts were not very clear on the issue:

As a woman, I was always very confident that I would make a difference in society. I always believed that Turkey needs self-confident women who would fight for their rights and take an active part in society. When I removed my headscarf, I realized that it is very difficult to mingle as a woman. I do not know. Maybe I cannot express myself very clearly... The bottom line is that I lost a little bit of my self-confidence as a woman, which was my raison d'etre in society, as a result of unveiling.

All in all, in this chapter, part-time unveilers perceived numerous ways in which the policy impacted their identities as Turkish citizens, Muslims, and females. They shared their perspectives in order to show the various ways in which unveiling affected them. Even though there were some part-time unveilers who perceived that their identities (or part of their identities) were not influenced to a great extent, most part-time unveilers perceived that their multiple identities were challenged because of their experience of complying with the policy and removing their headscarf.

7

Discussion and Reflections

This book examined the perceptions of 30 part-time unveilers vis-à-vis the impact of the headscarf ban policy on their educational and cultural experiences in Turkish public universities. Part-time unveilers who participated in the study had diverse backgrounds in terms of age, SES, family life, and the schools they attended as well as with respect to their personalities and citizenship, religious, and gender identities. Part-time unveilers who first dropped out of university as a result of the headscarf ban but later returned to complete their studies were also included. This diversity added to the strength of the sample and the power and usefulness of the findings.

The systematic analysis of the perceptions of the part-time unveilers has two main contributions. Data analysis unpacks who the research participants were and how they lived and highlights some of their distinct features as undergraduate students and covered women. In other words, the accounts of the students familiarize readers with the lives and identities of 30 part-time unveilers and provides the reader with a portrait that seems not to have been depicted in a detailed way in discussion of the higher education headscarf ban up to now. Also findings indicate that, according to the part-time unveilers in this study, the headscarf ban is not merely an access policy that appears to attempt to regularize students' entrance to universities, but also a multilayered higher education policy that seems to deeply impact and have serious repercussions on both the academic experiences and identities of the research participants together with the campus climate of Turkish universities they attended. Political and educational debates about the headscarf ban have always framed the policy from the access-to-higher education point of view, linking the policy to the social and political contexts of Turkey. From this perspective the issue seems to have been approached from a narrow viewpoint as it appears to disregard the bigger picture of the ramifications and implications of the policy with regard to the lives and personalities of the part-time unveilers, the higher education system, and the society in the long run. Thus, it appears that discussions around the issue of the policy need to be reframed, and their scope broadened, to better comprehend the long-term consequences of the policy for the education system and the country.

With these two main contributions of the study in mind, this section first portrays the part-time unveilers and their multifaceted lives and personalities and then tackles the complexity of the higher education headscarf ban policy and its tensions. Later it highlights the campus life of part-time unveilers and reveals the impact of the headscarf ban policy on their sense of identity.

Part-Time Unveilers and Their Multifaceted Lives and Personalities

Part-time unveiler is a term coined for a woman who chooses to cover her hair in her private life in line with her understanding of the tenets of Islam, but removes the headscarf to go to college. This particular group of women are unique in the sense that they experience both what it means to be covered and uncovered for a long period of time, at least during their undergraduate studies, as a result of the headscarf ban.

The part-time unveilers in this book, were distinct individuals both as covered women and as undergraduate university students. As covered women, they seemed to have strong but multifaceted personalities, and their religious identity seemed to be the dominant identity that governs their personalities and lifestyles. As students, they were similar to other undergraduate students with all the feelings and emotions of youth. However, they were distinguished from other students in the way they had to physically appear on campuses—that is, with wigs, hats, or non-genuine exposure of hair. The ban seemed to force research participants to negotiate it in various ways. They first considered their possible options—that is, complying or not complying with the policy—then rationalized their reasons for compliance, decided on the type of unveiling, and dealt with the various reactions they received from family and friends with regard to their decision. Their negotiation process and compliance with the policy seemed to indicate that they were strong and resilient women who tried to adjust their lives according to the changing circumstances in which they lived. One main reason for their flexibility likely stemmed from the value they attach to higher education. However, as a consequence of the headscarf ban policy, they appeared forced to make strategic, not always voluntary, choices about the academic programs they would like to pursue.

One interesting observation about the findings concerning the negotiation process of the part-time unveilers in this book is that they appeared more resistant to the idea of unveiling as compared with their parents. When some part-time unveilers initially refused to comply or were hesitant about complying with the policy, their parents, who one might have expected to be more conservative and resistant to the idea of unveiling as compared with their children, encouraged them to unveil so that they could attend university. In addition, it was apparent that some parents became enthusiastic when their daughters, who had dropped out as a result of the ban, decided to comply with the policy and go back to university. According to the accounts of the part-time unveilers presented in this book, several parents supported the decision of the participants to remove their headscarves and in the case of a couple of parents, they even expressed a preference that their daughters would choose to expose the hair as their style of unveiling. Based on the perceptions of the part-time unveilers about the supportive and encouraging role of some of these parents for their children to comply with the ban, it is possible to deduce that the parents of these part-time unveilers are quite liberal when it comes to the idea of their daughters unveiling to continue in higher education. This may be as a consequence of parents recognizing the role that higher education plays in creating successful individuals in society or it could even be that these parents were "children" of the 1970's, when most women veiled in a traditional way without knowing Islamic teachings in depth (Göle, 1996). In such an instance, the parents may have been more willing to compromise on the issue of the headscarf as they had no claims of great knowledge and consciousness about Islamic teachings and thus may not have the same dedication to the headscarf as their daughters did.

An alternative explanation as to why parents of the part-time unveilers appeared more liberal than their daughters regarding unveiling may lie in generational differences as to what the headscarf was perceived by them to mean. As discussed in Chapter 2 (Arat, 2005; Göle, 1996), some argue that in its traditional form, the headscarf, before the 1980s, represented the submission and subservience of women. Women wore it as a means of following traditions. On the other hand, some argue with the emerging *türban* style of veiling, the headscarf, after the 1980s, symbolized liberation (Göle, 1996). Furthermore, almost half of the participants stated that they wore the headscarf voluntarily, without any external pressure. So, based on these arguments, it is possible to claim that participants appeared more conservative because it may be easier for the mothers to "give up" a traditional garment that may have restricted them than for the participants who wore it by choice and perceived it as liberating.

Part-time unveilers seemed to identify themselves as members of the Muslim community who were introduced to the tenets of Islam by their parents and/or during their school years. About one-third (nine) of the participants reported that they decided to cover their heads because they were encouraged or influenced by their peers, teachers, or acquaintances in schools. Three women were at university when they were attracted to Islam, and two were at the test centers for university exam preparation when they were asked to wear headscarves in return for financial support. I would argue, this shows that educational sites might be venues where individuals are exposed to ideologies, in this instance, Islamism, akin to the situation in Turkish universities prior to the 1980's, although then the dominant ideologies were leftist or nationalist. At universities, students can decide to use the headscarf and influence others to do the same. This lends credence to the concern of policymakers over the use and spread of headscarves on campus (Arat, 2005). Nevertheless, the accounts of the students indicated that one challenge of the headscarf ban policy was that the prohibition seemed to provoke the part-time unveilers and honed their will to fight the system.

Findings highlighted that part-time unveilers had strong but multi-faceted socially constructed identities as Turkish citizens, Muslims, and women. Although each component of their overall identity appeared to be an important part of the self, the responses of the part-time unveilers signalled that their religious identity was the aorta that fed other identities that constitute their "self" as covered women.

Part-time unveilers in this book were proud of being Turks and also of being Muslims. They considered themselves different from Muslims in the Arab world and appreciated the secular values Turkey provides them. Their accounts reflected the amalgamation of the influence of the Islamist belief system and worldviews and the secular nature of the education system they received and the system they lived in. In other words, their identity, akin to the traditional Turkish identity (Ayoob, 2004; Gülalp, 2003) was shaped by both Islam and secularism. I would argue that these women are different from many other Muslim females in the world in that the principles and customs of a secular nation-state shape their religion (Arat, 2005).

However, even within Turkish Muslims, these women differentiated themselves as conscious Muslims in contrast to those who blindly followed Islam as a result of tradition, a finding which is in line with the extant literature (Acar, 1995; Göle, 1996) explored in Chapter 2. As discussed in Chapter 2, the choices of these women implied a rejection of the model provided by their parents "who are perpetuating traditions and traditional religion within their domestic lives" (Göle, 1996, p. 5). As I mentioned previously, based on my observation during interviews and the accounts of the part-time unveilers, the part-time unveilers did not use the old small headscarves tied under the chin that their mothers use. Instead, they wore large and colorful *türbans* that framed their head and cover their neck and sometimes shoulders. Their new style of unveiling and their definitions of themselves as Muslims with extensive knowledge about Islam, as opposed to traditional Muslims, were two distinct features of part-time unveilers that came out of this research. In addition to the influence of Turkish feminism and the rising power of Islam in the Turkish public sphere, I would argue that, these features of the part-time unveilers also highlighted the influence of Islamic feminism, a movement of Muslim women whose ultimate goal is "freedom of choice and a full exercise of identity" (Masood, 2004, p. 2). These features signalled waves of change and new religious identities in the world of covered women (Arat, 1995). I agree with Göle (1996) that the message this new emerging profile of Muslim women tries to convey to both secular and Islamist communities is that Islam is not associated with backwardness or traditionalism, but rather with modernism and improvement. Yet, with reference to the arguments of the scholars in Chapter 2, the challenge they seem to face is that secularists generally perceive this novel representation of Muslim identity as a political and ideological movement that brings a threat of religious radicalism and fundamentalism (Göle, 1996).

As for their identity as females, these part-time unveilers aspired to be women who wanted education, prosperous careers, gender equality, and economic freedom. They wanted to take an active role in both social and business spheres. They did not want to become dependent on male power; rather, desiring emancipation and liberation from patriarchal values. They sought recognition as self-asserting and independent women. They believed that they had the power to change future generations as mothers of their sons and daughters. This idea of educating children who would potentially shape the future of the country seemed to empower their identities as women and gave them a sense of self-importance and superiority over men. In my view, Turkish and Islamic feminism encouraged them to make their own choices, to assert their identity and visibility, to gain more power and dominance, and to create waves of change in the gender equilibrium. The new portrait of these women seems to be an attempt to diminish or if possible eliminate the perception of the female as the other "within the context of hierarchical and bureaucratic relations of patriarchy" (Prasad & Prasad, 2002, p. 57) in a predominantly male-dominated society. In other words, part-time unveilers in this book, akin to other covered women wearing the *türban,* tried to make a transition to the position of being subjects rather than objects (Göle, 1996) by means of a process of active self-formation that transformed them "into subjects who secure their meaning and reality through identifying with a particular sense of their own gender" (Bruni & Gherardi, 2002, p. 35). Furthermore, the part-time unveilers have made attempts to establish the modern image of assertive, career-oriented, and educated Muslim women as emerging actors within Turkish society and have been particularly instrumental for Islamists in trying to change the perceptions of the secularists who consider the Islamist community to be a male-dominated environment where women do not have many rights (White, 2002).

The part-time unveilers also indicated that family was a very critical institution. This is in line with mainstream Islamic and Turkish opinion that suggests a critical role for the family in life (Tekeli, 1995). Most participants enjoyed family life and aspired to have a family of their own where husbands and wives have equal rights. Their social life was family-oriented and predominantly shaped by their understanding of the dictates of Islam since they preferred to have relatively limited relationships with men, and did not drink or go to places where alcohol is consumed. These accounts provide further evidence of the apparent dominance of religion over the personalities and social lives of part-time unveilers.

As students, part-time unveilers were full of energy and dynamism with personalities ranging from responsible and relaxed to anxious and quick-tempered. Most identified themselves as conscientious, industrious, and productive, with great hope for the future. These characteristics of the students seemed to be indicative of the fact that these women are just like other college students, full of ideals, goals, and excitement for life. However, they differed in terms of their physical appearance, not through their headscarf or conservative clothes, but instead through the way they conformed to the headscarf ban policy, that is, by wearing hats, using wigs, or exposing their hair. This inability to portray their genuine physical appearance, that is, wearing the headscarf, necessitated them leading a double life, one on and one off campus. This enforced double life differentiated part-time unveilers from other university students.

However, this double life did not appear to make the participants victims of the ban. Rather, the accounts of the part-time unveilers suggested strength and resilience and an ability to adapt to changing circumstances thus allowing them to be in control of their lives. They were very realistic as to what they could and could not change, understood their circumstances as a result of the headscarf ban policy, recognized their options, and took actions strategically and rationally. Instead of acting with emotions based on hopes and dreams, it seemed that they acted with minds based on the real world in which they live.

Additionally, the accounts of the part-time unveilers demonstrated a respect for higher education as a means toward social and economic mobility. The positives to be gleaned from further education seemed to outweigh any negatives associated with the headscarf ban policy. I believe this strong desire to continue higher education in pursuit of a better life is rational and in line with scholars' findings showing that women who had a good education have frequently had prestigious and lucrative jobs in Turkey (Öncü, 1979).

Part-time unveilers in this book made strategic choices about the academic programs they would like to pursue based on their university exam scores, the number of part-time unveilers in the program, and the extent to which the academic program contributes to the formation of a successful career for a covered woman to overcome some challenges presented by the general and higher education headscarf ban policies. They seemed to make a decision that ensures a support structure while attending university and a future career path. I believe that this rational approach to choice of areas to study may have led them to study in areas they are not passionate about and ultimately could impact their long-term achievement. This may lead to long-term dissatisfaction with, and a lack of success in, the careers that these part-time unveilers chose.

In addition, part-time unveilers shared the ongoing negotiation process that they had with the headscarf ban policy. They considered complying or not complying with the ban, rationalized compliance, welcomed positive comments and disregarded negative comments, considered different types of unveiling, and even consciously chose not to engage with friends that may negatively influence their decision. The heuristic they employed seemed to be one that allows them to make well-informed decisions about their future. I believe these choices were symbolic decisions that explained how they thought about the headscarf ban policy especially with regard to their religion. It was a negotiation between education and career options, and religious duty, and also often meant disregarding some of the comments of their relatives or friends that they may not have been subjected to in other circumstances. These tough internal battles were fought in the formative teenage years and these students consequently were being forced to grow up very quickly. This has the potential to have a negative long-term impact on these students and may even serve to over-politicize part-time unveilers.

To sum up, although some part-time unveilers appeared to be quiet and passive, most of them seemed to be active, confident, outspoken, and ambitious women who sought higher education, opposed traditional and domestic roles of women, and aspired to take active roles in society. They tried to reconcile how to be a Muslim woman in a contemporary and modern society. These self-conscious Muslims tended to seek full integration into society, better social and economic status, and more respect for their rights. Their vibrant personalities, strong feelings of citizenship, religious, and female identities, and their determination to continue university, suggested a desire for change, to create a new image of an covered woman who would both alter the public visibility of Islamists, and eradicate the negative perceptions of secularists about Islamists. In my opinion, it is these part-time unveilers who will determine the direction of the Islamist community with a voice and influence within the Turkish society, as opposed to those who choose not to comply with the policy, stop their education, and limit their options for the future.

Complexity of the Higher Education Headscarf Ban Policy and Its Tensions

Findings highlighted that the headscarf ban policy is a complex and intriguing issue that can be debated from various starting points. Part-time unveilers in this book perceived the headscarf ban policy to be intertwined with the social and political context of Turkey. They thought the policy was a limitation on their basic right of access to higher education, restricted the freedom of religious expression, hindered the relationship between religion and education, and discriminated against women. Also the ban appeared as a catalyst for their politicization, an instrument that categorizes and classifies female students, and a vehicle that made some of them passive. They perceived that secularists use the ban as a change agent to modernize the Islamists and the ban perpetuated the message that covered women symbolized the backwardness.

The accounts of the part-time unveilers highlighted that the policy had emerged as a direct result of the Turkish political tensions and politicization of Islam. I believe part-time unveilers are part of a power struggle between secularists and Islamists in Turkish politics where the headscarf has been *victimized* or compromised to enable the Turkish ruling elite to get certain messages across to the future leaders of society. Another issue is that just as Islam was politicized and used to attract votes in the 1970s as discussed in Chapter 2, it seems that now the headscarf has been politicized, making the headscarf ban policy an instrument in strategy formulation for political parties to win elections.

Linked to the sociopolitical situation of Turkey, the part-time unveilers perceived the ban as a policy that restricted their freedom of religious expression in contrast to their understanding of the principles of Turkish secularism and democracy. This seems to highlight a tension between secularism and democracy in theory and secularism and democracy in practice in the context of Turkish higher education and create conflict and confusion in the minds of students as discussed by Seggie (2007b) and Mabokela and Seggie (2008).

In addition to its appearance as a restriction on religious freedom, the ban also appears to hinder the relationship between religion and education (Arat, 2005). According to the part-time unveilers interviewed in this book, Islam advises its followers to both wear a headscarf and pursue education, but the ban left them face-to-face with a situation where they couldn't do both and had to give up one even if it was only temporary.

Within the context of education, the research participants perceived the ban as a limitation on their basic right of access to higher education. The ban was an obvious and long-term barrier for their future lives. Their decision about whether to unveil or not seemed to be a turning point which determined the direction of their lives. I propose that their compliance with the policy hinted at their willingness to choose the opportunities provided by education over the challenges resulting from unveiling. This meant that part-time unveilers considered higher education as a means that empowered them and equipped them with the necessary tools to challenge the current headscarf ban policy in force.

Some of the part-time unveilers also understood the ban as an attempt to make students passive at universities. According to them, by forcing covered women to uncover their hair on campuses, the Turkish higher education system attempted to prevent Islamist women from becoming political activists. This use of the ban as a means to make students passive made the issue of the ban more complex for two reasons. One the one hand, both the literature (Arat, 2005; Göle, 1996) and accounts of some of the part-time unveilers indicated that some women covered their hair to make a political statement. These women covered their hair not because they considered the headscarf as a tenet of Islam, but because they believed that the headscarf contributed to the visibility of Islamism on campuses. On the other hand, based on the literature (Human Rights Watch, 2004; "Mazlumder," 1998) and the accounts of some others of the part-time unveilers, there were also women who covered their hair because of their religious beliefs. I would argue that their voices also need to be heard to foster the diverse nature of the campus. So, from the perspective of equal human rights, the existence of the ban violated social justice, limited the freedom and religious and educational rights of the part-time unveilers, and restricted the promotion of diversity.

The part-time unveilers also explained how the ban had a direct impact on their worldview and hinted at the possibility of the ban becoming a catalyst for their politicization due to their being victims of the political context of Turkey. It is ironic that the headscarf ban policy, which was implemented as a way to depoliticize the higher education context (Sunar, 2004; Sunar &

Sayari, 2004), may have had the opposite effect on some and become an instrument that politicizes part-time unveilers. This politicization may even perpetuate the categorization between secularists and Islamists. Also, politicized women may be driven enough to mobilize and politicize other students they encounter on campus, re-politicizing the higher education context. Thus in the long run, the policy that was intended to depoliticize the Turkish university could actually perpetuate politicization.

From a feminist perspective, the part-time unveilers perceived the ban as discriminatory against women, placing them below men. Men with beliefs similar to covered women may enter universities freely while women are forbidden. Therefore, I would argue that the headscarf ban policy discriminates against covered women not only due to their belief systems, but also because they are female (Arat, 2005). In essence there exists a struggle against male dominance. This shows that the Turkish higher education system seems to extend privilege to men. Therefore, the higher education headscarf ban is a policy that reiterates sexism and perpetuates male dominance on campuses, which may negatively influence the psychological well-being of the discriminated (Schmitt et al., 2002), in this case, the part-time unveilers.

In addition to gender discrimination, the ban appears to create several layers of categorization within the same sex. Part-time unveilers perceived that the policy classified female students as covered or uncovered with the insinuation that covered was in some way inferior. Also, covered women were separated into compliers and noncompliers, with the category of compliers further broken down into hat wearers, wig users, and those with hair exposed. Within compliers there was also a level of acceptance or nonacceptance of the different methods of compliance. I believe all these various classifications may create multiple levels of difference, lead to the generation of subcultures, and encourage feelings of alienation, opposition, and/or superiority among female students: all of these being problematic in the context of higher education.

Framing the policy through the views of the secularists as perceived by the part-time unveilers, the ban appeared to be an instrument for the secularists to label covered women as "anachronistic" with the intention of modernizing them through the act of unveiling on campuses. According to the part-time unveilers, secularists perceived covered women as backward and narrow-minded people who were lower class and not open to development (White, 2002). Part-time unveilers believed that secularists wanted to educate the covered women and considered the ban to be a change agent intended to modify part-time unveilers in the long run by making them live a campus life where they were different, that is, unveiled. According to part-time unveilers, the secularists wanted to move covered women toward a more secular existence and, in addition to secular education that automatically contributed toward that aim (Göle, 1997). The ban was used as an instrument toward that goal. However, the ultimate change seemed to take place in two different directions; in some cases, the part-time unveilers interviewed noted that some women may have ended up removing the headscarf for good while others became more attached to their headscarves. In this sense, following the accounts of some of the part-time unveilers, one could argue that the ban might either "secular-ize" or further "islamicize" part-time unveilers in the long run. Then, the emerging question is, what is the percentage of those who are "secularized" or further "islamicized"? The answer to this question may reveal the extent to which the ban achieves its goal for the purposes of secularists. To fur-ther complicate matters, one could argue that secular education secularizes covered women to a certain extent anyway and the policy may not add anything further to that process.

Furthermore, the voices of the part-time unveilers indicated that, in their opinion, the ban perpetuated the message that Islamists were the rep-resentatives of the religious law and a threat to the existing regime. In other words, the ban appears to be an indicator of the fact that secularists contin-ued to perceive the headscarf or *türban* as a "symbol of opposition to the Republic" (Arat, 2005, p. 26) and threat to secularism even if women wore it for only religious purposes.

In addition, paradoxically, based on the accounts of the part-time unveilers in this book, the ban seemed to serve as an instrument for covered women to express themselves, explain who they were, and tell their "life stories." I think the policy, framed from this perspective, *de-victimized* the participants—that is, it removed its perceived victimization effect ("Mazlumder," 1998)—and so empowered them, enabling them to make statements about the ideologies of the Islamist community and the role of Islam and the covered women in secular Turkey.

To sum up, on the one hand, the headscarf ban seemed to be a policy that challenged, discriminated, and disadvantaged covered female students in this book who were already disadvantaged as women. It seemed to cat-egorize, stigmatize, and politicize them on campus. This may result in resentment and bitterness from Islamists against secularists and perpetuate the polarization of secularists and Islamists, which might have some long-term implications for the Turkish society. However, on the other hand, the ban seemed to problematize the role of religion in a secular country, centralize the covered woman, and create a platform for covered women to narrate their stories and make political and nonpolitical statements about themselves, Islamism, religion, and secularism. From this perspec-tive, the policy seemed to empower the part-time unveilers in this book, and, through the ways they handled the policy, become a vehicle through which the women explicitly avoided being victims.

Additionally, the ban impacted the lives of the part-time unveilers and made them choose between continuing to veil or unveil after graduation. Some women may continue covering their hair while some others may continue unveiling after graduation. Following the viewpoints of some of the research participants in Chapter 4 with regard to the policy intending to secularize covered women and assuming that those who choose to continue unveiling after graduation have become fully secularized, based on the viewpoints of some of the research participants in Chapter 4, if the aim is to secularize the covered women then one could argue that the policy achieves, to a certain extent, what it intends to achieve from the point of view of the higher education policymakers.

Campus Life of Part-Time Unveilers and Its Challenges

Analysis of the data, as documented in Chapter 5, revealed opportunities and challenges as a result of part-time unveilers unveiling. The opportunities occured when unveiling acted as (1) an instrument that opened doors to campuses and academic experiences, and (2) a protector from academic discrimination and marginalization. The challenges appeared when (1) unveiling created problems, and (2) as a result of unveiling, a majority of the participants spent little time on campus, had infrequent contact with faculty, and experienced hostility.

In terms of opportunities, all part-time unveilers perceived unveiling as the key to enter Turkish campuses and some of them, as protection from academic discrimination and social marginalization. However, is unveiling really an opportunity, or merely a temporary solution that allows part-time unveilers to continue higher education?

There were some part-time unveilers who perceived some specific advantages of unveiling, such as enhancing their campus activities, extracurricular activities or motivation for studying. Thus, whether these students complied with the policy reluctantly or not, it is apparent that they discovered some positive outcomes of unveiling for themselves and decided to take full advantage of these specific opportunities to become as involved in the higher education experience as possible.

Coupled with the opportunities came challenges, and based on the accounts of the part-time unveilers, it appeared that ultimately, unveiling created problems and negative outcomes that outweighed any positive outcomes. Sooner or later the type of unveiling (e.g., wig or hat), outfit (e.g., constant use of turtlenecks even under the heat in the summer), or behavior (e.g., shying away from men or not drinking alcohol) gave away who part-time unveilers really were and this led to some part-time unveilers becoming subject to discrimination, harassment, marginalization, or isolation, not only because they were covered but also due to their type of unveiling, outfit, or behavior. Thus, in many cases, it appeared as if the act of unveiling exacerbated biases and prejudices of other undergraduate students and perpetuated feelings of discrimination and intolerance.

The accounts of the part-time unveilers showed that most, if not all, of these women tended to spend little time on campus as a result of unveiling, in an effort to avoid attention or minimize the discomfort of being uncovered. This resulted in students not using campus facilities and not attending extracurricular activities, thus losing out on educational and cultural experiences that might have strengthened their connection to the academic life and created a sense of belonging.

In addition, the accounts of the part-time unveilers highlighted that they had infrequent contact with faculty. They may have missed class or made purposeful curricular choices by avoiding certain electives even when they were useful for their education just to stay away from certain professors who they believed were opposed to their type of unveiling. I would argue that these findings implied that part-time unveilers may not have received enough academic support, may have lacked faculty guidance, and made curricular decisions that may not have contributed to their area of specialization. Coupled with their strategic choice of disciplines mentioned earlier, their intentional course selection reinforced the fact that some part-time unveilers may have followed a curriculum that they were not fully committed to or were not passionate about. In my opinion, this might hinder their learning, achievement, and intellectual maturity, which are critical elements in student success and development (Evans et al., 1998; Kuh et al., 2005; Pascarella & Terenzini, 1991, 2005) and which could ultimately have an impact upon their future success and satisfaction in their chosen careers.

Moreover, on various occasions, some part-time unveilers indicated they suffered hostility. This included verbal abuse and harassment. They felt challenged while making friends, which may have contributed to their becoming antisocial and suffering from isolation, exclusion, and marginalization. The staring and scrutiny of others both in class and campus challenged them further. These challenges were likely to result in a situation where they did not develop the social network which college attendance is expected to strengthen, or establish the kind of connections they need during and after their university lives as explained in the literature (Evans et al., 1998).

In my opinion, these perceived feelings of marginalization and tokenism as a result of their hurdles around the issues of socialization may have caused frustration, anxiety, and concern about whether these part-time unveilers mattered to people on and off campus. To feel that one matters is particularly important because research findings indicate that a sense of mattering facilitates growth and learning, encouraging the development of self-esteem, self-confidence, and a sense of fitting in (Evans et al., 1998; Schlossberg, 1989). What emerged from the data was that students perceived a lack of opportunities to be noticed, appreciated, cared about, needed, and rewarded in university. Furthermore, these part-time unveilers felt unable to develop a sense of mattering as a consequence of the headscarf ban policy and how it impacted their academic experiences. Based on the part-time unveilers' reported GPAs and their accounts about their numeric success in classes, unveiling did not seem to drastically affect their exam grades. As a result of becoming more ambitious and determined to graduate and prove that they were smart and studious women, several of the part-time unveilers appeared to devote considerable energy to their studies. The perceived challenges in their relationships with faculty, administrators and peers, and the quantity and quality of the time spent on campus, suggested that the part-time unveilers may not have been fully involved in campus life. In my opinion, this is particularly important because research (Astin, 1984; Kuh & Love, 2000) indicates that the degree of involvement in the campus environment is an important indicator of the extent to which a student learns and develops. Scholars explain that a high level of involvement—that is, studying effectively and efficiently, spending time on campus, participating actively in extracurricular activities, using campus facilities, and interacting frequently with faculty and peers—results in a higher amount of student learning and growth (Astin, 1984). These arguments are based on research conducted in the United States but I believe that the findings hold in other settings as well. However, I think in the case of part-time unveilers, apart from some degree of studying (which may be a solitary effort as well), an active engagement in the campus environment did not seem to take place. This implied that (a) the campus did not present a fully healthy environment for participants, and (b) the student learning, development, and growth expected to take place during their undergraduate studies may not have fully taken place. In other words, the headscarf ban policy appeared to create a "chilly" campus climate which may not have provided the kind of faculty, administrator, and peer support part-time unveilers needed, and which seemed to be uncomfortable, unsafe, and excessively challenging so that part-time unveilers preferred to spend only a minimal amount of time on campus. All these negative experiences may have resulted in institutional dissatisfaction. Also, both the unwelcoming environment and organizational dissatisfaction may have had a negative effect on the educational outcomes of the part-time unveilers, which would have long-term implications.

Furthermore, this unsupportive-looking campus climate for the part-time unveilers may hinder the development of their self-esteem, which would normally be improved in a supportive campus climate (Green, 1989; Hale, 1991; Tinto, 1993; Watson et al., 2002). Enhancement of self-esteem is important because it enriches teaching and learning and encourages individuals to take advantage of the special experiences and opportunities offered on higher education campuses. This suggests that part-time unveilers may not have had enough opportunities to develop their confidence to fully benefit from the academic life at universities.

Impact of the Headscarf Ban Policy on the Identities of the Part-Time Unveilers

As young undergraduates who were at the final stages of their adolescence or at the beginning of their adulthood, the part-time unveilers seemed to experience challenges to their identities on two different levels as a result of unveiling. On one level, their core identities (i.e., personalities and psychology) were challenged while negotiating the policy in terms of considering their options, exploring the kind and extent of compromises they needed to make during their compliance with the policy, deciding on whether they preferred the wig, hat, or exposing the hair, and negotiating the campus life in terms of educational and cultural experiences at university. On another level, their socially constructed identities (that is, identities as Turkish citizens, Muslims, and women) were challenged while negotiating others' understanding of them as part-time unveilers, exploring how others perceived their identities as women who were unveiled on campus and veiled outside campus, and trying to find ways in which they could become accepted and convey their personalities as part-time unveilers on campus.

Research findings presented in Chapter 6 revealed that the act of unveiling impacted the identities of the participants as students and as Turkish citizens, Muslims, and females in numerous ways that had various implications for identity formation and development. Based on the perceptions of the part-time unveilers about how unveiling impacted their identities, key findings were as follows: Because of unveiling, part-time unveilers in this book seemed to experience psychological problems, felt like second-class citizens in Turkey, felt ugly and naked, and thought that they were making concessions from their religious beliefs.

The accounts of the women indicated that unveiling created psychological problems such as anxiety, depression, anger, guilt, and feelings of paranoia. Similar findings are also highlighted in Seggie and Austin (2010) who also discuss the impact of the headscarf ban policy on the identity development of the part-time unveilers based on the same study presented here. Some part-time unveilers appeared to manage or overcome these negative emotions, but the impact of simply experiencing such intense psychological feelings at such young ages on the health of their long-term identities needs careful examination. Other part-time unveilers did not seem to manage or overcome these negative emotions, which might have hindered the psychosocial development that contributes to the formation of identity (Chickering, 1969; Chickering & Reisser, 1993).

Also, the findings highlighted that as a result of the headscarf ban policy, some part-time unveilers consider themselves to be second-class citizens. With feelings of second-class citizenship, they felt restricted and not valued. This implied that the headscarf ban policy may have obstructed the further development of their citizenship identity, an important component of their identity as part of Turkish society, making them feel like restricted second-class citizens who were not valued. In my opinion, this might mean that their identities as citizens became politicized and polarized. This is because the policy appeared to produce and reproduce ideologies, and create class issues based on their physical appearance and the way they lived their religion as citizens. Furthermore, in a country where there is democracy and equality of citizens in the eyes of the law, the ways in which the policy impacted the citizenship identities of these participants might have impaired the way they perceived themselves and acted as citizens in the long term. Moreover, a sense of not being valued may not only have impacted their learning and academic development as indicated in the earlier sections, but also their overall identity formation and development as active citizens of Turkey.[1]

Findings highlighted that the students, as Muslims, felt they made concessions from their belief systems and religious lifestyles. From a religious perspective, participants seemed to negotiate unveiling within the framework of it being a sin and tried to understand and rationalize the extent to which their unveiling under the current circumstances might have been a sin or not. This created fears and dilemmas in the minds of some of the participants. I would argue that from an identity development perspective, these feelings may have made them question their religiosity, destabilized their religious identity, which is an important part of their socially constructed identities, and hindered the establishment of their overall identity. In addition, from a religious perspective, this is likely to create new understandings of Islamic teachings, which might cause hot debates about unveiling and its consequences, which might exacerbate the instrumentalization of Islam within the social and political contexts of Islam.

As women, the findings indicated that unveiling challenged the gender identities of part-time unveilers and made them feel ugly or naked, which led to a loss of confidence or a sense of passiveness. In my opinion, this might have damaged their comfort with their appearance, self-concept, and self-respect and impaired their personal stability and integration, which are crucial for their identity formation and development (Chickering, 1969; Chickering & Reisser, 1993).

In short, the challenging impacts of unveiling on students suggested that the headscarf ban policy seemed to attack their personal and social identities. This means that the policy appeared to threaten the stability of personalities and trouble the identity formation of part-time unveilers in this book.

To sum up, even though the headscarf ban policy may have been seen as a barrier in their pursuit of higher education opportunities, part-time unveilers tried to proceed rationally and flexibly, adjusting themselves to the existing circumstances in order to gain access to university, which they viewed as a hope for a better life or a step up the social ladder. However, their decision to comply with the policy and their act of unveiling seemed to be accompanied by several challenges that impact their educational and cultural experiences in their undergraduate studies. Following from insights the part-time unveilers shared in the study, the policy seemed to impair their relationship with faculty, administrators, and peers, compromise their social skills and socialization opportunities, interfere with the way they are treated in class and on campus, and challenge them in different ways while they are making attempts to engage socially, intellectually, and affectively on campus. Furthermore, the policy seemed to impact the development of part-time unveilers affecting their identities as young undergraduates, Turkish citizens, Muslims, and women. It appeared to encumber them with numerous psychological challenges at early periods of their lives, defy their personalities by making them doubt their value and place in society as citizens and women, and question the extent of their religiosity. These perceived challenges, lack of support, and feelings of not mattering or being welcome indicated that they may not have been fully involved in campus life and that their learning, growth, and identity development may suffer, which has some implications for themselves, higher education, and the society in general.

Implications for Practice and Future Research

The findings imply issues and concerns for part-time unveilers, the higher education system in Turkey, and Turkish society. In this section, I discuss some of these broader issues that researchers and higher education stakeholders—educational leaders, administrators, policymak-ers, students, and citizens in the society—need to consider.

Implications for Part-Time Unveilers

First, based on their experiences on campus, part-time unveilers did not seem to be fully involved in the campus environment and as a result they may drop out of college before graduation. Research on college attrition of undergraduate students (Astin, 1975, 1977, 1997) indicates that college environment has a significant impact on a student's successful comple-tion of university. Positive factors such as participation in extracurricular activities, student-faculty interaction, and joining student communities are likely to increase student involvement and contribute to student persistence whereas noninvolvement is likely to contribute to dropping out. Based on the study's findings, the part-time unveilers do not seem to be significantly engaged in the campus environment and suffer from a lack of involvement, so they may drop out before they graduate. It is important to examine and understand the attrition rate of part-time unveilers to realize the extent to which the concerns raised in this discussion are valid.

Furthermore, the educational and cultural experiences of the part-time unveilers indicated that the university may not have completely provided an environment where they could fully grow, progress, or increase their developmental capabilities. As a result, enhancement in learning, intel-lectual growth, and affective and behavioral changes that are expected to happen in university, may not have taken place to the fullest extent possible. So in my opinion, even if these part-time unveilers persisted and did not drop out, they could graduate without developing as much as they might have and may not become as mature, sophisticated, productive, and active citizens as they otherwise could. This means that the country may not be able to utilize the talents of these women as fully as possible.

There is research evidence (Cabrera & Nora, 1994; Cress & Ikeda, 2003; Guthman, 1994; Lagdameo et al., 2002) that suggests that students who are not fully integrated in college life might develop psychological and emo-tional identities which might destabilize their personalities and generate anger, bitterness, ill feelings, animosity, and opposition. These negative feelings and instabilities have the potential to negatively impact their future lives and the lives of those who are involved with them when they take different roles such as wives, professionals, friends, and perhaps most importantly mothers in society.

Also, the perceived challenges of part-time unveilers, their constant struggle, and the search for creative and reactive coping strategies to survive for a couple of years may have exhausted and demotivated the participants and drained their energy in their undergraduate years. As a result, they may feel too worn out to participate positively in the workforce, particularly if they perceive the general headscarf ban policy to be creating an uncomfortable work climate. Even if they join the workforce, they may not be as constructive in their professional contributions as they could be. This would be a significant loss to both the students who would not make good use of their academic degrees, but most significantly, a loss for Turkey where an educated group of people would either avoid contributing or only contribute marginally to the civic and economic development of the country.

Moreover, the experiences of the part-time unveilers as demonstrated by the research findings implied that some of the key factors (e.g., extensive and varied interaction among faculty and part-time unveilers, respect for the individual differences of participants, meaningful friendships) that exert significant influence on student development (Astin, 1997; Evans et al., 1998; Pascarella & Terenzini, 1991, 2005) were not fully in place. As existing literature explains (Chickering & Reisser, 1993; Pascarella & Terenzini, 1991, 2005; Watson et al., 2002) the absence of these factors may hinder the development of confidence, interconnectedness with others, mature interpersonal relationships, and integrity and management of emotions; the existence of which would promote psychosocial development of the part-time unveilers and contribute to the establishment and growth of identity. The lack of meaningful developmental experiences may prevent participants from forming a healthy identity, and participants may not have the opportunity to strengthen their self-esteem, intellectual and interpersonal competency, network, social, and leadership skills and interdependency, which can often be strengthened as a result of college attendance (Astin, 1984; Evans et al., 1998).

Finally, based on the study findings, the experiences articulated by the part-time unveilers implied that they, instead of focusing on their studies, enjoying their undergraduate years, taking full advantage of the academic life, and preparing themselves to become active citizens and professionals, were spending time and energy on the negotiation of the policy and outcomes of unveiling. This meant that they seemed to miss out a lot of developmental experiences and may not have fully benefited from the opportunities the higher education system offers in Turkey.

Implications for Higher Education

First, if all policies are to be evaluated in terms of the degree to which they increase involvement, based on the ways in which the higher education headscarf ban policy affects the time and amount of effort part-time unveilers devote to their educational experiences, findings from the study suggest that this policy may have had unintended outcomes. Framed from the perspective that the effectiveness of an educational policy is directly linked to the capacity of that policy to increase student involvement and because the experiences of part-time unveilers indicated otherwise, one might conclude that the policy unintentionally had a negative impact on this group of students. It is therefore critical to explore those elements of the higher education system that have been most supportive to help students reach their full potential and contribute to society's betterment.

Second, the social function of higher education is to preserve, transmit, and enrich cultural and political values (Evans et al., 1998; Gök, 1995). Considering the experiences of the part-time unveilers, the emerging questions are (1) what kind of social and political values are transmitted to the part-time unveilers and (2) to what extent do part-time unveilers internalize society's values during their higher education years? In addition, the main responsibility of higher education to society is to prepare students in such a way that they become active citizens and contribute to economic development. Considering their experiences, does the university equip all students with the necessary knowledge and skills to realize its responsibilities? Also, higher education has an emancipating potential (Gök, 1995). With a policy that restricts the actions, thoughts, and ideals of some students, to what extent is higher education liberating? What is the role of the university in Turkey?

Third, the higher education headscarf ban policy seemed to have the potential to influence and also politicize Turkish higher education in two different ways. First, it seemed to directly influence, politicize, and polarize the covered students and their academic experiences. Second, it appeared to indirectly influence, polarize, and politicize the campus climate, faculty, administrators, and other students. Faculty, administrators, and students took sides and reacted one way or another to the policy through part-time unveilers or (even perhaps noncompliers). Therefore, the campus climate became affected as a result of the reaction to the policy by part-time unveilers, administrators, faculty, and peers. From this perspective, the policy had the potential to polarize and politicize the higher education system.

Finally, findings imply an extensive variation in the interpretation and implementation of this policy across state universities. Even though the policy was the same for all state universities, it seems that different universities, departments and even professors interpreted the ban in different ways and implemented it accordingly, which resulted in a nonsystematic and inconsistent implementation across universities, departments and even classrooms. The emerging questions that require investigation are as follows: What does this variation in implementation highlight about Turkish higher education? What kind of understandings can we garner about the way the policy works in different universities, departments, and classrooms? What are the perceptions and reactions of students toward this inconsistency?

Implications for Society

The headscarf ban policy seemed to have the potential to exclude some talented women, the noncompliers of the policy, and create an outcome that may perpetuate the disadvantaging of women. This means the country loses many potential members of the workforce, especially considering the role of women in economic development and the nation-building process of countries, since scholars argue that the number of women in the workforce contributes to the economic development and social welfare of a country (Gök, 1995). This may slow down the process of Turkey becoming a developed country, especially when it is preparing itself for full membership of the European Union. From this perspective, is the current interpretation and implementation of the policy truly in the best interest of the country? What are the long-term consequences of the policy? These are important questions that require attention and careful examination.

Also, the policy may generate negative feelings toward "the other" and perpetuate the further polarization of Islamists and secularists in the society. The ban had the potential to polarize covered women according to their type of unveiling on campus or decision of continuing veiling or unveiling. So the policy added extra layers in categorization and further polarized the society to different social and political camps, a development that may negatively impact the sociocultural structure of Turkey.

Finally, emerging from the findings, the headscarf ban seemed to hinder the equal participation of one group of female students and force them to make critical decisions about their appearance related to their beliefs in order to gain access to higher education. Furthermore, the ability of women to become active participants both on campus and in the Islamic milieus was compromised as a result of the decision to unveil. This raises important questions about democratic participation, equal rights, and opportunities and the extent of social justice in the society.

Conclusion

This book has examined the impact of the higher education headscarf ban policy on the educational and cultural experiences of the part-time unveilers. The diverse findings allow for certain conclusions to be reached.

First, based on the findings, one conclusion is that the headscarf ban policy appears to be more than just a policy of access. Instead it appears to be a value-laden, multifaceted, and complex policy with many layers, interpretations, and implications. It seems to have several dimensions and multiple (un)intended outcomes. Additionally, it is also possible to conclude that the ban impacts part-time unveilers in this book at different levels. It seems to affect their daily life on campus, their personalities, and their identity development in a variety of ways. The effects of the ban on the part-time unveilers have long-term and short-term implicit and explicit implications for higher education and society in Turkey. In turn these may impact the social, political, and economic contexts of the country.

Based on the perceptions of the part-time unveilers, the headscarf ban policy also appears to have an impact upon issues of power among covered women. Specifically, the policy seems to produce new power dynamics within covered women differentiating between policy compliers, noncompliers, wig wearers, hat users, and those who expose their hair. The ban also appears to reproduce the existing power struggle among Islamists and secularists by perpetuating the concepts of covered and uncovered women. Additionally, the ban seems to make part-time unveilers negotiate their belief systems and future lives and discriminates against women by preventing them from entering campuses in the way they want while men are not subjected to such restrictions.

The policy appears to be full of tensions and juxtapositions in terms of the ways in which it impacts part-time unveilers in this book. On the one hand, it seems to create a platform for veil politics and to empower part-time unveilers by enabling them to make political and/or apolitical statements about themselves, the role of religion in Turkey, and the their community. On the other hand, it appears to challenge their identity and diminish their educational and cultural experiences on campuses. At the educational level, it seems to influence their motivation for study in a negative way, while it appears to make them ambitious and determined for success. Furthermore, at the identity level, it seems to weaken and destabilize their psychology and their citizenship, gender, and religious identities. In contrast, it appears to strengthen their personalities by making them mature and strong. In addition, while it appears to make them passive on campuses, it seems to motivate them to be assertive in their future lives and in their commitment to advance in society. And finally, in the long run, on the one hand, it may devalue the headscarf wearing in the eyes of the part-time unveilers and make them consider unveiling for good. On the other hand, it may empower veiling in the eyes of the part-time unveilers and make them more attached to their religion and headcovering. With such a list of opposing consequences, how one interprets and makes meaning out of the impacts of the headscarf ban policy may relate to one's position (e.g., Islamist or secularist) in society.

Finally, based on the findings, the headscarf ban policy can be argued to be a reflection of the very significant battle occurring concerning how to reconcile issues of religion, democracy, and secularism, the place of men and women in society, and the power struggle between Islamists and secularists in the social and political context of Turkey. Taking its intended and unintended outcomes, impacts, and implications into consideration, the higher education headscarf ban policy seems to be a challenging and conflicting issue for the higher education institutions in Turkey.

The case of the impact of the headscarf ban policy on the cultural and educational experiences of 30 part-time unveilers at university is an example of how higher education policies can be intertwined with the social and political contexts of the countries where such policies exist and how they may have intended and unintended outcomes which might have numerous repercussions for the society and for workforce development. Thus, it is critical for policymakers to approach the issue of policymaking from a comprehensive perspective and for policy researchers to consider politics as part of their analysis to better understand the dimensions and the extent of the impacts of higher education policies.

The results presented in this book are snapshots of the picture in Turkish higher education based on the accounts of 30 part-time unveilers interviewed in 2006 while they were attending 5 different state universities; they cannot be generalized to the entire higher education sector in this country. One snapshot, while important, is not enough to grasp the complexities of the whole system. Therefore, it is crucial to conduct additional research around the headscarf ban policy in order to have a bigger picture of the impact of the headscarf ban policy on covered (compliers and non-compliers of the policy) female women.

Reflections

Work on the research was a rewarding experience that helped me grow both intellectually and personally. It challenged some of my core beliefs and opinions and made me reconsider the ways in which I analyze and evaluate the outside world and "the other", and it broadened my perspective about issues I had not tackled before.

As a scholar, I also faced challenges. The struggle to use proportionally balanced Western and Turkish references, to understand what Western research findings might mean for the Turkish context, if applicable at all, and to explore the relevance of a theoretical framework about student identity development constructed in an American context, were intellectual challenges.

On a personal level, trying to find a balance between objectivity and subjectivity and considering the extent to which my identity as an unveiled Turkish woman could, and did, impact the research challenged me in different ways throughout the study. In particular, while writing the final chapter in which I interpret and discuss the findings, I experienced some internal conflicts and tensions which turned out to be transformational for my personality. These challenges showed me the complexity and delicacy of dealing with sensitive issues both for the researcher and those studied. While, as a qualitative researcher, I impacted this work, this work also affected me and my identity in numerous ways all throughout the process.

Appendices

Appendix A

Aggregated Data (Statistical Description) of the Participants

Tables AI and AIV do not take into account the language preparatory years students attended during their secondary education and/or at university if the medium of instruction of the school they attended was not Turkish. So if a student is in her second year, this is her year of study in her program regardless of whether she did or did not attend the preparatory class at university. In addition, these tables do not show the interruptions students had during their education as a result of health problems, dropping out of school, or not becoming successful in the national university exam.

Table A.I Distribution of participants according to age groups

Age	Number of participants
19 years	2
20 years	4
21 years	7
22 years	3
23 years	5
24 years	2
25 years	1
26 years	2R
27 years	2R
29 years	1R
30 years	1R
	TOTAL: 30

Note: Since I conducted the research in the summer of 2006, their year of study is recorded taking the upcoming 2006–2007 academic year, that is, the year of study of a student who finished her second year in the summer of 2006, for example, was recorded as the third year.
R: Returning students

Table A.II Distribution of participants according to student type

Student type	Number of participants
Traditional	24 (1 married)
Returning	6 (2 married)
	TOTAL: 30

Table A.III Distribution of participants according to their field of study

Field of study	Number of participants
Applied Social Sciences	8
Technical Sciences	5
Math & Natural Sciences	6
Health Sciences	5
Arts	1
Social Sciences	3
Language & Literature	2
	TOTAL: 30

Note: Applied Social Sciences: This group includes disciplines such as Educational Administration, Business Administration, International Relations, and Teacher Education.
Technical Sciences: This group includes Engineering and Architecture.
Mathematics and Natural Sciences: This group includes disciplines such as Mathematics, Biology, Chemistry, Astronomy, and Physics.
Health Sciences: This group includes disciplines such as Medicine, Dentistry, and Nursing.
Arts: This group includes Art and Music.
Social Sciences: This group includes disciplines such as Political Science, Sociology, Psychology, and Philosophy.
Language and Literature: This group includes all language- and literature-related disciplines, such as Turkish Language and Literature and German Language and Literature.

Table A.IV Distribution of participants according to the time they started veiling

Time the participant started veiling	Number of participants
Grade 1	1
Grade 5	1
Grade 6	9
Grade 7	3
Grade 8	2
Grade 9	4
Grade 10	2
Grade 11	2
University	5
	TOTAL: 29
	(1 non-respondent)

Table A.V Distribution of participants according to their reasons for veiling

Reason for her veiling	Number of participants
Voluntary	14
Influence of other parties	7
Financial	1
Family pressure	2
Other (imitation, fear of God etc.)	4
	TOTAL: 28
	(2 non-respondents)

Table A.VI Distribution of participants according to their type of unveiling

Type of unveiling	Number of participants
Expose the hair	16
Hat	11
Wig	3
	TOTAL: 30

Note: There were some students who predominantly wore hats. When their professors did not let them wear hats in class, they wore wigs or exposed their hair during those classes. I considered such students as hat wearers since their primary choice of the type of unveiling was the hat with the exception of special circumstances that made them wear wigs or expose their hair. There were also some students who started the unveiling process with a wig or hat, but were uncomfortable with it, and they decided to expose their hair as their style of unveiling. I categorized these students' type of unveiling as "expose the hair" since they only wore a wig or hat for a short time and decided to expose their hair as their final style of unveiling. Finally, some participants reported that they wore versions of a hat such as bandana or beret. For the purpose of reporting and analysis, I grouped all students who wore bandana, beret, hood, or hat under the same category called "hat." Two participants in the study reported that recently, when professors did not accept students with hoods, some students took their case to the Judiciary. The decision was that a hood did not carry an ideological meaning and it could be worn on campus. However, according to these students, this was not a decision widely known by students and professors yet. I have not been able to find the original document of the decision taken by the Judiciary with regard to the hood via a Google search or document analysis to report in this book.

Appendix B

Profile of the Part-Time Unveilers

Table B.I Profile of all the research participants

Participant	Age	University	Year of study	Field of study	Place of residence	GPA
Gamze	21	University of West	3	Applied Social Sciences	Off campus	High
Fatma	24	University of East	2 *2-year degree	Technical Sciences	Off campus	High
Leyla	22	University of West	3	Math & Natural Sciences	Off campus	High
Zeynep	20	University of West	3	Applied Social Sciences	On campus	Average
Hale	23	University of South	5	Health Sciences	Off campus	
Reyhan	29 R	University of North	2	Math & Natural Sciences	Off campus	Low
Nurten	27 R	University of North	4	Applied Social Sciences	Off campus	High
Sezen	27 R	University of North	4	Language & Literature	Off campus	
Sevgi	22	University of Center	2	Technical Sciences	Off campus	Average
Sevda	19	University of East	2	Social Sciences	Off campus	Average
İpek M	26 R	University of South	4	Applied Social Sciences	On campus	
Buket	23	University of East	4	Health Sciences	Off campus	Average
Sevtap	23	University of West	2	Arts	Off campus	High
Suzan	21	University of Center	3	Math & Natural Sciences	Off campus	
Alara	21	University of East	4	Social Sciences	Off campus	Low
Dilara	21	University of Center	3	Technical Sciences	Off campus	High

Name	Age	University	Year	*2-year degree	Field	Campus	Level
Mine	19	University of East	2	*2-year degree	Applied Social Sciences	Off campus	Average
Bahar M	20	University of North	3		Language & Literature	Off campus	High
Semra	21	University of West	3		Math & Natural Sciences	On campus	Average
Sema	20	University of West	3		Math & Natural Sciences	Off campus	High
Sevim	22	University of South	4		Health Sciences	Off campus	Average
Elif M	26 R	University of South	4		Applied Social Sciences	Off campus	Average
Beyza	23	University of South	4		Social Sciences	Off campus	High
Berna	24	University of South	6		Health Sciences	Off campus	High
Burcu	20	University of Center	2		Technical Sciences	Off campus	Average
Melek	23	University of South	6		Health Sciences	Off campus	High
Yeliz	25	University of West	4		Applied Social Sciences	Off campus	High
Merve	30 R	University of South	4		Applied Social Sciences	Off campus	High
Seda	21	University of South	3		Math & Natural Sciences	Off campus	Average
Selma	21	University of Center	3		Technical Sciences	Off campus	Average

Note: This table does not take into account the language preparatory years students attended during their secondary education and/or at university if the medium of instruction of the school they attended was different than Turkish. So if a student is in her second year, this is her year of study in her program regardless of whether she did or did not attend the preparatory class at university. In addition, this table does not show the interruptions students had during their education as a result of health problems, dropping out of school, or not becoming successful in the national university exam.

M: Married;   R: Returning student

Table B.II Profile of all the research participants—continued

Participant	City she is from	Mother's job	Father's job
Gamze	Small city	Housewife	Retired
Fatma	Small city	Housewife	Worker
Leyla	Big city	Housewife	Professional
Zeynep	Big city	Housewife	Professional
Hale	Small city	Worker	Worker
Reyhan	Small city	Housewife	Businessman
Nurten	Big city	Housewife	Businessman
Sezen	Big city	Housewife	Deceased
Sevgi	Big city	Housewife	Retired
Sevda	Big city	Worker	
İpek M	Small city	Housewife	Businessman
Buket	Small city	Housewife	Worker
Sevtap	Small city	Housewife	Businessman
Suzan	Big city	Housewife	Retired
Alara	Small city	Housewife	Businessman
Dilara	Big city	Businesswoman	Businessman
Mine	Big city	Businesswoman	Businessman
Bahar M	Big city	Housewife	Businessman
Semra	Big city	Housewife	Retired
Sema	Small city	Housewife	Retired
Sevim	Big city	Professional	Professional
Elif M	Small city	Housewife	Businessman
Beyza	Big city	Professional	Professional
Berna	Big city	Professional	Professional
Burcu	Big city	Housewife	Professional
Melek	Small city	Housewife	Businessman
Yeliz	Big city	Housewife	Professional
Merve	Big city	Housewife	Retired
Seda	Big city	Professional	Professional
Selma	Small city	Worker	Worker

Table B.III Profile of all the research participants—continued

Participant	School(s) attended before university	Women in the nucleus family with regard to veiling	Time/age the participant started veiling
Gamze	İmam Hatip high school	Mother and all sisters: veiled	Grade 6
Fatma	Vocational high school	Mother: veiled	Grade 6
Leyla	İmam Hatip high school (Grades 6-7) Public school (Grades 8-9-10-11)	Unveiled	Grade 9
Zeynep		Unveiled	At university
Hale	Public high school	Mother: veiled	Year 1 at university
Reyhan	Public high school for girls	Mother: veiled	Grade 9
Nurten		Mother: veiled	Grade 11
Sezen			
Sevgi	İmam Hatip high school	Mother and all sisters: veiled	Grade 6
Sevda		Mother: veiled	At university
İpek M	İmam Hatip high school	Mother: veiled	Grade 10
Buket	Vocational school	Mother and all sisters: veiled	Year 1 at university
Sevtap	İmam Hatip high school		Grade 7
Suzan	Public primary school İmam Hatip high school (Grades 6-7-8) Public high school (Grades 9-10-11)	All sisters: veiled	Grade 1
Alara	İmam Hatip high school (Grades 6-7-8) Private high school (Grades 9-10-11)	Mother and all sisters: veiled	Grade 5
Dilara	Public high school	Mother and all sisters: veiled	At the end of the first year at university

Table B.III (Continued)

Participant	School(s) attended before university	Women in the nucleus family with regard to veiling	Time/age the participant started veiling
Mine	Vocational high school	Mother and one sister: veiled Two sisters: unveiled	Grade 9
Bahar M	Private high school	Mother: veiled	Grade 6
Semra	Science high school (boarding) (for girls)	Mother and all sisters: veiled	Grade 10
Sema	Public high school	Mother: veiled	Grade 8
Sevim	Public primary school İmam Hatip school (Grade 6) Private school (Grades 7 and 8) Anatolian high school	Mother: veiled	Grade 7
Elif M	İmam Hatip high school	Mother and all sisters: veiled	Grade 6
Beyza	İmam Hatip school (Grades 6-7-8) Private high school (for girls)	Mother: veiled	Grade 6
Berna	Public primary school İmam Hatip school (Grades 6-7-8) Private high school (Grades 9-10-11-12) (for girls)		Grade 8

Burcu	Anatolian İmam Hatip school Private high school (coeducational)	Mother: veiled	Grade 6
Melek	Anatolian İmam Hatip school (Grade 6) Private school (Grades 7-8) Private high school (for girls)	Mother: veiled One sister: veiled One sister: unveiled	Grade 6
Yeliz	Science high school (coeducational)	Mother: veiled Sisters: veiled	Grade 9
Merve	Public high school (coeducational)	Mother: veiled Older sister: unveiled	Grade 11
Seda	Private school (Grades 6-7-8) Anatolian high school	Mother: veiled Sister: veiled	Grade 7
Selma	Public high school (for girls)	Mother: veiled Sisters: veiled	Grade 6

Table B.IV Profile of all the research participants—continued

Participant	Reason for her veiling	Type of unveiling at university
Gamze	Voluntary	Expose the hair
Fatma	Voluntary	Expose the hair
Leyla	Voluntary	Expose the hair
Zeynep	Influence of a girlfriend—a decision made with a girlfriend	Expose the hair
Hale	Financial and encouragement from the test center she attended	Expose the hair
Reyhan	Voluntary, when she felt ready, a conscious decision	Hat (wig when necessary)
Nurten	Voluntary	Hat (expose the hair when necessary)
Sezen		Expose the hair
Sevgi	Qur'an course, teachings of her family, her reading about Islam	Hat
Sevda	To imitate other veiled women in her family and encouragement from students and teachers in a test center	Expose the hair
İpek M	Voluntary	Hat
Buket	Influence of friends at university	Hat
Sevtap	Influence of friends at secondary school	Hat (with a wig and use of wig when necessary)
Suzan	Voluntary after listening to the veiling experiences of her sisters	Hat (expose the hair when necessary)
Alara	Voluntary after spending some time in a boarding Qur'an course	Expose the hair
Dilara	Influence of friends and religious readings	Expose the hair
Mine		Expose the hair
Bahar M	Voluntary	Expose the hair
Semra	Voluntary	Expose the hair
Sema	Fear of God during the earthquake in 1999	Expose the hair
Sevim	She thought she was mature and adult enough to start veiling, a voluntary decision	Wig
Elif M	Influence of the father	Hat
Beyza	Voluntary	Expose the hair
Berna	Influence of friends	Wig

Burcu	Influence of the İmam Hatip school and voluntary	Hat (wig when necessary)
Melek	Voluntary	Expose the hair
Yeliz	Pressure of the father	Expose the hair
Merve	Voluntary	Hat
Seda	Wanting to imitate veiled women around her	Wig
Selma	Pressure of the father	Hat

Appendix C

A Summary of the Turkish Education System

The Turkish education system consists of preschool, primary, secondary, and tertiary education ("The Republic of Turkey," 2001; "The Republic of Turkey Ministry of National Education Research," 2001). Until the academic year 1997–1998, the compulsory primary education lasted five years and the secondary education (lower secondary and high school) at least six years. In 1997, the system changed in such a way that the compulsory primary education lasted eight years and secondary education at least three years ("The Republic of Turkey," 2001). The tertiary education lasts between two and four years depending on the type of university students attend.

Primary education is compulsory for all Turkish children, starting at the age of six, regardless of gender, and is free of charge in public schools. In addition to public primary schools, there are numerous private Turkish, foreign, minority, and international primary schools where students have to pay for tuition ("The Republic of Turkey," 2001; "The Republic of Turkey Ministry of National Education Research," 2001). At the end of the primary education, students take a national exam that tests their knowledge in Turkish, mathematics, sciences, and social sciences. Students are placed in different kinds of schools according to their scores.

Secondary education includes general schools and vocational and technical schools. The most popular types of general schools are public schools, Anatolian schools, science schools, and private (Turkish, foreign, minority, or international) schools. High schools, Anatolian schools, and science schools are public-funded institutions and free of charge. Anatolian schools are famous for preparing students for the national university exam in a generally successful way. Science schools, which prepare students to succeed in the university exam, are science focused. Anatolian and science schools are very competitive and difficult to get into ("The Republic of Turkey," 2001; "The Republic of Turkey Ministry of National Education Research," 2001).

Vocational schools give education according to profession. Some of the vocational schools include technical schools, vocational schools, Anatolian technical schools, Anatolian vocational schools, vocational schools for girls and boys separately, technical schools for girls and boys separately, İmam Hatip schools, and Anatolian İmam Hatip schools ("The Republic of Turkey," 2001; "The Republic of Turkey Ministry of National Education Research," 2001). These vocational and technical schools are free and public-funded institutions. As discussed in the literature review section at greater length, the graduates of vocational and technical schools are at a disadvantage if they decide to pursue a program that is different from what they have studied during high school. Should such a case arise, the points of the graduate students of these schools are deducted, affecting their overall score in the university entrance examination (Gorvett, 2004). With reference to the headscarf ban policy, during primary and secondary education, students are not allowed to cover their hair while going to school, regardless of the type of school they attend.

Appendix D

Translations of the Surah an-Nur and Surah al-Ahzab

Translation of the Surah an-Nur (Light) verse 31 from the Qur'an reads:

> And say to the believing women that they should lower their gaze and guard their modesty; that they should not display their beauty and ornaments except what (ordinarily) appear thereof; that they should draw their veils over their bosoms and not display their beauty except to their husbands, their fathers, their husband's fathers, their sons, their husbands' sons, their brothers or their brothers' sons, or their sisters' sons, or their women, or the slaves whom their right hands possess, or male attendants free of sexual desires, or small children who have no carnal of women; and that they should not strike their feet in order to draw attention to their hidden ornaments. And O ye Believers! turn ye all together towards Allah in repentance, that ye may be successful.
>
> (The Holy Quran, n.d.)

Translation of the Surah al-Ahzab (the Confederates) verse 59 from the Qur'an reads:

> O Prophet! Tell thy wives and daughters, and the believing women, that they should cast their outer garments over their persons (when out of doors): that is most convenient, that they should be known (as such) and not molested. And Allah is Oft- Forgiving, Most Merciful.
>
> ("The Holy Quran," n.d.)

Notes

Chapter 2

1. *İmam* means a person trained to lead the prayer in a mosque.
2. A review of the literature can also be seen in Austin and Seggie (2010), Mabokela and Seggie (2008), and Seggie (2007b).
3. *Şeriat* means the compilation of Islamic holy laws.
4. A *tarikat* is a religious brotherhood that follows Islam in a particular way. Each *tarikat* has a different religious mission and follows the tenets of Islam in a distinct way.
5. These issues are also in Seggie and Austin (2010), Mabokela and Seggie (2008), and Seggie (2007b).
6. *Medrese* is a college where teaching and learning revolve around law and theology (Berkes, 1998).
7. There is also a ban on beards and moustaches.

Chapter 5

1. Data presented in this chapter represent some of the several perceptions of part-time unveilers with regard to the impact of the policy on part-time unveilers' campus experiences. Other perceptions of part-time unveilers that indicate similar findings and conclusions specifically with regard to their educational opportunities and challenges as a result of unveiling was presented at the Fourth Conference of the Mediterranean Society of Comparative Education (MESCE) in Rabat, Morocco in 2010 and at the Association for the Study of Higher Education, International Forum, in Jacksonville, FL in 2008.

Chapter 6

1. Data presented in this chapter represent some of the several perceptions of part-time unveilers with regard to the impact of the policy on part-time unveilers' identities. Other perceptions of part-time unveilers that indicate similar findings and conclusions specifically with regard to the impact of the ban on their identities as a result of unveiling can be seen in Seggie and Austin (2010) and

were presented at the Fourth Conference of the Mediterranean Society of Comparative Education (MESCE) in Rabat, Morocco, in 2010 and at the Association for the Study of Higher Education, International Forum, in Jacksonville, FL, in 2008.

Chapter 7

1. See Seggie and Austin (2010) for similar findings.

References

Acar, F. (1995). Women and Islam in Turkey. In Ş. Tekeli (Ed.), *Women in Modern Turkish Society: A Reader* (pp. 46–65). New Jersey: Zed Books.

Aksoy, M. (2005). *Başörtüsü-türban: Batılılaşma-modernleşme, laiklik ve örtünme.* Istanbul: Kitap Yayınevi.

Altıntaş, M. (2002). *YÖK ve hukuk.* Ankara: Eğitim Sen Yayınları.

Anon. (2008). Country Profile: Turkey. Retrieved March 04, 2011, from http://lcweb2.loc.gov/frd/cs/profiles/Turkey.pdf.

Arat, Y. (1995). Feminism and Islam: Considerations on the journal *Kadın ve Aile.* In Ş. Tekeli (Ed.), *Women in Modern Turkish Society: A Reader* (pp. 66–78). New Jersey: Zed Books.

Arat, Y. (2005). *Rethinking Islam and Liberal Democracy: Islamist Women in Turkish Politics.* Albany: State University of New York Press.

Astin, A. (1975). *Four Critical Years.* San Francisco, CA: Jossey-Bass.

Astin, A. (1977). *Preventing Students from Dropping Out.* San Francisco, CA: Jossey-Bass.

Astin, A. (1984). Student involvement: A developmental theory for higher education. *Journal of College Student Personnel, 25*(3), 297–308.

Astin, A. (1997). *What Matters in College: Four Critical Years Revisited.* San Francisco, CA: Jossey-Bass.

Avcı, C. (1990). Atatürk, din ve laiklik. *Atatürk Araştırma Merkezi Dergisi, 6*(18), 479–492.

Ayoob, M. (2004, Summer). Turkey's multiple paradoxes. *Orbis,* 451–463.

Bacık, G., & Aras, B. (2002). Exile: A keyword in understanding Turkish politics. *The Muslim World, 92*(3/4), 387–406.

Barrows, L. C. (1990). *Higher Education in Turkey.* Monographs on higher education. Ankara: Student Selection and Placement Center.

Berg, B. L. (2001). *Qualitative Research Methods for the Social Sciences* (4th ed.). Needham Heights, MA: Allyn & Bacon.

Berkes, N. (1998). *The Development of Secularism in Turkey.* New York: Routledge.

Bruni, A., & Gherardi, S. (2002). En-gendering differences, transgressing the boundaries, coping with the dual presence. In I. Aaltio & A. J. Mills (Eds), *Gender, Identity, and the Culture of Organizations* (pp. 21–38). New York: Routledge.

Cabrera, A. F., & Nora, A. (1994). College students' perceptions of prejudice and discrimination and their feelings of alienation: A construct validation approach. *Review of Education, Pedagogy, and Cultural Studies*, 16(3–4), 387–409.

Cherry, M. (2003). When a Muslim nation embraces secularism. *The Humanist*, 62(3), 21–23.

Chickering, A. W. (1969). *Education and Identity*. San Francisco, CA: Jossey-Bass.

Chickering, A. W., & Reisser, L. (1993). *Education and Identity* (2nd ed.). San Francisco: Jossey-Bass.

Clark, J. A. (2006, July). Field research methods in the Middle East. *Political Science & Politics*, 417–424. Retrieved October 23, 2006, from http://www.apsanet. org/imgtest/PSJul06Clark.pdf#search=%22Field%20research%20methods %20in%20the%20middle%20east%22.

Cress, C. M., & Ikeda, E. K. (2003). Distress under duress: The relationship between campus climate and depression in Asian American college students. *NASPA Journal*, 40(2), 74–97.

Creswell, J. W. (2003). *Research Design: Qualitative, Quantitative and Mixed Methods Approaches* (2nd ed.). Thousand Oaks, CA: Sage.

Crotty, M. (1998). *The Foundations of Social Research: Meaning and Perspective in the Research Process*. London: Sage.

Dagi, I. D. (2004). Rethinking human rights, democracy, and the West: Post-Islamist intellectuals in Turkey. *Critical Middle Eastern Studies*, 13(2), 135–151.

Demirer, T., & Özbudun, S. (1999). Egemen eğitimin üniversite(ler) gerçeği. In F. Alpkaya, T. Demirer, F. Ercan, H. Mıhçı, İ. Önder, S. Özbudun, & M. Özuğurlu (Eds), *Eğitim: Ne için?, Üniversite: Nasıl?, YÖK: Nereye?* (pp. 122–225). Ankara: Ütopya Yayınevi.

Derry, S. J. (1999). A fish called peer learning: Searching for common themes. In A. M. O'Donnell & A. King (Eds.), *Cognitive Perspectives on Peer Learning* (pp. 197–211). Mahwah, NJ: Erlbaum.

Downey, L. D. (1988). *Policy Analysis in Education*. Calgary, Alberta: Detselig Enterprises.

Dumanlı, E. (2004). *Imam-Hatip Schools and Social Balance*. Retrieved February 13, 2006, from http://www.zaman.com/?bl=columnists&trh=20041202&hn= 3721.

Edmondson, J. (2005). Policymaking in education: Understanding influences on the Reading Excellence Act. *Education Policy Analysis Archives*, 13(11), 1–18. Retrieved May 1, 2005, from http://epaa.asu.edu/epaa/v13n11/v13n11.pdf.

Ernest, P. (1999, March 23). *Social Constructivism as a Philosophy of Mathematics: Radical Constructivism Rehabilitated?* Retrieved December 20, 2006, from http://www.ex.ac.uk/~PErnest/soccon.htm.

Evans, N. J., Forney, D. S., & Guido-DiBrito, F. (1998). *Student Development in College: Theory, Research, and Practice*. San Francisco, CA: Jossey-Bass.

Fuller, G. E. (2004). Turkey's strategic model: Myths and realities. *The Washington Quarterly*, 27(3), 51–64.

Gök, F. (1995). Women and education in Turkey. In Ş. Tekeli (Ed.), *Women in Modern Turkish Society: A Reader* (pp. 131–137). New Jersey: Zed Books.

Göle, N. (1996). *The Forbidden Modern: Civilization and Veiling*. Ann Arbor, MI: The University of Michigan Press.

Göle, N. (1997). Secularism and Islamism in Turkey: The making of elites and counter elites. *The Middle East Journal,* 51(1), 46–58.

Gorvett, J. (2004). *Secular Anger Over New Turkish Law*. Retrieved May 3, 2005, from http://english.aljazeera.net/NR/exeres/92FBAD44-4870-4CE2-81FA-28157E29734C.htm.

Green, M. (1989). *Minorities on Campus: A Handbook for Enhancing Diversity*. Washington, DC: American Council on Education.

Gülalp, H. (2003). Whatever happened to secularization? The multiple Islams in Turkey. *The South Atlantic Quarterly,* 102(2/3), 381–395.

Guthman, J. C. (1994). *Faculty-Student Interaction, Alienation and Other Correlates of Achievement and Attrition of Minority and Majority Undergraduates*. Dissertation Abstracts International: Section B: The Sciences & Engineering, 54(11-B), 5926.

Hale, H. (1991). *Institutional Effectiveness*. Columbus: Ohio State University Press.

Hatiboğlu, M. (2000). *Türkiye üniversite tarihi* (2nd ed.). Ankara: Selvi Yayınevi.

Hooglund, E. (1996). The society and its environment. In H. C. Metz (Ed.), *Turkey: A Country Study* (pp. 71–146) (5th ed.). Washington, D. C.: GPO for the Library of Congress. Retrieved March 5, 2005, from http://www.marines.mil/news/publications/Documents/Turkey%20Study_2.pdf.

Human Rights Watch. (2004). *Turkey: Headscarf Ban Stifles Academic Freedom*. Retrieved June 20, 2005, from http://hrw.org/english/docs/2004/06/29/turkey8965.htm.

Human Rights Watch. (2008). *Turkey: Constitutional Court Ruling Upholds Headscarf Ban*. Retrieved July 12, 2009, from http://www.hrw.org/en/news/2008/06/05/turkey-constitutional-court-ruling-upholds-headscarf-ban.

Hurtado, S., Milem, J., Clayton-Pedersen, A., & Allen, W. (1999). *Enacting Diverse Learning Environments: Improving the Climate for Racial/Ethnic Diversity in Higher Education*. ASHE-ERIC Higher Education Report, Volume 26, Number 8. Washington, D.C.: The George Washington University, Graduate School of Education and Human Development.

Jones, S. R., & McEwen, M. K. (2000). A conceptual model of multiple dimensions of identity. *Journal of College Student Development,* 41(4), 405–414.

Kim, B. (2001). Social constructivism. In M. Orey (Ed.), *Emerging Perspectives on Learning, Teaching, and Technology*. Retrieved December 20, 2006, from http://www.coe.uga.edu/epltt/SocialConstructivism.htm.

Kongar, E. (1999). *21. Yüzyılda Türkiye* (25th ed.). Istanbul: Remzi Kitabevi.

Kotan, B. (2004). Katsayı kâbusu sona erdi. Retrieved June 10, 2010 from http://www.radikal.com.tr/Radikal.aspx?aType=RadikalHaberDetay&ArticleID=992867&Date=22.04.2010&CategoryID=97.

Kuh, G. D., Kinzie, J., Schuh, J. H., Whitt, E. J., & Associates (2005). *Student Success in College: Creating Conditions That Matter*. San Francisco, CA: Jossey-Bass.

Kuh, G. D. & Love, P. G. (2000). A cultural perspective on student perspective. In J. M. Braxton (Ed.), *Reworking the Student Departure Puzzle* (pp.196–212). Nashville: Vanderbilt University Press.

Kukla, A. (2000). *Social Constructivism and the Philosophy of Science.* New York: Routledge.

Kuran kursları icin anayasal tartışma. (2005). Retrieved January 15, 2006, from http://www.sabah.com.tr/2005/01/02/siy106.html.

Labi, A. (2006). A symbol of oppression, or a sign of faith? *The Chronicle of Higher Education,* 52(22), A44.

Lagdameo, A., Lee, S., Nguyen, B., Liang, C. T. H., Lee, S., Kodama, C. M., & McEwen, M. K. (2002, Spring). Voices of Asian American students. *New Directions for Student Services,* 97, 5–10.

Lee, R. M. (1993). *Doing Research on Sensitive Topics.* London: Sage.

Mabokela, R. O., & Seggie, F. N. (2008). Mini skirts and headscarves: Undergraduate student perceptions of secularism in Turkish higher education. *Higher Education,* 55(2), 155–170.

Mardin, Ş. (1983) Tabakalaşmanın tarihsel belirleyicileri: Türkiye'de toplumsal sınıf ve smif bilinci. Istanbul: *Yazko Felsefe Yazıları Dizisi:* 5.

Marshall, C., & Rossman, G. B. (1999). *Designing Qualitative Research* (3rd ed.). Thousand Oaks, CA: Sage.

Marshall, G. A. (2005). Ideology, progress, and dialogue: A comparison of feminist and Islamist women's approaches to the issues of head covering and work in Turkey. *Gender and Society,* 19(1), 104–120.

Masood, M. (2004). At the crossroads of Islamic feminism: Negotiating the gender politics of identity. *Al Nakhlah,* 5, 1–7. Retrieved September 13, 2005, from http://fletcher.tufts.edu/al_nakhlah/archives/spring2004/masood.pdf.

Mazlumder insan hakları ve mazlumlar icin dayanışma derneği. (1998). *Bütün yönleriyle başörtüsü sorunu: Olaylar, belgeler, anılar (1981–1998)* (2nd ed.). Istanbul: Mazlumder Istanbul Şubesi Yayınları.

McCosker, H., Barnard, A., & Gerber, R. (2001, February). Undertaking sensitive research: Issues and strategies for meeting the safety needs of all participants. *Forum Qualitative Sozialforschung/Forum: Qualitative Social Research,* 2(1). Retrieved January 13, 2007, from http://www.qualitative-research.net/fqs-texte/1-01/1-01mccoskeretal-e.htm.

Mızıkacı, F. (2006). *Higher Education in Turkey.* UNESCO/CEPES. Bucharest.

National Education Statistics: Formal Education 2008–2009. (2009). Retrieved July 14, 2010, from http://sgb.meb.gov.tr/istatistik/meb_istatistikleri_orgun_egitim_2008_2009.pdf.

Nauck, B., & Klaus, D. (2005). Families in Turkey. In B. N. Adams & J. Trost (Eds.), *Handbook of World Families* (pp. 364–388). Thousand Oaks: Sage.

Navaro-Yashin, Y. (2002). The market for identities: Secularism, Islamism, and commodities. In D. Kandiyoti & A. Saktanber (Eds), *Fragments of Culture: The Everyday of Modern Turkey* (pp. 221–253). New Brunswick, NJ: Rutgers University Press.

Öncü, A. (1979). Uzman mesleklerde Türk kadını. In N. A. Ünat (Ed.), *Türk toplumunda kadın* (pp. 271–286). Ankara: Türk Sosyal Bilimler Derneği.

Öniş, Z. (2006). The political economy of Islam and democracy in Turkey: From the Welfare Party to the AKP. In D. Jung (Ed.), Democracy and development: New political strategies for the Middle East (pp. 103–128). New York: Palgrave.

Pascarella, E. T., & Terenzini, P. T. (1991). How College Affects Students: Findings and Insights from Twenty Years of Research. San Francisco, CA: Jossey-Bass.

Pascarella, E. T., & Terenzini, P. T. (2005). How College Affects Students: A Third Decade of Research (Volume 2). San Francisco, CA: Jossey-Bass.

Prasad, A., & Prasad, P. (2002). Otherness at large: Identity and difference in the new globalized organizational landscape. In I. Aaltio & A. J. Mills (Eds.), *Gender, Identity, and the Culture of Organizations* (pp. 57–71). New York: Routledge.

Republic of Turkey, Ministry of National Education. (2001). *The Turkish Education System and Developments in Education.* Retrieved September 21, 2006, from http://www.ibe.unesco.org/international/ice/natrap/Turkey.pdf#search=%22Turkish%20%20education%22.

Republic of Turkey, Ministry of National Education Research, Planning and Coordination Board (RPCB). (2001). *National Education at the Beginning of 2002.* Retrieved September 21, 2006, from http://www.meb.gov.tr/english/indexeng.htm.

Robinson-Fischer, A. (n.d.). *Education in Turkey.* Retrieved February 19, 2006, from http://socialscience.tyler.cc.tx.us/mkho/fulbright/1998/turkey/amy.htm.

Schlossberg, N. K. (1989). Marginality and mattering: Key issues in building community. In D. C. Roberts (Ed.), *Designing Campus Activities to Foster a Sense of Community* (New Directions for Student Services, No. 48) (pp. 5–15). San Francisco, CA: Jossey-Bass.

Schmitt, M. T., Branscombe, N. R., Kobrynowicz, D., & Owen, S. (2002). Perceiving discrimination against one's gender group has different implications for well-being in women and men. *Personality and Social Psychology Bulletin, 28*(2), 197–210.

Seggie, F. N. (2007a). The headscarf ban in the Turkish university: Educational and cultural Experiences of part-time unveilers. Michigan State University, East Lansing. Available from ProQuest Dissertations and Theses database (Publication Number: 3282198).

Seggie, F. N. (2007b). Graduate student perceptions of secularism in Turkish higher education. In R. O. Mabokela (Ed.), *Soaring Beyond Boundaries: Women Breaking Educational Barriers in Traditional Societies* (pp. 37–54). Rotterdam: Sense Publishers.

Seggie, F. N., & Austin, A. E. (2010). Impact of the headscarf ban policy on the identity development of part-time unveilers in Turkish higher education. *Journal of College Student Development, 51*(5), 564–583.

Sieber, E., & Stanley, B. (1988). Ethical and professional dimensions of socially sensitive research. *American Psychologist, 43*(1), 49–55.

Sunar, İ. (2004). State, society and democracy in Turkey. In İ. Sunar (Ed.), *State, Society and Democracy in Turkey* (pp. 97–119). Istanbul: Bahçeşehir University Publications.

Sunar, İ., & Sayarı, S. (2004). Democracy in Turkey: Problems and prospects. In İ. Sunar (Ed.), *State, Society and Democracy in Turkey* (pp. 65–96). Istanbul: Bahçeşehir University Publications.

Sunar, İ., & Toprak, B. (2004). Islam in politics: The case of Turkey. In İ. Sunar (Ed.), *State, Society and Democracy in Turkey* (pp. 155–173). Istanbul: Bahçeşehir University Publications.

T. C. Yükseköğretim Kurulu. (n.d. a). *The Law on Higher Education System*. Retrieved June 13, 2005, from http://www.yok.gov.tr/english/law/art4.html.

T. C. Yükseköğretim Kurulu. (n.d. b). *The Law on Higher Education System*. Retrieved June 13, 2005, from http://www.yok.gov.tr/english/law/art5.html.

T. C. Yükseköğretim Kurulu. (n.d. c). *The Turkish Higher Education System (Part 2- Governance)*. Retrieved June 13, 2005, from http://www.yok.gov.tr/english/part2.doc.

T. C. Yükseköğretim Kurulu. (n.d. d). *The Law on Higher Education System*. Retrieved June 13, 2005, from http://www.yok.gov.tr/english/law/art43.html.

Tekeli, Ş. (1995). Introduction: Women in Turkey in the 1980s. In Ş. Tekeli (Ed.), *Women in Modern Turkish Society: A Reader* (pp. 1–22). New Jersey: Zed Books.

The Holy Quran. (n.d.). Retrieved July 15, 2010 from http://www.kuranikerim.com/english/m_indexe.htm.

Tinto, V. (1993). *Leaving College: Rethinking the Causes and Cures of Student Attrition*. Chicago: University of Chicago Press.

'Türban' *tartışmaları ve bilimsel araştırmalar*. (2007, December 14). Milliyet. Retrieved July 14, 2010, from http://www.milliyet.com.tr/-turban—tartismalari-ve-bilimsel-arastirmalar/guncel/haberdetayarsiv/14.07.2010/261778/default.htm.

Türbanın hızlı yükselişi. (2007, December 3). Milliyet. Retrieved July 14, 2010 from http://www.milliyet.com.tr/turbanin-hizli yukselisi/guncel/ haberdetayarsiv/14.07.2010/261685/default.htm.

Turkey, education. (n.d.). Retrieved January, 14, 2006, from http://www.countrydata.com/cgi-bin/query/r-13955.html.

Yağcı, A. (2008). Kemalist söylemde türban: Bir milli kimlik meselesi. Retrieved July 14, 2010 from http://www.birikimdergisi.com/birikim/makale.aspx?mid=441.

Yükseköğretim Kanunu. (n.d.). Retrieved June 13, 2005, from http://www.yok.gov.tr/mevzuat/kanun/kanun2.html.

Watson, L. W., Terrell, M. C., Wright, D. J., & Associates (2002). *How Minority Students Experience College: The Implications for Planning and Policy*. Sterling, VA: Stylus Publishing, LLC.

White, J. (2002). *Islamist Mobilization in Turkey: A Study in Vernacular Politics*. Seattle, WA: University of Washington Press.

2008–2009 öğretim yılı vakıf üniversitelerinde okuyan öğrenci sayılarına ilişkin bilgiler. (n.d). Retrieved June 25, 2010, from http://yogm.meb.gov.tr/Vakifogrenci.htm.

2008–2009 öğretim yılı devlet üniversiteleri öğrenci sayıları. (n.d). Retrieved June 25, 2010, from http://yogm.meb.gov.tr/devletogrenci.htm.

2009-ÖSYS Merkezi Yerleştirme Sonuçları. (2010). Retrieved June 25, 2010 from http://www.osym.gov.tr/Genel/BelgeGoster.aspx?F6E10F8892433CFFD4 AF1EF75F7A796823BE6F87556AA8A4.2009-ÖSYS Merkezi Yerleştirme Sonuçları. (n.d). Retrieved October 31, 2005, from http:// www. yok. gov. tr/webeng/current.html.

Index